# Civil-Military Relations
## in Sierra Leone

# Civil-Military Relations in Sierra Leone

A Case Study of
African Soldiers in Politics

Thomas S. Cox

Harvard University Press
Cambridge, Massachusetts, and London, England
1976

**Library of Congress Cataloging in Publication Data**
Cox, Thomas S          1944-
   Civil-military relations in Sierra Leone.

   Bibliography: p.
   Includes index.
   1. Sierra Leone—Politics and government.
2. Sierra Leone. Army—Political activity.
I. Title.
DT516.8.C69   1976          322'.5'09664          75-17940
ISBN 0-674-13290-4

*To Molly and my parents, who made this book possible*

# PREFACE

Within the last decade, military involvement in the political process has become an increasingly salient feature of the African scene. In this book, I analyze this involvement at the country level, using the West African state of Sierra Leone as a case study. The primary emphasis of the book is upon the rules and parameters that have governed and will necessarily continue to govern the interaction between military and civilian leaders in Sierra Leone. In this respect, the book seeks to expand our understanding of civilian control of an army establishment and the diverse processes that may render that control inoperative over extended periods of time. The book then is not simply an account of the whys and hows of coups d'état in general and attempted coups in an African state, but rather a study of political disintegration and its relation to changing patterns of civil-military relations.

The research for this book was conducted while I was a Visiting Research Student at the Institute of African Studies of Fourah Bay College, Freetown, Sierra Leone between November 1969 and December 1970. During that period, unstructured interviews were held with a number of Sierra Leone army and ex-army officers on the understanding that, for those officers still resident in the country, names would not be revealed. An attempt was made to secure government permission to conduct systematic interviews of a large sample of army officers as a means of acquiring insights into the officer corps's socio-economic origins and political biases. However, this permission was not granted, and therefore I had to content myself with such biographical and other pertinent data as could be gleaned from newspaper accounts, publications of the government information services, and unofficial sources.

A number of civilian leaders closely associated with the former SLPP Government were also interviewed, and I can only underline my gratitude at the willingness of these individuals to discuss matters which were unquestionably politically sensitive. Most of those whom I did interview have deliberately been left unnamed if only because they are still involved in the affairs of their country and because the subject of our conversations was rather delicate. Certainly without the unbounding encouragement of several key personalities my study could never have been accomplished. I should especially like to thank Dr. Edward Blyden III, the former director of the Institute of African Studies at Fourah Bay College, and his assistant, Jonathan Hyde, for their invaluable assistance and hospitality while I was attached to the Institute.

My own study has also greatly benefited from the views of a number of students of African politics. Martin Kilson of the Harvard University Department of Government, whose own work on political modernization in Sierra Leone to some extent foreshadowed my study, offered helpful advice at various stages during the drafting of the manuscript. W. Scott Thompson, Associate Professor of International Politics at the Fletcher School of Law and Diplomacy, supervised the doctoral dissertation which eventually led to this book. Others to whom I am gratefully indebted for their useful comments include Claude E. Welch, Jr., of the State University of New York at Buffalo, Valerie P. Bennett, John Cartwright of the University of Western Ontario, and John Colas, formerly of the American University, Washington, D.C. However, such errors of fact and judgment as may exist in this study are solely my own responsibility.

T.S.C.

# CONTENTS

# Civil-Military Relations in Sierra Leone

# 1
# CIVIL-MILITARY RELATIONS THEORY AND SUB-SAHARAN AFRICA

The rapid substitution of military officers for men in civilian garb, within the last decade or so, has constituted *the* political reality for much of sub-Saharan Africa. The Gowons, the Afrifas, the Acheampongs, and even the Juxon-Smiths have replaced the first generation of civilian leaders in independent black Africa with frightening and sometimes ludicrous regularity. "Want to get ahead faster?" quipped a recent advertisement in the British magazine *Punch;* well then, enlist in the army, complete your training at Sandhurst, and soon you may be in charge of entire countries. Thus "Yakubu Gowon joined the British army to see the world, and now owns 357,000 square miles of it."[1] To put it another way: "Get the keys of the armoury; turn out the barracks; take the radio station; . . . and you arrest the state."[2] For better or for worse, the fate of many African states is now firmly in the hands of the men on horseback, and it is the interaction of the civilian and military sectors that constitutes the essential dynamic of political change in these states.

The statistical frequency of military intervention or attempted intervention in the new states of Africa has already been well-documented. Kenneth Grundy, in a survey of various acts of political violence carried out on the African continent between 1955 and 1967, mentions some seventy-five incidents. These include successful army coups, military-led secessions (that in some cases led to outright civil wars), and other military actions that were instrumental in fostering a change of regime. Also included in this survey are attempted army putschs that were thwarted by the civilian authorities as well as assorted coup plots where, either because of the incompetence of the conspiratorial cohort or the intelligence-gathering capabilities of the target governments, it was not possible for the coupmakers to reach the actual implementation phase.

Claude E. Welch, Jr. gives us a similar listing of several hundred "political events in black-ruled African countries in which violence and/or military involvement has occurred."[3] As with Grundy, Welch includes the North African states in his sample but, in addition, mentions generalized instances of low-level political violence—that is, violence that falls short of interstate conflict and that ranges from arrests of opposition political leaders through coups d'état to internal wars such as that experienced in Nigeria. Military men can, of course, involve themselves in all such manifestations of political instability. In October 1970 the civilian regime in Sierra Leone thus relied almost exclusively upon army officers to arrest the leaders of a newly formed opposition party, and as Ruth First attests, in speaking of Nigeria, "if the armed men of Africa's military governments have an ultimate achievement, it was this wretched war."[4]

For purposes of this study, discussion of the military's role in African politics will be restricted to that role as personified by the coup d'état which, in our view, simply involves the forceful seizure of the government apparatus by armed establishments or by cliques within those armed establishments. Limiting our queries in this fashion should permit us to maintain a certain amount of conceptual clarity in our discussions of that military activity undertaken for the purposes of dislodging civilian leaders or, similarly, activity in the form of countercoups against existing juntas. Therefore we shall not have any reason to consider the involvement of army officers in the more traditional forms of military operations except as the experiences gained in such operations—the participation of African contingents in the United Nations Congo exercise comes to mind—affected trends in domestic civil-military relations.

From a theoretical point of view it would seem preferable to exclude references to North African civil-military relations in any survey of the African scene. Limiting the framework of study to sub-Saharan Africa recognizes the special characteristics of the North African tradition of military intervention perhaps best exemplified by the Nasserite Society of Free Officers in Egypt and more recently by Colonel Qaddafi in Libya. Military intervention in those countries belongs more appropriately to patterns of civil-military relations in Latin America and the Middle East which so often involve acute interclass conflict and ideological polarization—phenomena which, as we shall note later, are somewhat alien to the African milieu. If one excludes the Egyptian, Libyian, and Algerian coups as well as the numerous attempted coups in Morocco while at the same time including examples of military intervention in the Sudan, Somalia, and Ethiopia; then sub-Saharan Africa, by my estimation, has experienced some seventy-five to one hundred successful coups, attempted coups, as well as coup plots, between 1958 and 1974. Within that period, the years 1965 through 1967 were characterized by especially widespread and intensive coup activity, a large proportion of it successful. As Africa entered the decade of the 1970s the number of successful coups abated somewhat, perhaps because of the increased ability of governments to detect early symptoms of military discontent. Nevertheless, the volume of coup plots uncovered by existing civilian regimes did not noticeably slacken, and there were of course continuing opportunities for the staging of countercoups. Thus whereas 1973 recorded only one successful coup—that of Rwanda in June—various plots were uncovered by the military governments in Ghana and Dahomey and by the civilian regimes in Liberia and the Ivory Coast.

Nineteen seventy-four proved to be a boom year for coups in black Africa. There was the February coup in Upper Volta, the April coup in Niger, and the so-called "creeping coup" in Ethiopia which began in February as an army mutiny in Asmara and culminated seven months later, on September 12, with the Armed Forces Committee announcement of Emperor Haile Selassie I's deposition and the installment of a provisional military government. In that same year, there were also several countercoup attempts in Uganda, an attempted coup in the Central African Republic and an alleged coup plot in the Sudan which was made public by President Nemeiri in October.

In January 1975, Dahomey experienced an attempted overthrow of its military government by Captain Janvier Assogba who was himself the Minister of Civil Service and Labor in that government. On February 11, the Malagasy Head of State, Colonel Richard Ratsimandrava (who had succeeded General Gabriel Ramanantsoa only 6 days earlier in a peaceful transfer of power) was assassinated by members of the Mobile Police Group, a paramilitary force, although the military government which had ruled the Malagasy Republic since May 1972 was not overthrown. The Chad civilian government of President Ngarta Tombalbaye was toppled in a coup on April 13 and a nine-member Military Higher Council headed by Brigadier General Félix Malloum was established.

As of mid-1975, among the some thirty-six independent states in sub-Saharan Africa (including Guinea Bissau, Equitorial Guinea, the Sudan, Somalia, Ethiopia, the Malagasy Republic, and Mauritania), eighteen or

exactly 50 percent are governed by full-fledged military regimes or by regimes such as those in Togo and Zaire which are no longer ostensibly military but where army officers remain the dominant political force. There can
be little doubt that this is a rather impressive track record for a continent
where the average country has enjoyed its independence for only slightly
over one decade and where the colonial armies inherited by the African
states were supposedly trained to be the servants of these states rather than
their masters.

On the most general theoretical plane, the intense, often frantic, intrusion of African armies into the process of political change represents no more
than a special variation in a broader theme of political instability. Viewed in
this way, army intervention or attempted intervention demonstrates along
with other examples of internal disorder the failure of most African states to
preserve even a modicum of political stability. In fact, a great deal of the
recent literature on the comparative politics of instability includes the military coup within a larger typology of civil unrest. For example, in a three-
fold typology developed by Ted Gurr, the coup is shown to fall somewhere
between spontaneous mass strife at one end—that is street riots—and large-
scale civil war at the other. The act of military intervention normally belongs
to the intermediate category of conspiracy, a category that includes political
assassination and purges.[5]

Samuel Huntington, in his seminal "Political Development and Political
Decay" published in 1965, traced increased instability to situations in which
the rates of political mobilization and participation far exceeded the rates of
organizational institutionalization. As regards Africa per se, James
O'Connell referred to the "inevitability of instability" noting that for all
their pretensions of social progress and "civilizing burdens," the colonial
governments were essentially autocratic and coercive and only managed to
introduce "democracy" at a very late hour to legitimize the processes of
decolonization. The net effect of the absence of an appropriate gestation
period for democracy was that "the successor authorities . . . were not only
ill-schooled in the politics of representation, participation, and conciliation,
but they were quick to resent the imposition of constitutional and other
restraints by the departing metropolitan state, which left them with apparently less power than the colonial officials had enjoyed."[6]

Certainly the fact of political instability in black Africa and elsewhere—of
which the coup d'état is merely one of the more salient indices of the use of
force to achieve political goals—has finally gained the importance due to it.
Thus whereas in the early 1960s scholars proclaimed the institutionalization
of political parties, the rise of the charismatic leader, and the formation of
indigenous bureaucracies (even while recognizing that colonial-inspired
structures were often modified to suit the particular exigencies of African

regimes); widespread rioting, civil wars, and increased military praetorian-ism called into question earlier assumptions about the reality behind the rhetoric. No doubt the ease with which Nkrumah and the Convention Peoples Party (CPP) were swept aside by the army in Ghana forced us to reconsider the prevailing wisdom—that the ruling party there had managed to cope successfully with political demands and to distribute political rewards while simultaneously creating a relatively unified nation of Ghana-ians.

Just as the subject of political instability was generally ignored in early accounts of African development, so too was the political role of African armies in mediating competition or in displacing civilian regimes neglected. Herbert Spiro, for example, wrote in early 1965 that "the most important feature of the role of the military in sub-Saharan Africa is that their role has generally been insignificant" and advised scholars to recognize the "significance of their insignificance."[7] Rupert Emerson stated that "because they are so young, inexperienced, and, in many instances, almost nonexistent, the military forces, which have played so large a role in other nations, cannot be expected to be of much significance in Africa for some time to come."[8] While William Foltz hinted that army intervention could not be entirely ruled out as a possibility for the future, the "inherent strengths" of the political order would most likely serve as an effective, institutional counterpoise:

Above all, it is usually the politician, not the soldier, that brought independence and that profits from the revolutionary aura. Whoever the leader of the national military establishment may be, he is certain not to match the president or party leader in terms of prestige or charisma. Frequently the political demands of the preindependence nationalist period obliged the party to organize widely throughout society, to find ways of including or silencing a wide variety of social groups, and to enforce some form of discipline over its members and the most politically relevant sectors of society.[9]

The list of those who questioned the political relevance of African armies could, of course, be extended indefinitely.

With the benefit of hindsight much is revealed to us, and it is therefore not particularly difficult to understand the rather widespread neglect of the African military in the early pioneering studies of political change. From the point of view of scholars, African armies, unlike the often "innovative" single-party regimes of charismatic leaders, served no particularly interesting or worthy function except perhaps to mount a guard of honor upon the arrival of some visiting head of state. In none of the sub-Saharan African states had military men contributed to the liberation of the national territory from metropolitan control, although it is true that ex-servicemen, especially in Kenya and Ghana, helped to raise the level of political consciousness among the native population of those territories. As such the military was a purely colonial vehicle, devoid until the very last moment of an indigenous officer corps, and as preoccupied as the police in enforcing the imperial version of "law and order." With the advent of independence, most of these tiny poorly equipped African armies were simply handed over to the respective local governments as part of the general symbolic paraphernalia that accompanied the transfer of power from whites to blacks. In practically every sense, the African military establishments were largely marginal or peripheral institutions, and, as such, generally ignored by outside observers and by the ruling elites themselves. The latter for their part had little time to devote serious attention to these unproductive relics of the colonial heritage, given the more serious questions of social and economic development that confronted the new states. Many leaders, of course, ignored these armies at the cost of their political careers and, in some instances, their lives as well.

The frequent intrusion of army officers into an arena heretofore monopolized by African politicians has required the scholar to devote greater attention to the more destabilizing elements in a political system, including labor unions, student groups, revolutionary movements, and above all, the military. Armies demand special attention given the frequency with which they have managed to topple civilian regimes throughout Africa. The military's resort to actions that are decidedly unbecoming to professional officers must call into question many of the assumptions writers have entertained about the nature of political development, including the notion of a linear progression from the traditional to the modern. The coup d'état, perhaps more than any other instrument for altering a given political order, suggests neither the structural nor the institutional development, which many came to associate with certain African political systems, but rather a structural and institutional void. Aristide Zolberg, the first in an emerging line of political scientists who have adopted a somewhat revisionist perspective on Africa, articulates the need for present and future research to examine the irrational and formless elements in any synthesis of comparative political change. He suggests that "in our pursuit of scientific progress, we have learned to discern such forms [for example, the modernizing political party] as regular features of behavior which constitute structures and institutions; but the most salient characteristic of political life in Africa is that it constitutes an almost institutionless arena with conflict and disorder as its most prominent features."[10] It is within just such an arena that political activity by military officers can flourish.

Students of civil-military relations in the non-African areas of the third world generally have pursued several paths in an endeavor to explain political behavior on the part of army officers. One group especially prominent during the early 1960s favors explanations of both the disposition to intervene and the military's capacity to govern in terms of the "internal organization of the military profession." Those who would consider the politicization of armies as an outgrowth of the specificity and rationality inherent to military organizations tend to regard the influence of "civilian values and institutions . . . as qualifying or complicating factors rather than as an elaborated part of the theory."[11] Morris Janowitz, a sociologist at the University of Chicago, whose *Military in the Political Development of New Nations* contributed immensely to the growing scholarship in the field, looks for the causes of a military political role in terms of a cluster of variables readily discernible in most armies. These include, among others, skill structure and career lines, social recruitment and education, and military ideologies such as puritanism or asceticism.

Many writers have argued that not only do organizational characteristics explain military intervention but also the "special nature" of armies in developing societies facilitates constructive and reformist governments. The army's devotion to technical skills and its insistence on an administrative, apolitical approach to problem solving give it a special sense of how to manage the affairs of state. In writing of the Burmese army, Lucian Pye notes: "Many of the skills commanded by the army are peculiarly relevant to civilian, and particularly administrative abilities. The army thus takes considerable pride in its ability to develop modern skills and believes that it is well fitted to manage all aspects of government."[12] Others have postulated a kind of symbiotic relationship between "modernizing" military and "good" government. Thus Edward Shils believes that all developing countries aspire to modernity, that it is the "technical-executive intelligentsia" who can best effect social and economic change in the desired direction, and finally that by dint of their training—much of it overseas—army officers have become the "major representatives of modernity in technology and administration."[13] Given their modern attributes, armies that had previously remained in the barracks become political since they stand in marked contrast to the civilian sector that so often lacks a technologically innovative capacity and frequently evidences signs of fragmentation and disorientation. Intervention therefore is said to result from an unequal rate of modernization between the military subsystem and its civilian environment. Pye, Halperin, and others often regard military rule as a kind of middle way between feudal oligarchies, on the one hand, and leftist regimes on the other.

Linkages between the military and the political system, occasionally hinted at by organizational theorists, are usually described as an alliance between army officers and the so-called new middle class or "emerging middle sectors,'' particularly when the latter group is juxtaposed against such tradi-tional ruling elites as the propertied bourgeoisie. Army officers, said to possess a modernizing outlook, will tend to rely on the middle class as a sup-port mechanism in order to fashion bureaucratic rule and execute adminis-trative decisions. This, according to many scholars, is essentially the Nas-serite experience in the Middle East. John Johnson believes that in Latin America the military favors ''industrial development and technological change'' and will employ ''large numbers of civilian advisers, who will in most cases hold middle-sector convictions.''[14]

If some scholars seek to construct a political sociology of military elites to explain the phenomenon of intervention, others have eschewed this method to probe in greater depth the civilian side of the civilian-military relation-ship. S. E. Finer, for example, equates military intervention with the level of ''political culture'' in a particular state. Societies of high political culture, where there exists ''wide public recognition as to who or what constitutes the sovereign authority, and a corresponding belief that no other persons or center of power is legitimate or duty-worthy,''[15] rarely have to confront either the specter or reality of military takeovers. In societies of low political culture, one finds neither agreement on the mode of political intercourse nor the presence of highly institutionalized structures such as churches, industrial associations, and political parties. In such societies, found throughout the developing world, military intervention is not only ex-tremely likely but will also tend to encourage outright displacement of the ruling civilian groups.

Finer's approach has been refined by Samuel Huntington, Amos Perlmut-ter, and others to include the general notion of praetorianism whereby the military will tend to intervene and potentially come to dominate the politi-cal system. In this way, the army is viewed as one of several groups compet-ing for scarce political resources without necessarily adhering to peaceful methods of competition. One group after another becomes involved in efforts to influence the balance and maintenance of political power; in the process of heightened conflict, the more general issues of socioeconomic development recede to the background:

In such societies, politics lack autonomy, complexity, coherence and adapt-ability. All sorts of political forces and groups become directly engaged in general politics. Countries which have political armies also have political clergies, political universities, political bureaucracies, political labor unions and political corporations. Society as a whole is out-of-joint, not just the military.[16]

Political concerns become less and less the monopoly of formal political institutions such as legislative assemblies. The goal of staying in power becomes paramount in the minds of the "ins"; the goal of acquiring power, by whatever means necessary, whether through bribery or coups d'état, becomes paramount in the minds of the "outs." It is into this vortex of uncertainty that the military may feel compelled to intervene, and, by dint of its control over the instruments of violence, it is in a particularly advantageous position to do so.

To summarize, the basic difference between the "organizationalists" and the "praetorianists" may be considered as follows. The first group focuses almost exclusively on the special characteristics of military organizations that set them apart from other nonmilitary organizations in the society. This sense of being different from other groups fosters a particular army mystique, and the officer corps begins to regard itself as an exclusive repository of modernizing values and devotion to the ideal of the state as opposed to the regime in power.

The praetorianists place a much greater emphasis upon the process of interaction between army and society. The military, in their view, can no more be expected to remain autonomous or neutral with respect to political issues than can any other group within the system, particularly during a time of rising expectations by all groups. Perhaps the question of military cohesion most clearly dramatizes the qualitative difference between the two approaches to our understanding of civil-military relations. Both a Huntington and a Janowitz would agree that cohesive armies are far more capable of undertaking collective action against existing regimes than are armies lacking internal solidarity particularly at the level of the officer corps. Huntington would no doubt accept Janowitz's observation that "lack of cohesion leads to unstable and fragmented involvement and to the likelihood of countercoups d'état after the seizure of power."[17] However from the standpoint of the political sociologists, an absence of cohesion within the officer corps will tend to reflect disputes over rates of promotion and scales of pay. These disputes may, in turn, indicate an underlying generational cleavage between the junior and the senior officers. The junior officers may expect to receive swift promotions on such bases as their educational qualifications and direct-entry backgrounds. The senior officers, many of whom probably "paid their dues" through long service in the ranks, may act to thwart the ambitions of their junior colleagues—all of this contributing to a breakdown in cohesion.

The praetorianists are also concerned with this question of intra-army cohesion, but differ from the political sociologists by emphasizing correlations between the absence of cohesion in the organization and political fragmentation within the larger system. According to Perlmutter, for example, cohesion has never been realized in the Argentinian, Iraqi, and Syrian armies because, more often than not, internal army rivalries are continually mixed with politics. In Syria, "there are many examples of ambitious Syrian army officers, especially the Ba'thist . . . who have eliminated their army rivals by allying with a Ba'th faction that these rivals opposed, or, especially since the left Ba'th party's rise to power in 1966, who have created a wedge between rival Ba'th factions to advance personal causes and have finally achieved a complete takeover of the Ba'th by the army, which represents the extreme wing of the Ba'th.''[18] It is true that Janowitz suggests that younger officers "are less involved in the social and political status quo and more involved in contemporary political currents, with the result that they are inclined toward a more radical outlook.''[19] However, apart from hinting at the possibility that younger officers may entertain certain political ideas and by so doing receive an additional external reinforcement for their specific "target goals" within the military hierarchy, Janowitz really tells us very little about the dimension and quality of interaction between these army men and the environment beyond their barracks. Only vaguely are we told that society may penetrate the upper echelons of the military organization or vice versa. The boundaries between the army and the society of which the army is a component are assumed to be fairly well defined, at least in the precoup stage.

The praetorianists are relatively unimpressed by the military's performance while holding office. While Huntington can argue that armies once in power possess the ability to "de-praetorianize" the society—at least in the short run—and to "generate order," he is far less hopeful about their ability to move beyond a "non-political model of nation-building.''[20] In short, while military intervention may succeed in imposing a kind of artificial order where before there was only chaos, army men generally have little inclination to work to reconcile or to mediate conflicting political interests. Furthermore, the failings of both charismatic civilian leadership and of military juntas may be qualitatively similar when it comes to attempts at creating viable political institutions. Nasser's repeated efforts to construct a mobilization party in Egypt to some extent paralleled those undertaken by Nkrumah to create a CPP which could remain truly in touch with the aspirations of the populace. However, neither the so-called Liberation Rally and its successor organizations nor the Convention Peoples Party ever evolved into the institutionalized mass parties envisaged by their respective founders.

Huntington's view of the marginal impact of the military on nation-building and political development is shared by others such as Henry Bienen who argues that in many cases the "military does not mobilize," does not succeed in "organization- and institution-building," and "fails as well to increase economic development, political participation and other aspects of the modernization process.''[21] Perhaps the most damning evidence on the question of the impact of army rule on political and economic development is presented by Eric Nordlinger. Nordlinger draws upon extensive cross-national data and concludes that the much vaunted army-middle-class alliance that was often held out by some Washington policymakers in the early 1960s as the salvation of the developing areas does not in most cases contribute to economic growth or progressive political change. On the contrary, Nordlinger finds negative and zero order correlations between the presence of officer-politicians and modernization.[22] Military regimes are shown to oppose the demands of lower class groups for an increased distribution of economic rewards since even the so-called reformist coupmakers simply use the "call for economic and social change for the realization of their own class and status interests." As a result of research of this type, there remain few who are prepared to defend the thesis of the army as a modernizing agent.

What does this brief view of civil-military relations theory tell us about the cumulative African experience? Can we in fact readily transpose the lessons learned from the study of non-African systems to that hodgepodge of coups and coup plots so endemic to the African continent? Certainly, on a general level, the praetorian models favored by Perlmutter and others, whereby armies are seen as but one of many actors engaged in political competition, would seem to have considerable relevance. Given the swift undermining in Africa of western traditions of regulated competition involving a respect for nonviolence and acquiescence to certain democratic norms, it would seem logical that the African military with its monopoly over the means of violence finds itself involved in the "I win—you lose" zero—sum approach to power acquisition and retention. Nevertheless, some caution is in order.

In the first place, whereas in the Latin America setting the present-day man on horseback is often but the modern cousin of the nineteenth century caudillio, African officers have evolved from no such praetorian traditions. On the contrary, the colonial experience emphasized the apolitical role of the armed forces. The colonial armies were considered apolitical in that they were asked to support the government of the day, usually by suppressing urban riots and chiefdom uprisings. While it is true that the record shows isolated instances of small-scale mutinies by African enlisted men over conditions of pay and service, African army officers must have been grilled thoroughly by their colonial mentors in the tradition of army noninvolvement in things political. Furthermore, the total absence of participation by most black African armies in wars of national liberation—unlike some of their North African and Latin American counterparts—meant that coupmakers in Bangui, Lomé, Freetown, and elsewhere could not hark back to the earlier days of direct military involvement in the ouster of the imperialists. In short, army intervention in sub-Saharan African politics has been taking place in a historical and sociocultural vacuum.

There is a second difficulty in attempting to draw upon explanations of military praetorianism in non-African regions to explain African development. Based on the available evidence, interclass conflict in which the army is either a participant or a mediator is generally not found in black Africa. Mauricio Soláun and Michael Quinn, in a comparative study of military intervention in Latin America, refer to the "participation-problem" interpretation of a coup d'état. Thus, the coup becomes a "response to the mounting pressures brought to bear when traditionally deprived groups begin to demand a greater role in deciding how goods and services are allocated in their society."[23] Armies may therefore intervene either on behalf of a rightist or leftist-oriented civilian group or may try to separate the warring classes and to impose a middle-of-the-road solution—in any case, a solution which involves the restoration of order. In black Africa, however, coups are generally reflections of disputes within the ruling group as opposed to disputes between classes.

A concomitant of the above is the ideological polarization that may color civil-military relations in non-African regions. Coup leaders in Latin America, North Africa, and the Middle East continually allude to the overthrow of "reactionary" forces at one extreme or "communism" at the other. While it is true that some of these mutterings lack substance and may serve as window-dressing designed to conceal the army's corporate interest or the personal ambitions of the principal contestants, nevertheless it is reasonable to assume that given the demonstrable class orientation of some Latin American and Middle Eastern armies, ideological factors can and do play a major role in setting the tone of armed intervention in those areas.

However, such considerations are as yet relatively absent in black Africa, and efforts to view intra-army or military-civilian fissures through ideological lenses may only mislead. For example, one observer of the Uganda coup of January 1971 has described the Amin takeover as a military "class action." The Uganda army, so the argument goes, although "not an economic class in the strict sense of the term" (at the time of the coup it exercised no control over the means of production) nevertheless by reason of the high salaries paid to its officers aligned itself with the Ganda civil service and coffee growers to topple the socialist Obote.[24] However there is almost no empirical evidence to support Michael Lofchie's claim, and most would accept the view that the Amin coup was primarily an attempt to "re-align the factions controlling the Uganda armed forces" by eliminating the threat posed by the alliance between Obote and his Acholi and Langi supporters in the officer corps.[25] As I intend to demonstrate with respect to Sierra Leone, it is the growth of cleavages *within* armies which probably forms the basis for most coups in sub-Saharan Africa.

Furthermore, and much to the annoyance of a number of western governments who themselves regard the ouster of Obote as a class action on behalf of the privileged and thus "friendly" elements, Amin in a number of respects has proved to be substantively more radical than his civilian predecessor both by his expulsion of Uganda's Asian population and through the development of relations with Libya and other Arab socialist states. Nevertheless these actions have served primarily a legitimizing and regime-maintenance function and cannot be really compared to the revolutions wrought by the Boumediennes and Qaddafis whom Amin so admires. The departure of the Asians has helped Amin to project himself as a man of the people while his chumminess with Qaddafi has been primarily self-serving as it has resulted in an influx of modern weapons for use by the Uganda army and the admission to training facilities in Libya for Ugandan officers. Certainly in most of black Africa the notion of a class polarity in its purest sense— peasantry, urban proletariat, urban bourgeoisie, and landowning aristocracy—does not as yet conform to sociological realities and thus should not be permitted to intrude into scholarly discussions of civil-military relations.

Aristide Zolberg in fact notes that military takeovers have not occurred "within a context of well-defined institutions anchored in a social structure with a clearly-defined stratification system." In most African states, the military rarely constitutes "an *elite* or *stand* which is clearly differentiated in terms of socialization, recruitment, and behavior, from other groups which contain potential rulers."[26] It is true that with a growing discrepancy in Africa between the life styles of the elite and those of the masses, class as opposed to primordial, ethnic, and regional loyalties will become undoubtedly more important. In a time of rising unemployment and other dislocations brought upon by the unwillingness of the politicians to meet the welfare needs of the comman man (as opposed to satisfying their own special needs for conspicuous consumption), African armies conceivably could become far more aware of their society's inequities and prepare themselves to strike against those held responsible for socioeconomic disequilibrium. This appears to have been the case in Ethiopia where the military intervention of 1974 resulted at least partially from the widening gap between a traditional aristocracy and the peasantry—a gap rendered all the more acute by prolonged drought in the Ethiopian countryside. In view of the feudal nature of Ethiopian society—unique in sub-Saharan Africa—and in view of the relatively sophisticated nature of the army's officer corps, further research on civil-military relations in that country should take a very serious look at the avowed intention of the Provisional Military Administrative Council to transform Ethiopia into a socialist state.[27]

Nevertheless, in the foreseeable future, the revolutionary pretensions of most African military establishments which have seized power should continue to be treated with considerable skepticism, and the concept of such establishments as purveyors of class interests will contain little relevance to the African dialectic. Certainly this seems a valid observation for a country such as Dahomey where the latest in a continuing succession of military governments recently has declared itself to be in favor of Marxism-Leninism and has formed "Defense of the Revolution Committees." According to one source, the sudden "conversion" of the army regime of General Mathieu Kerekou to Marxism and the formation of the revolution committees was simply a pretext for spying on civil servants who had objected to the imposition of economic austerity measures.[28]

Finally it is questionable whether the ideal-type organizational models can contribute much to our understanding of African civil-military relations and specifically the modalities of army rule since this approach begins with the assumption that armies are cohesive, integrated, nationalistic organizations capable of transmitting western value systems to disorganized societies. One lone defender of this view as regards sub-Saharan Africa is Ernest LeFever:

African armies tend to be the most detribalized, Westernized, integrated, and cohesive institutions in their respective states. The army is usually the most disciplined agency in the state. It often enjoys a greater sense of national identity than other institutions. In technical skills, including the capacity to coerce and communicate, the army is the most modernized agency in the country.[29]

LeFever's description of the African military, however, hardly seems to be supported by the evidence. Not only are most of these armies tiny in proportion to the overall population of the various states but rarely have their officer corps displayed a sense of unity placing them safely beyond the reach of the forces of fragmentation and decay that manifest themselves in the civilian sector. All too often, the so-called military establishments are usually little more than heterogeneous collections of men in arms under the command of officers whose sense of belonging to an honorable profession guided by well-established norms and regulations is as yet only dimly perceived. In many cases, the initial decision to preserve these ex-colonial armies and to rapidly Africanize their officer corps had its origins in the urge of the first generation of ruling civilian elites to attach symbolic content to their newly acquired political independence.

Eschewing attempts to explain army intervention in Africa in terms of the inherent characteristics of military organizations, most of the current writing on the subject tends to emphasize the political origins of the coup d'état. The military is said to intervene in reaction to events *x, y,* and *z* which are taking place in the civilian sector. J. M. Lee, for example, in his *African*

*Armies and Civil Order,* favors the "army in society approach" in his discussion of the reasons for the sudden spate of coups d'état. The term "civil order" is meant to refer to the acceptance by all the various political actors of "certain norms within a broader definition of the state than that provided by the formal institutions of government, which help to remove the higher degree of uncertainty that might otherwise prevail in political negotiations."[30] In the absence of civil order—a condition Lee finds prevalent throughout black Africa—it is rare for the "political leadership at the territorial level . . . [to] renounce the opportunity to reach a solution by violent means."[31] Political competition on the basis of the rules of the game is soon discarded in favor of open, nonregulated competition with the first one past the gate "taking all." The transfer of formal political power from the metropole to the successor elites resulted in the most tenuous acculturation of Westminister parliamentarianism. It was into this environment of declining consensus that the military forces—so long merely an instrument of internal security—found themselves attracted as if metal to a magnet. In his analysis, Lee draws extensively upon the Zolberg notion of a "shift from power to force" in African states whereby the relative "value of political parties and of civilian administrative agencies has undergone a sort of deflation, while the value of the police, of the military, and of *any* organization capable of exercising force . . . has been vastly increased."[32]

Ruth First also adopts a power politics approach in her quasi-journalistic analysis of several "coup casebooks."[33] The army is viewed as one of three elite groupings in Africa—the others being the politicians and the civil servants—who are locked in a continuing struggle over the right to manage the system. Having little more than token access to the ownership of the means of production, the participants in that struggle seek to control the government machinery and therefore the key levers of the economy. Coups are thus to be interpreted as raw power grabs whereby the political influence previously exercised and in most cases monopolized by nonmilitary actors can now be enjoyed by army officers who choose to leave their barracks in the pursuit of higher ambitions. First's analysis is welcome in that it lays primary stress upon the competition among elites of roughly parallel socioeconomic backgrounds rather than the competition among classes that so often shapes civil-military relations in other parts of the developing world.

In an effort to avoid unicausal interpretations of military takeovers in black Africa, one scholar lists "significant factors" that helped precipitate military takeovers. Welch traces the appearance of the coup d'état in Africa to eight factors, not all of which, of course, are necessarily present at a given time. He identifies the "declining prestige of the major political party; . . . the schism among prominent politicians, thus weakening the broadly based nationalist movement that had hastened the departure of the former colonial power; . . . lessened likelihood of external intervention in the event of military uprising; . . . 'contagion' from seizures of control by the military in other African countries; . . . domestic social antagonism; . . . economic malaise, leading to 'austerity' policies most affecting articulate, urbanized sectors of the population; . . . corruption and inefficiency of government and party officials, a corruption especially noticeable under conditions of economic decline" and "heightened awareness within the army of its power to influence or displace political leaders."[34] Coups are therefore to be interpreted as a military response to political decay.

Given the obvious fact that African military governments scarcely have the wherewithal to rule without civilian support, the net effect of successful interventions is the creation of "administrative states" that may bear a marked resemblance to the colonial system of government. Military-civil service alliances are often forged in order to stress continuity and to proceed with the act of governing. With the removal of the political brokerage function previously carried out by political parties, the rights and privileges of the so-called traditional authorities are usually revived.

Most writers view such alliances as natural concomitants to a convergence of interests between groups who heretofore had been subjected to harassment by civilian rulers. Thus in Ghana, the military, the civil service, and the leading chiefs had all stood by as their respective spheres of influence were eroded by Nkrumah and his CPP lieutenants and thus were prepared to join hands in a common endeavor to restore a kind of quasi-colonial status quo in Ghana. The civil servant apparently admired the approach of the National Liberation Council to disciplined administration. Regarding the chiefs, the "lack of even a nominal base meant that the only political platform the NLC and its appointees had in the rural areas was that provided by the traditional authorities."[35]

It is one thing, of course, to establish a purely administrative state devoid of the mobilizing ideologies that characterized the previous civilian regime; it is quite another to foster political development and specifically political participation. Thus while it is true that the first military government in Ghana did succeed in restoring democratic rule of the multiparty type, a second coup in 1972 testified to the exceedingly fragile nature of the earlier restoration. In every other African state, a return to civilian rule usually has been followed by another successful coup or a series of coup attempts, as in Dahomey. Army regimes, possibly excepting that headed by Mobutu Sese Seko in Zaire, have not managed to create alternative political bodies that are more than paper organizations. The very imposition of a "no-party" state has meant that political power remains largely in the hands of military cliques in alliance with certain civilian administrators or technocrats who have found their positions relative to the nonelites and to the former political elites enhanced by the presence of men in uniform. While recognizing the capacity of the African military to work out seemingly stable relationships with some civilian actors, Welch, for one, nevertheless concludes that the African military "cannot build legitimate political institutions through the use of force; they cannot transplant their organizational style to the civilian realm; they are not equipped to bring stability, modernization or political participation; and they lack sufficient flexibility and innovativeness to govern effectively."[36] This view of the African military is now almost universal among academics.

The recent surge of interest in African civil-military relations no doubt has been useful for acquiring general insights into the subject matter at hand. At least some of the factors discussed by Welch could conceivably be quantified on a cross-national basis although no one has yet endeavored to do so in a systematic way. For example, it might be possible to determine to what extent coups were positively correlated with precoup indices of civilian elite instability. Comparisons of various rates of economic growth with the incidence and frequency of military intervention in a sample of black African states might yield some important data. On the other hand, it no doubt would be difficult to measure "declining prestige," or the "contagion effect," or for that matter the "inefficiency of government and party officials." One also would be confronted with the problem of determining which of these factors is the most significant in any given situation. Furthermore, while everyone would agree that there are probably inefficient officials in the Zambia government, that country has yet to experience a coup d'état. The Uganda coup of 1971 did not trigger similar coups in neighboring East African states.

One must also wonder whether in fact we are asking or even know the right detailed questions about the origins of military intervention in black Africa or about the conditions under which takeovers occur. One scholar, despairing over what he regards as the chaotic state of civil-military relations theory concerning sub-Saharan Africa, asks us to "try straight historical studies" on the belief that "at least the need for historical studies of the actual conditions of actual military intervention seems to be the implication of the many doubts that students have expressed about generalizations concerning military intervention."[37]

I believe that it is not sufficient to stress the praetorian syndrome or merely to list factors contributing to army intervention since this mode of analysis tends to perpetuate the scenario of precise boundaries between the civilian and military sectors. Armies are seen as lurking in the shadows waiting to pounce upon the politicians when "things fall apart." In this way, army officers are said to detect a general state of malaise or disequilibrium in their societies. This kind of rational juxtaposition of military and political systems may serve to conceal the more subtle interaction between officers themselves and, more importantly, between officers and civilians—especially politicians—over a distinct period of time. Perhaps it is within this rather complex spectrum of civilian and military intercourse that the actual preconditions for intervention are established despite the junta members' proclamation to the world that they have intervened to exorcise evil from the system and, by so doing, to restore "purity," "balance," and "good" as opposed to "corrupt" government.

In order to move beyond a basic praetorian model that traces the emergence of coup-minded armies to disequilibrium and/or stalemate in the civilian sector, the sociological characteristics of military hierarchies should be probed and their potential for cleavage determined. Generalized fragmentation which can manifest itself both within the military subsystem and within the larger political system may constitute the essential stuff of coups. A recognition of the phenomena of military takeovers as perhaps the end product of intraelite fissures cutting across fragile civilian-military boundaries should help to fathom the "story behind the story" so often overlooked in comparative studies of civil-military relations. Thus the covert rather than the more readily quantifiable overt factors behind military intervention in African politics can be analyzed more fully. One will also no no doubt become more wary of ex post facto explanations offered by some coupmakers who may find it politically expedient to blame their treason upon the various ills of civilian society. Finally, one should be able to discard the somewhat simplistic notion of "reactive militarism" whereby armies first diagnose the malaises in the polity and then act to remove them in the way a surgeon removes cancerous tissues.[38]

Once the complexity of the army's praetorian mission in black Africa is recognized, a number of more relevant questions about civil-military relations may be asked. First, one should begin distinguishing between "predisposing" causes of military intervention on the one hand and "precipitating" causes on the other. This distinction might also be considered in terms of primary versus secondary causes or between those that are chronic or endemic and those that operate as catalyctic, short-term agents. Thus while the rioting and thuggery associated with Nigeria's Western Region elections in October 1965 might have helped to trigger the January 1966 coup d'état, it was probably the interhierarchical cleavages in the Nigerian officer corps which constituted the predisposing incentives for the army to forsake its apolitical role.

One should also endeavor to comprehend the manner in which intramilitary disintegration relates to intracivilian disintegration and to explore the possibilities of cross-boundary linkages capable of reinforcing such fissures and rendering them overtly political. Thus while the idea of African military organizations conforming to the ideal-type of integrated, cohesive

entities can probably be dismissed, any study of civil-military relations cannot avoid altogether having to take a serious look at these organizations. As
most of these armies experienced a complete turnover in senior personnel
with the departure of expatriate officers, they can fail easily to perform up to
the expectations of their creators. They are especially susceptible to competition among the higher ranking officers for control of the military "turf"
and, perhaps at a later stage, for control of the political system as well. In
fact, the appearance of intraorganizational disequilibrium in the military
rather than the army's politicization or "growing awareness" of its special
position in a larger universe may be the most critical theme in the eventual
politics of the coup d'état. This should be particularly true when the society
fails to offer the military establishment any tangible or constructive role to
fulfill. Officers beginning to quarrel among themselves assert particularistic
claims to the few staff and command positions available. As civilian cliques
penetrate the organization and support the goals of military cliques, the
latter may choose to intervene on behalf of the former. When intraorganizational disputes, particularly at the senior levels, operate in conjunction with
disputes among civilian factions, military takeovers may be the preordained
outcome.

There is above all a need for a systematic examination of civilian control
mechanisms in sub-Saharan Africa to determine how such mechanisms function and why they so often break down. A number of countries such as
Tanzania (after the Colito barracks mutiny of 1964) and Guinea have sought
to create "political" armies by bringing them safely under the wing of the
party and its accompanying ideologies. Others including some of the Franco-
phone countries concluded arrangements with their former colonial patrons
whereby European troops could be called in to save the government in question from the wrath of its own army. These are of course the more obvious
methods of civilian control. Perhaps less intuitively perceived are those
methods found in African states that are neither guided by avowedly socialist single parties or that can rely upon an implicit or explicit threat of outside
intervention as a check against potential or actual military unrest. In country
after country of these categories civilian control has been sorely tested or else
has not managed to work at all. It is not altogether clear how such mechanisms have attempted or are attempting to cope with the specter of a rebellious army. Linkages of one kind or another were presumably formed between civilian and military leaders in order to facilitate a proper monitoring
of army sentiments. Elementary notions of reciprocity conceivably could be
called into play whereby army officers might agree not to intervene as long as
certain "rewards" were forthcoming from the civilian sector. In other words,
these officers might undertake rescue operations on behalf of the civilian
ruling group that finds itself under attack from its multifarious critics.

Such issues can be adequately explored only through a case study. Questions of the interaction of an army with its political environment over a period of years and under differing sets of circumstances—as opposed to the precise moment of the heralded coup d'état—require in-depth exploration at the microlevel. I would endorse the case-study method despite my recognition of its limitations, not the least of which, as Martin Kilson has pointed out, is that this approach can never "really prove anything general."[39] The case study, however, can reveal to us elements and especially nuances of political behavior that normally would be overlooked by the observer of such behavior on a cross-national scale. Hopefully and at the very minimum, a case study of civil-military relations in black Africa can yield the kind of data with which we can begin to wrest some conceptual order from out of the present theoretical confusion.

In order to accomplish the above task, I chose to focus upon the West African state of Sierra Leone. In the thirteen years from independence in 1961 to 1974, Sierra Leone has experienced a wide variety of attempts by its armed forces either to influence the political system or to dominate it altogether. These have included military plots which never moved much beyond the drawing board stage, attempted coups, successful countercoups, and a thirteen-month period of military rule. Certainly on anyone's ranking of states in Africa that have experienced chronic elite instability, Sierra Leone has become decidedly praetorian.[40] The most dramatic example of this occurred in March of 1967 when the current army force commander, Brigadier David Lansana, intervened on behalf of the ruling Sierra Leone Peoples Party (SLPP), declared martial law, and placed the leader of the just victorious opposition All Peoples Congress (APC) under house arrest. Two days after Lansana's takeover, the force commander was in turn arrested by a group of senior officers who immediately set up a military junta, the National Reformation Council. Overt military rule lasted only thirteen months before the army rank and file, themselves fully aware of the power behind the barrel of the gun, arrested all commissioned officers, gazetted police officers, and restored civilian rule.

Military coups d'état or attempted coups have since become an inevitable by-product of political change in Sierra Leone, especially during periods of heightened competition among civilian cliques. In March 1971, for example, at a time of renewed intraelite fragmentation and some four years after the Lansana intervention, the new force commander, Brigadier John Amadu Bangura, tried to overthrow the APC government. Bangura served as de facto head of state for a mere four hours prior to being arrested by his subordinates who disassociated themselves from the Brigadier's actions and remained loyal to the civilian ruling group. In July 1974, a civilian-army coup failed and the plotters were sentenced to death.

Military participation in Sierra Leone politics has at times suggested a kind of formless, random dynamic with no rules or structure. But this was not always the case. Prior to the Lansana "noncoup" in 1967 and the formation of a government by a group of army majors, Sierra Leoneans displayed a remarkable ability to make Westminster parliamentarianism work. Two political parties, the ruling SLPP and the opposition APC, represented the capital city, Freetown, and its provincial hinterlands in the House of Representatives; and neither party—contrary to trends elsewhere in Africa—appeared willing to go all out to eliminate the other. A significant measure of law and order prevailed in the country, and coercion of the kind experienced in Ghana and Nigeria prior to the military intervention there could rarely be discerned in Sierra Leone.

The army itself remained a low-profile institution at least until 1966 and never played a significant internal security or "Congo" role. One seminal account of Sierra Leone politics notes that "up to 1967 the little coastal state of Sierra Leone maintained a political system marked by vigorous competition between parties, and by numerous opportunities for the expression of diverse and discordant views, despite the fact that the pressures working against 'open' politics were no less severe than those found in neighbouring states."[41] A reporter for *West Africa* expressed similar sentiments in 1964: "Togo, Dahomey, Gabon—all these show that however tiny an army may be, it can still play a key role in a country's politics," but "above all, nobody can believe that Sierra Leone is in the slightest danger of political trouble from its army . . . partly because of the nature of Sierra Leone . . . but . . . also because the Sierra Leone officers and, above all, Colonel David Lansana are, and are known to be, dedicated professional soldiers."[42] None of this, however, really mattered in the long run. Military intervention and military rule came to Sierra Leone, albeit in a kind of half-hearted bumbling fashion; and while the country experienced only thirteen months of government by decree, the specter of the coup d'état was now firmly rooted in the body politic.

Our search for the underlying elements shaping the Sierra Leone experience in civil-military relations will require us to consider the nature of civilian control of the military prior to the Lansana coup. We shall pay special attention to the ways in which the political style of the ruling SLPP dictated the modalities of civilian control. In order to understand why the Party's executive proved ultimately incapable of maintaining a politically neutral army, we shall have to ponder the nature of civilian-military cross-boundary linkages, some of which were operative as far back as the late 1950s during the final era of the colonial army. Ours will be essentially an elite-oriented model of civil-military relations, squarely in the tradition of earlier studies of African politics that emphasized the primacy of civilian elites. However, we shall have to chronicle the swift rise of military elites, the formation of alliances of convenience between military clients and their civilian patrons, and the various primordial factors—ethnic, family, regional, situational—which in Sierra Leone's case determined the structure of these alliances. We hope to contribute to a broader understanding of the civilian control mechanism in sub-Saharan Africa, particularly in those states not led by radical or mobilizing parties.

Having traced the evolution of civilian-military linkages we shall then consider the impact of such linkages on the maintenance of cohesion within the military organization and more directly upon intra-army clique formation. We intend to demonstrate that intraorganizational weaknesses having begun to manifest themselves in late 1965 and early 1966 were soon exacerbated by both civilian in-groups and civilian out-groups. It shall be our principal contention that the predisposing causes of the 1967 intervention were to be found neither in the general disintegration of the political system nor in the declining legitimacy of the civilian regime. Rather it was as a result of the internal power struggles which were so characteristic of the Sierra Leone army from 1965 to 1967 and onto which were grafted disputes among civilian actors that the seeds of military praetorianism were planted.

True, at a later juncture as the stakes of the political game were raised, the system as a whole began to decay; and this decay culminated in an inept attempt to rig a general election following an apparent stalemate between contending political forces. However, system disintegration in the waning months of SLPP rule was at best the precipitating cause of the Lansana and later the Blake intervention. Analysis of civil-military relations in Sierra Leone during that period should demonstrate that army regime references to civilian corruption and economic collapse were simply devices seized upon by the junta to legitimize its rule. When, for example, the National Reformation Council stated that its intervention was motivated by the "almost total breakdown of law and order, bloodshed and imminent tribal war"[43] this was more a caricature of the Sierra Leone political situation than a description of reality and simply served as one among a number of "causes" presumably dished out for public consumption. It is interesting to note here that when Lieutenant-Colonel Etienne Eyadema, the Togolese army chief of staff, led a bloodless coup in that country on January 13, 1967, he stated that he had done so in order to stop the political confusion which had created a "psychosis of civil war."[44]

Consideration of the predisposing reasons for the breakdown in civilian control of the Sierra Leone military will be followed by a detailed examination of the Lansana and anti-Lansana coups from the perspective of interelite interaction. By so doing I intend to demonstrate the key involvement of civilian actors in these coups. At least in the Lansana coup, the civilian-military participation ratio was heavily weighted on the civilian side. This involvement of civilian cliques in military coups suggests a promising new area of enquiry particularly as it demonstrates the fact that civilians may be prepared to exploit their contacts with army officers either to retain power or conversely to obtain it. Recent coup plots uncovered in Ghana, the Ivory Coast, Liberia, and Dahomey apparently have all involved substantial participation by civilian opposition groups bent on inciting the overthrow of the government. Coup situations in fact may tend to strengthen preexisting civilian-military alliances and perhaps to create new ones.

Discussion of the March 1967 coups will then lead us to a consideration of the rule of the National Reformation Council. We intend to probe the formation of civilian support mechanisms based upon a convergence of special interests. Our study of the military regime in Sierra Leone will permit us to scrutinize some of the more fashionable theories about the method and content of army rule in black Africa to which we alluded earlier. Specifically we can test empirically the concept of a national alliance between the junta, the bureaucracy, and the traditional authorities. We shall also examine the relative impact of the regime upon the rural areas vis-à-vis the headier, more sophisticated atmosphere of Freetown. Finally we shall consider the army's efforts to achieve regime maintenance through the acquisition of a wider public acceptance of its right to rule. The success or failures of the NRC's efforts to be regarded as "legitimate" are shown to hinge ultimately on the regime's ability to foster a civilian-military dialogue and to convince all concerned that its much publicized plans for a return to civilian rule were actually credible ones.

Having studied in depth how a military regime works, we hope to be in a better position to assess the potential of African armies for contributing to political development in Sierra Leone and elsewhere. Specifically we should be able to determine whether Zolberg's somewhat pessimistic assessment of the situation—to wit that "the arrogant self-assurance of military officers that they can govern with greater wisdom and skill than their civilian countrymen leads them to come down with a heavy step where angels fear to tread"—is in fact the correct one.[45] This book concludes with an account of the so-called "privates' coup" of April 1968 and will offer some observations on Sierra Leone's civil-military relations in the post-NRC era.

# 2
# COLONIAL RULE AND THE SIERRA LEONE ARMY

## BACKGROUND

The forerunner of the present day Sierra Leone army was constituted in 1901 and named the Sierra Leone Regiment, West African Frontier Force (WAFF). The battalion consisted largely of former members of the disbanded Frontier Police, the force instrumental in suppressing the famous Hut Tax Rebellion of 1896. The WAFF itself simply provided an administrative umbrella for the preexisting constabularies in Nigeria, the Gold Coast, and Gambia.

The Sierra Leone Battalion like its sister units throughout English-speaking West Africa became upon its founding a purely colonial vehicle. African officers were therefore unknown—the African rank and file receiving all of its orders from Europeans. Throughout the decades prior to the outbreak of World War II, this battalion was engaged almost exclusively in the enforcement of the imperial version of law and order. Internal security operations involving troops of the Sierra Leone army were conducted in 1919 in Freetown against rioters discontented with Syrian traders believed to be hoarding large quantities of rice.

In 1926, a strike by the Railway Workers Union to protest wage scales and inadequate workmen's compensation broke out in Freetown and quickly spread along the main railway line to Pendembu on the Liberian border. Troops were called in as a "show of force," and serious incidents were avoided largely because of the prudence shown by British officers who resisted the demands of the rank and file to open fire on the strikers. Finally, in 1931, a Mahdist-type prophet by the name of Idara circulated throughout the Kambia district, emploring villagers not to pay their house tax on the grounds that Mohammed had replaced the British as "ruler of the world." Idara's followers quickly armed themselves, and several platoons of WAFF soldiers were despatched to the area; this action resulted in the deaths of the leaders of the uprising.

Only the intrusion of two world wars managed to upset momentarily the routine of barracks life and the occasional mounting of a small-scale internal security operation against dissident natives. With the outbreak of the first global conflict, the Sierra Leone army along with contingents of the imperial garrison based in Freetown assisted in securing the capture of Douala in what was then German Cameroon and took part in the final drive against German troops along the Cameroon-Spanish Guinea border. During World War II, the Sierra Leone Regiment reached a strength of three battalions, two remaining in Freetown for garrison duties with the third joining the Nigerian and Gold Coast Regiments as part of the 81st and 82nd West African Divisions. Sierra Leoneans were called upon to engage the Japanese in Burma either as carriers or as actual combat troops who participated in the decisive battle of Myohaung.

## THE ORGANIZATIONAL STATUS QUO

Several writers such as Valerie Bennett and Chester Crocker have considered in some detail the changing role of the Royal West African Frontier Force (the title of "Royal" was conferred on the WAFF in 1928) in the postwar years prior to independence and have pondered the transfer of military institutions from the War Office to self-governing states followed immediately by the Africanization of the officer corps. By the early 1950s, the Labor Government in Britain had reached the inevitable conclusion that, if for cost reasons alone, there would never be a West African army to replace the "loss" of the highly professional Indian Army. According to Valerie Bennett, "both the pressure on the pound and the pace of constitutional change in the Empire encouraged the British Government to give local personnel increased responsibility, to make their insistence that the colonial governments assume a greater share of the costs of colonial forces more palatable."[1] In line with these policies, a conference of War Office and West African government representatives met in Lagos in 1953 and, "impressed by the urgent need to provide for an increasing flow of African officers into the West African forces," set forth a number of recommendations.[2] These included plans for the formation of cadet training units, boys' companies, an increased number of openings for West African cadets at Sandhurst, and provision for a greater number of short-service commissions at the Eaton Hall and Mons Officer Training Schools in England. For their part, the governments of Gambia, Sierra Leone, the Gold Coast, and Nigeria agreed to increase the size of their contributions to the annual recurrent costs of maintaining their respective forces—the remaining balance of funds would continue to be provided by the United Kingdom. The Sierra Leone delegation offered to increase their country's contribution from £ 66,000 to £ 100,000 per annum, although this still represented less than 2 percent of the total cost of maintaining the entire RWAFF establishment in a given year.

The decisions taken at the Lagos Conference with respect to the West African Forces produced few substantive changes in the Sierra Leone Regiment. Bennett and N. J. Miners have documented the various factors that militated against rapid localization and Africanization in the Ghanaian and Nigerian military forces after 1953. These included the conservative mentality of British army officers which augured against rapid promotion of too many Africans so as to maintain "standards" and "efficiency" in the army. This exclusiveness would likewise isolate the War Office in London from local nationalist aspirations manifested in demands for more African faces in responsible positions.[3] All of these factors were operative in Sierra Leone.

Africanization of the Sierra Leone military forces was practically nonexistent throughout the 1950s. Of twenty places reserved at Sandhurst for West African candidates on a biannual basis after 1953, only one was set aside for a Sierra Leonean. Short-service commissions for serving NCOs and warrant officers offered another mode of entry into the officer ranks, but rigid selection criteria applied here as well as for Sandhurst candidates. Between 1951 and 1959, only three Sierra Leoneans demonstrated sufficient promise to be granted such a commission following a short course at Eaton Hall.[4] Of these only one eventually received a regular Queen's commission before independence in 1961. By that time four Sierra Leoneans, three of them Sandhurst graduates, held a regular commission in the army; however, it was not until August 1960 that there was a Sierra Leonean major. A pilot scheme for a cadet training unit did not become operational until 1961; and although a boys' platoon was established in 1955, only one member of that platoon eventually became an officer.

The rate of Africanization in the army officer corps contrasted dramatically with developments within the civil service. In 1949, for example, Sierra Leoneans accounted for 13 percent of the total number of senior pensionable posts. Ten years later, over half the posts in the senior service were held by

Sierra Leoneans; and, were it not for an increase in the overall establishment particularly in certain technical fields requiring further contracting of overseas officers, the percentage of posts held by Africans undoubtedly would have been even higher. Salaries in the army did keep pace with those in the civil service, although its prestige and the possibility for a relatively swift promotion made the civil service a far more desirable outlet for a young Sierra Leonean's aspirations than the army.[5] Thus even though a newly commissioned officer could expect to earn as much as, if not more than, a university graduate upon appointment to the civil service, the "glory of wearing an academic hood," as Miner notes with respect to Nigeria, "was unbeatable."[6] In Sierra Leone, there was only one officer during the 1950s, Andrew T. Juxon-Smith, who had acquired a reasonably good record in secondary school and who therefore might have sought a university degree. This officer eventually was persuaded to join the army. However, his choice of a military career was considered somewhat odd, given the usual aspirations of his contemporaries.

## POLITICAL TRANSFORMATION AND THE SIERRA LEONE MILITARY

The nature of political change in Sierra Leone throughout the pre-independence period has been discussed by Martin Kilson and John Cartwright. Both scholars emphasize the traditio-modern origins of the Sierra Leone political elites who came to power in 1951 under the banner of the Sierra Leone Peoples Party. Their rise followed the introduction of certain constitutional arrangements that allowed for an unofficial African majority in the Legislative Council and, some time later, the assumption of ministerial portfolios by Africans on a limited scale in the Executive Council. Unlike their counterparts in the CPP in Ghana and the NCNC in Nigeria, the SLPP leaders acted out the "leading roles in the modern political system," on the strength of their ties with the traditional ruling class and on the basis of educational and occupational achievements. Kilson notes that "whereas the average rate of literacy for the country was between five to ten percent, some 30 percent of the SLPP members had attained higher education, and 61 percent secondary education."[7] The bourgeois nature of the SLPP colored their attitudes toward the colonial dialectic and resulted in a go-slow approach to the dismantlement of empire in Sierra Leone. The gradualist posture favored by the SLPP and, in particular, its older, more conservative members such as Dr. Milton Margai, probably contributed to a lack of interest in military affairs especially with respect to the issue of Africanization. Furthermore many Sierra Leoneans, particularly those "men of learning" who monopolized the bureaucratic, judicial, and political roles, viewed the army with contempt—a necessary institution to keep handy in case the mob rioted, but hardly a suitable place for a young man with ambition.

The local press, for example, seems to have paid little or no attention to the careers of those Sierra Leoneans who undertook military training in Great Britain; this in stark contrast with the often excessive attention lavished on those who went overseas for academic studies. The *Daily Mail* editorialized on 13 April 1956 on the way in which Sierra Leoneans, particularly those with "all the letters" after their name, tended to disparage things military: "All soldiers are considered to be of the same category, that is, 'they are a menace to education.' In all respects, ex-servicemen and serving soldiers are looked upon as worthless beings. There is no public interest in the Sierra Leone army." While this kind of attitude was embraced with special zeal by the Creoles, there is little reason to doubt that such views were shared by the SLPP ruling group—which included a number of Creoles—as well.

Those few Sierra Leoneans who embarked upon a military career during the 1950s tended to be regarded by prominent civilians as "small boys" even in those cases where the officer in question could claim a "big man" as his relative. David Lansana, the first Sierra Leonean and fourteenth West African to be commissioned in the RWAFF offers a case in point. Born in March 1922, the son of a farmer-trader who happened to be related to the local chief in Mandu Chiefdom, Eastern Province, Lansana received only a primary school education, although he was enrolled for a brief time at Union College, Bunumbu, which served as a training institute for primary school teachers. During World War II, Lansana worked as a clerk for the Admiralty in Freetown; and after enlisting in the RWAFF in August 1947, he was assigned to the Military Records Office. Following a course at the Eaton Hall Officer Cadet School, he became a second lieutenant in February 1952. Given his limited education and humble origins, Lansana's receipt of a commission scarcely rendered him an influential in Sierra Leone society. Nevertheless, the *Daily Mail* was somewhat hopeful on this score and in an editorial published in 1956 about Captain Lansana asked: "What has the future in store for this very much alive 34-year-old Sierra Leonean who has broken through all the taboos by making a career in the Army in this country worthwhile."[8]

Lansana's sole mode of access to elite status came as a result of his marriage in 1957 to the sister of a prominent Paramount Chief, Madam Ella Koblo Gulama, herself the daughter of P. C. Julius Gulama, a benefactor of Albert Margai. Madam Gulama was an avid supporter of the SLPP and later would serve as minister without portfolio under both Sir Milton and his brother. Yet even with his marriage to Komeh Gulama, Lansana remained a peripheral figure in Sierra Leone ruling circles. He was subservient by and large to the whims of his superiors, the civilian leadership, who eventually would call upon him as their chosen servant to help ensure the survival of a political dynasty. In a society where elite status flowed from educational background and occupational achievement, a military career was thought to be reserved for those who just couldn't make the grade in civilian life.

Only a handful of Sierra Leoneans took much of an interest in matters that could be construed as bearing on civil-military relations. In June 1949, the African mayor of Freetown, Dr. E. H. Taylor-Cummings, addressed the Sierra Leone Ex-Servicemen's Association (SLESA) on the occasion of its second annual rally and stated that he hoped to see Sierra Leoneans training as officers as was the case in the Gold Coast and Nigeria.[9] In 1954, one African member of parliament expressed "disappointment" that so few Sierra Leoneans were being trained at Sandhurst. He also noted that "those who are being sent are mostly those who have passed through the rank and file in the R.W.A.F.F." and asked "that steps are taken by this Government to get boys from our secondary schools who are interested so that we will have more Africans as Cadets and as Commissioned Officers in our Armed Forces."[10] Two years later, I.T.A. Wallace-Johnson, a fiercely nationalistic MP, discussed racial discrimination in the battalion: "Is Government aware that there is at present existing a feeling of dissatisfaction among African personnel in the Army in regard to what is considered to be either racial or colour discrimination in the award of the privileges of training for promotion to the rank of officer?"[11] Johnson further noted that African NCOs were being issued third-class warrants for travel by train to the provinces while Europeans of similar rank were permitted to travel first class. Though valid, these criticisms were only rarely voiced as few, if any, SLPP leaders felt inclined to probe into military affairs or to make an issue of them on the floor of the House of Representatives. It was not until 1958 that a SLPP member requested detailed information on the rate of Africanization in the Royal Sierra Leone Military Forces, and Milton Margai's revelation that the army contained only three African captains out of an overall officer establishment of sixty provoked little discussion. It also must be remembered that the size of the Sierra Leone contribution toward the annual recurrent costs of the Regiment amounted to only fifteen percent of the total cost of maintaining the establishment. For this reason, Sierra Leone's leverage in military matters was strictly circumscribed.

Throughout the 1950s circumstances required the participation of the Sierra Leone Regiment in times of political confrontation. Except for one important instance, however, this participation became increasingly marginal and secondary as the police force developed more of a paramilitary capability. While the need for War Office economies in the late 1940s and early 1950s ruled out any increase in the manpower of the 1,300-man army, such increases were far more feasible for the police force since the costs involved could be charged entirely against the Sierra Leone vote without subventions by the British taxpayer. Accordingly, after 1952 the Sierra Leone force was doubled to equal the size of the army, equipped with rifles and other non-lethal weapons such as tear gas, trained extensively in riot control, and in 1954 stationed in the provinces. The greater prominence accorded the police in Sierra Leone enabled the governor to engineer a more flexible response to political disorders than previously.

The first use of the battalion in any concerted way during the postwar period occurred on February 11 and 12, 1955 following an outbreak of rioting and looting in Freetown preceded by labor union unrest. Clashes between policemen and rioters near the Ross Road Police Station in Freetown's east end prompted a request by the commissioner of police for military assistance, and two companies from the battalion were dispatched from Wilberforce Barracks at 2:25 PM on the afternoon of the eleventh. The deployment of police and troops—some of the latter armed with automatic weapons—eventually resulted in an estimated 139 civilian casualties including eighteen deaths. In one instance three African civilians who were looting a Syrian shop were killed by automatic rifle fire from an army platoon although a Commission of Enquiry later held that the RWAFF had acted responsibly. In a number of cases of confrontation between rioters and soldiers, "a mere appearance of armed and disciplined men in strength at a crucial moment" had "a sufficiently awe-inspiring effect upon the mob to restore law and order for the time being without the use of force."[12]

Rural unrest also posed a threat to the maintenance of civil order in the pre-independence decade. The government response to the disturbances that spread throughout many northern districts in late 1955 and early 1956—largely in protest against the levying of a whole range of new taxes by paramount chiefs—differed somewhat from that employed during the Idara uprising in 1931 when a primarily military operation was undertaken. Now that the Sierra Leone police were stationed at various points in the Protectorate, there remained little need for actual military intervention except where the situation became drastic. While the police were ostensibly in the Protectorate to cope with increased crime in the larger towns near the principal mining centers, a government commission of enquiry into the anti-tax rioting stressed that the rural population tended to regard the police and army as one in the same:

. . . the first view of the Sierra Leone Police Force which most people in the disturbed areas have had is of steel-helmeted men armed with tear-gas and rifles in addition to the normal (and acceptable) batons. It must have been a considerable shock to see police in place of the unarmed constabulary of the previous days whose strength had been in their power of persuasion more than in weapons. Witnesses have referred to the Force as "soldiers."[13]

While the Regiment itself was placed on alert during the tax riots, clashes between the army and the civilian populace of the type observed in Freetown never materialized, and the twenty-three deaths recorded during the disturbances were as a result of police actions. The government did post a static guard at the Lungi airport, a signals unit in the Kambia District (the scene of some of the worst rioting) and in mid-December 1955, dispatched a company of soldiers on a "four-day tour of the provinces by motor vehicle and train" in order to "show the flag."[14] Members of the commission of enquiry, however, warned all Sierra Leoneans not to deceive themselves "into believing that the absence of military intervention indicates that only a minor disturbance has occurred."[15]

Apart from the continuing threat of urban unrest and anti-tax disturbances in the rural areas, the Sierra Leone government after 1954 faced a number of difficulties in the rich diamond-producing areas of Kono in the Eastern Province. Well-organized groups of "illicit diamond miners," many of them financed by wealthy Lebanese merchants and consisting by and large of tribes not indigenous to the province, attempted to conduct their diggings on lands held in concession by the Sierra Leone Selection Trust (SLST). Clashes between gangs of African miners and police became a commonplace occurrence particularly after 1957, and as many as 600 police including an auxiliary force and the SLST security guards became involved in the Kono operations.

Contingents of the Sierra Leone Regiment were posted to the Kono District as a kind of static guard in order to allow the police greater freedom to conduct highly mobile actions against the illicit diamond miners. At the peak of the disturbances in late 1957 and early 1958, two companies of the battalion, one from Moa Barracks in Daru and the other from Freetown, were assigned to the area. The first lorry load of troops arrived in Kono on August 30, 1957 and took up defensive positions around the SLST plant at Koidu which had been occupied and, thus, considerably damaged, by a group of miners six days previously. On September 14, more soldiers moved into the area, this time to guard other SLST installations. According to the colonial secretary: "The army was sent in order to safeguard lives and property and to allow the police to extend their operations whilst the army was on guard duties. . . . The role of the army in Kono has been of a non-combatant nature."[16] In at least one instance, army units were used to conduct arrests of chiefs thought to be sympathetic to the rebel miners. For the next several years, SLST officials, the commander of the Sierra Leone Battalion, and the commissioner of police coordinated security arrangements in the Kono area;

but although the army was placed on continual alert, it rarely saw any action.

The use of army and police forces to deal with the problems of rural and urban populism in Sierra Leone was apparently with at least the tacit approval of SLPP ministers and did provide a possible issue of contention for those groups objecting to the hegemony of the SLPP. Cartwright suggests that "the uprisings in both urban and rural areas of Sierra Leone, and the SLPP government's reluctance to deal with their root causes, indicated bright prospects for an opposition party that could transform this discontent into political support."[17] Two political parties, the United Sierra Leone Progressive Party (UPP) founded in 1954 and the Peoples National Party (PNP) founded in 1958 by several younger ex-SLPP members, offered a considerable challenge to the ruling SLPP. Although their efforts were never sustained, these two parties endeavored to establish their radical, modernizing credentials with revelations of SLPP complicity with the British in calling out the army and the police.

The UPP was led by a Freetown barrister, Cyril Rogers-Wright, who made a name for himself as general council for the Sierra Leone trade unions during the Shaw Commission hearings. According to the report of that commission, Rogers-Wright "fulminated" against the security forces and mentioned in particular the "wild, indiscriminate, and vengeful shooting, including the promiscuous use of automatic weapons, a callous disregard for the lives of unarmed and innocent civilians, and indifference to the sufferings of the wounded."[18] Three years later, an editorial in the newspaper *Shekpendeh* (which was personally owned and operated by Rogers-Wright) portrayed the army as a political tool of the ruling group.

A Government which depends on guns and blood to make its authority felt is worthless and grossly incompetent. In our recent history, innocent blood has been shed on account of the incompetence and inactivity of the S.L.P.P. Government. No more blood must be shed at Kono or elsewhere and the money spent in maintaining the police and military forces there must be more usefully spent otherwise. The S.L.P.P. Government stands condemned for the blood of many Sierra Leoneans.[19]

A member of the PNP executive committee blamed the SLPP for "shooting people:" "It was the SLPP that killed so many people at Kono on account of diamond smuggling. They are also responsible for the killing of people during the northern riots . . . and souls were again lost in Freetown, when soldiers were called in by the SLPP."[20] Question time in the House of Representatives afforded an additional opportunity for members to criticize the government's internal security policies. T. S. Mbriwa, leader of the Kono-based Kono Progressive Movement (KPM), spoke of the SLPP-SLST alliance to exploit the people of that district and condemned the use of "terrorist and repressive means to maintain law and order."[21] A police report mentioned "political elements" in the Kono district "who issued a weekly news sheet in which individual police officers and their men were vilified and held up to ridicule," resulting in "increasing hostility to the police throughout the distict."[22] Where the army itself carried out arrests in Kono, there was a marked increase in support for the KPM and its left-of-center challenge to the SLPP.

While opposition charges of SLPP "militarism" reflected a good deal of sheer opportunism, there is little evidence to indicate a discrepancy of views between members of the SLPP and their colonial overlords on the subject of internal security. Just as the elitist nature of the African ruling group militated against demands for a swift replacement of white with black faces in the army, so did the SLPP hierarchy, in its distrust of mass politics and "disruption," favor a law-and-order approach to unrest fomented from below. During the early 1950s, SLPP leaders such as Milton Margai and his younger brother Albert worked ceaselessly to persuade their allies, the paramount chiefs, that it was in the interest of both groups to support the introduction of armed police from the Colony into the Protectorate. Dr. Margai (as he was called prior to being knighted in 1959) explained to members of the Protectorate Assembly in 1951 that "disorders are becoming prevalent in the Protectorate" and "it is essential that we safeguard the property and lives of the individuals in the country." He recalled that in a chieftaincy dispute in Kailahun District, the district commissioner and his court messengers ". . . were really unable to stop people from looting the whole town and doing irreparable damage to the Chief's compound."[23] Many chiefs feared that by stationing armed police throughout the rural districts, their chiefly prerogatives might be infringed upon, particularly those that applied to the administration of native law. Intensive lobbying by the Margai brothers both within the Protectorate Assembly and in the Legislative Council, however, succeeded in persuading the chiefs as to the efficacy of the police in helping to suppress political disorder.

The deployment of police and army units in Freetown, the northern province, and in the Kono area failed to provoke any negative response by SLPP ministers; and, although no one is guilty merely by association, it should be relatively easy to postulate a convergence of interests between colonial officials and their African partners on the necessity for such deployment. In 1955, the SLPP had particularly good reason to favor the mustering of armed police and troops since the houses of several ministers including one owned by Sir Albert Margai had been looted by mobs. Eight years later, in an independent Sierra Leone, the Council of Labor hinted that it would stage a general strike in the absence of the prime minister in England. The acting prime minister, Dr. John Karefa-Smart, announced that should such a strike occur, the Government would take the "strongest measures to protect all citizens." On his return from Great Britain, Sir Milton suggested that the Sierra Leone labor leaders had decided eventually against calling a general strike because "they knew how we dealt with them in 1955."[24] As for the anti-tax disturbances, the government expressed "its appreciation of the admirable mixture of restraint and resolution with which the Police Force discharged its duty" and "wished to record its approval of the Police action taken and its undiminished confidence in the officers concerned."[25]

Joint army-police actions in Kono also received the support of SLPP leaders. Thus, in early 1959, the SLPP went on record as follows:

In Kono illicit mining has got worse during the last two months and has now reached the point where if it is not stopped it will imperil the whole economic and constitutional future of the country. The Government intends to take whatever measures may be necessary to stamp out this crime against the country.[26]

In March of 1959, the Sierra Leone envoy in London, A. B. Cotay, a close personal associate of Sir Milton and an SLPP stalwart, told a gathering at the Royal Commonwealth Society that "the Army is in Sierra Leone solely to protect the commercial interests of Great Britain."[27] Actually, the SLPP had a considerable stake in the suppression of illicit diamond mining and smuggling as exports of industrial diamonds accounted for a substantial percentage of Sierra Leone's foreign exchange earnings. Cotay explained that the army was "under readiness for the area and this had had a *sobering* effect."[28]

Some debate ensued within the ruling party as to a postindependence role for the Sierra Leone army—much of the discussion centering on financial considerations. The cost of maintaining military forces in a small, economically unviable state may divert scarce resources away from the more urgent task of economic development. This is especially the case if one takes into account the "administrative tail" required to support even a single-infantry battalion and the salaries paid out to seconded British NCOs and commissioned officers. These burdens became the formal responsibility of the Sierra Leone government on January 1, 1959 with the relinquishing of War Office administrative control and the transfer of the Tower Hill Barracks (which had served as headquarters for the Sierra Leone and Gambia Districts, RWAFF) to the local authorities.[29] In the speech referred to earlier, A. B. Cotay maintained that Sierra Leone lacked the financial base to support any military forces no matter what the size of the establishment. The government subsequently issued a statement explaining the system of British subventions designed to offset purely local revenues for the purposes of meeting regimental expenses.

The former secretary-general of the SLPP told me that some of Sir Milton's advisers sought to expand the battalion and "make it more important."[30] If this were in fact the case, their views never became public at least through the medium of the local press. Others apparently favored a "Gambian solution" involving disbandment of the army and creation of a de jure paramilitary police.[31] According to Gutteridge, Dr. Karefa-Smart, who assumed the portfolio of External Affairs and Defense immediately following independence in April 1961, was "prepared to discuss openly the pros and cons of military nakedness."[32] Sir Milton, for his part, is said to have had an eye for the ceremonial and to have understood the importance of ceremony in the wider process of gaining independence. At the time of an army exhibition of military hardware, the prime minister explained to the audience how "sorry that he was not able to be at the Trooping of the Colour ceremony" of the week before.[33] Sir Milton also wanted to make a Sierra Leonean contribution to the defense of the Commonwealth. Delegates attending the London Constitutional Conference held in April and May 1960 learned that "Her Majesty's Government and the Sierra Leone Government had agreed that a Defence Agreement providing for mutual cooperation in the field of defence should be negotiated, to be signed after independence."[34]

The presence of the militant Sékou Touré as an immediate neighbor raised the specter of interstate friction, and in October 1960 there were rumors in Freetown of troop movements on both sides of the Sierra Leone-Guinea border.[35] The problem of internal security, of course, could not be wished away simply because of continuing unrest in Kono, and more importantly, the growing prospect of an opposition group that might not be willing to play the game of politics according to the rules. In September 1960, a new party was formed, the All Peoples Congress, led by the former trade unionist and SLPP Labor Minister, Siaka Probyn Stevens. The APC espoused a moderately radical line and, in particular, opposed any kind of postindependence defense arrangements between Sierra Leone and Britain. Just prior to independence, the APC "turned to more violent means of persuasion" and one APC leader, M. O. Bash-Taqi was alleged to have urged his supporters to attack ministers, "stop traffic, sink launches, stop trains" and to break up meetings of SLPP supporters.[36] The prime minister declared a State of Emergency on April 18, 1961, called out the military, and detained a number of APC leaders. According to Haywood and Clarke, "this involved the provision of patrols, piquets and extra-guards, so that every officer and other rank was fully employed."[37]

In the final analysis, it is highly unlikely that the SLPP gave much consideration to the future role of the tiny Sierra Leone army. The absence of parliamentary discussion on military affairs during this period supports such a thesis. The acquisition and maintenance of political power and not the rather mundane affairs of the military—the connection between the two was as yet unperceived—became the prime focus of concern for the elites. Those who held political office at the time of independence no doubt still believed that the army represented the state of Sierra Leone rather than the personal interests of any special group of individuals. No one challenged the notion of the military as the selfless servant of the country, and, as long as British officers remained in positions of control, the army could be isolated effectively from the political divisions which prevailed at the time. To the extent that the army served any legitimate purpose at all, it was to mount an honor guard at the airport for some visiting Head of State or to assist the police in suppressing popular discontent. Beyond that, the Sierra Leone battalion was a rather unimportant organization with little or no influence on political developments.

The Sierra Leone Regiment of the Royal West African Frontier Force became the single battalion army of an independent Sierra Leone in April 1961. For some sixty years, that battalion had acted out a largely marginal, perfunctory role in the general scheme of things—namely as the ultimate trump card in the enforcement of the rule of law. Throughout the interwar period the army periodically came to the aid of the civil power. In the postwar decade, a strengthened police force, trained in the performance of internal security duties as opposed to the mere detection of crime, gradually replaced the battalion itself as the most thoroughly operational deterrent to political unrest. Nevertheless, the army remained at Wilberforce Barracks on a hill with a magnificent view of Freetown; and, when the occasion warranted, came down into the city to "rescue" the police as in 1955 or to perform static guard duties in the provinces, thereby releasing the police for paramilitary operations of their own.

In no sense could the Regiment be regarded as a productive institution. As if to break the monotonous routine of an army mounting a guard over its own barracks or trooping the colors for some visiting dignitary, army days were held and the people of Freetown invited to witness marching units and the firing of mortar shells. In 1960, a government report called attention to the "noticeable feats" performed by two companies of the Regiment "in making jeep tracks through dense bush . . . "[38] In that same year, the army "in addition to normal training carried out a number of company marches 'showing the flag' throughout most of the districts of the Protectorate.''[39] ''Showing the flag,'' as we have observed had become perhaps the army's major preoccupation throughout the colonial period ever since the last of the so-called punitive expeditions was conducted against the Kissi tribe in 1907.

In the next Chapter we shall demonstrate that while colonial patterns of civil-military relations were scarcely tampered with during the first few years after independence, nevertheless the army did experience certain internal changes that would eventually render it more susceptible to penetration from without. The influence of ethnicity upon civil-military relations will also be considered although it will be seen that the ethnic factor did not assume any special importance until after the accession of Albert Margai to power in April 1964. It was only then that the ethnic consciousness of certain officers was definitely heightened as perhaps the first step in the transformation of the Sierra Leone military from a politically sterile organization into an activist but fragmented and coup-minded body of men.

# 3
# *THE ARMY UNDER*
# *SIR MILTON MARGAI*

ROLE CONTINUITY

In a passing-out parade held for new recruits at Juba Barracks in March 1961, the governor of Sierra Leone, Sir Maurice Dorman, offered some cogent advice to a platoon of soldiers who, in a month, would serve in the army of an independent state. The governor focused most of his attention on the relationship between the African enlisted man and the hierarchical command system—both civilian and military—of which he was an integral part. Dorman warned the African rank and file that the accession to an independent status for the Colony and Protectorate of Sierra Leone carried with it fundamental responsibilities and noted in passing the example of the former Belgian Congo where "many soldiers thought that Independence meant freedom to do whatever they wanted, and that has brought great confusion to their country and great harm to the soldiers themselves."[1] Unquestioned obedience and service to the Queen, Country, and Government—these qualities should guide the behavior of the men who would constitute the Sierra Leone military forces.

Dorman's speech to the Kaladan platoon at Juba Barracks prompted one Freetown newspaper to comment on possible patterns of future civil-military relations in Sierra

Leone. The editorial suggested that Dorman's advice "should be passed on to the whole Sierra Leone Military Forces, and the attention of the Officers in both the Army and Police should be especially called to it." Part of this editorial deserves quotation in full:

When Sierra Leone becomes independent it is important that members of the police and military forces clearly understand that whatever might be their polititical complexion or outlook their duty lies with the legitimate government.

Nothing could be more dangerous than tribalism and politics entering the ranks of the army or police force.

No military or police force riddled with tribalism or politics can effectively protect its country, thus the Governor's advice though very simple, is of great importance and should not be taken lightly if members of both the army and police are to fulfill their obligations to their country."[2]

Though in retrospect, much of this exposition displays remarkable predictive powers both for Sierra Leone as well as for other West African states, analysis of the tone of civilian-military interaction during the formative years of independence in Sierra Leone suggests continuity rather than any sharp breaks with the colonial past. Military praetorianism generally has its roots in the designs of civilian authorities to restructure the colonial army.[3] However, throughout the period of Sir Milton Margai's premiership—from April 1961 through April 1964—efforts at redefining the existing system of civil-military relations to conform with the needs of an independent country do not seem to have unduly preoccupied the attention of the ruling elite. The Sierra Leone army remained a shadowy institution whose role or status in the developing polity attracted little public interest.

Under the provisions of an Ordinance promulgated on April 27, 1961 and modeled after one governing the operation of the Nigerian army, the Royal Sierra Leone Military Forces became an independent organization.[4] The mere legalization of an independent Sierra Leone army scarcely precipitated any special excitement. Newspaper accounts—such as there were—recalled the "glorious victories" achieved by the battalion throughout the Burma campaign rather than sketching out a vision of the "new" Sierra Leone army. The palm tree insignia of the RWAFF became the Regiment insignia while the battlefields of Burma were enshrined in the Myohaung officers mess and the Kaladan and Arakan platoons. The annual celebration of Myohaung Day on January 24th helped preserve the mystique of the past. Finally, the traditional red fez and cumberbund remained the ceremonial uniform of the battalion.

In strictly financial terms, the battalion continued to rely heavily upon military assistance from Great Britain, partly in the form of provisions for

Sierra Leone cadets to receive officer training in that country. The two governments, under agreements reached at the London Constitutional Conference of 1960, also concluded arrangements for financial subventions on a tapering basis to cover the capital and recurrent expenditures required to maintain the Sierra Leone army. Of a total of £ 829,000 provided for defense expenditures in 1959, the British government contributed £ 590,000. By fiscal year 1963-64, this subvention still represented almost one-fourth of the total expenditure on the army, although in the following year Sierra Leone assumed full financial, as opposed to merely managerial, responsibility for her armed forces.

The maintenance of RWAFF insignia, uniforms, and nomenclature evidenced the role continuity for the Sierra Leone army which undoubtedly helped foster an impression that the army would never become "important," at least not by eschewing subordination to civilian authority in the pursuit of decidedly nonmilitary goals. It is true that in strictly formal terms, the SLPP government paid a ritualistic deference to the role of the army as defender of the state against external enemies and as a member of the United Nations peace-keeping force in the Congo. An official policy statement in November 1962 explained that "in order to be on the alert against aggressive attacks on Sierra Leone, Government maintains the Royal Sierra Leone Military Forces." The statement added that "these forces will also help us to fulfill certain international responsibilities which may become obligatory on us as a member of the United Nations."[5] The traditional notion of a military establishment as a bulwark against external aggression, however, does not seem to have applied seriously to the Sierra Leone case. The bourgeois SLPP leadership in Freetown, along with their Creole allies in the civil service and the judiciary, shared a community of interests with the Americo-Liberian ruling group in neighboring Liberia, so that by no stretch of the imagination could the government have been alluding to Liberia as an aggressor.

The breakaway Republic of Guinea posed a different problem. Sékou Touré's militant Pan-Africanism could not be reconciled easily with Sir Milton's pro-British, "functionalist" approach to inter-African political issues. Guinea had since become a member in good standing of the Casablanca bloc while Sierra Leone's sympathies lay with the more moderately disposed Monrovia grouping. Allegations in late October 1962 of Guinean financial assistance to the opposition All Peoples Congress augured against any substantive rapprochement between the two states. It is worth noting that Sir Milton's reference to the possibility of aggression from without followed immediately upon revelations in the press of a Conakry-APC axis. Sékou Touré, however, had yet to evince an interest in such interventionist stratagems favored by Kwame Nkrumah; so that he, unlike Nkrumah, was more favorably disposed to respect the sovereignty of his immediate neighbors. That Sir Milton never lobbied for military expansion or for new weaponry also might suggest that the prime minister did not regard the Guinean army as a serious threat to Sierra Leone sovereignty.[6] Border disputes, traditional sources of friction between states with overlapping ethnic groupings, never became a major issue in Guinean-Sierra Leone relations. Population movements—largely consisting of Fulani traders—rarely were impeded by the authorities on the border although there were occasional incidents of smuggling. In the final analysis, it seemed highly unlikely that Guinea's 5,000-man army would ever clash with Sierra Leone troops.

In light of the remote possibility of West African interstate warfare involving fixed battles between national armies, the United Nations Congo Operation in the early 1960s afforded a singular opportunity for a number of states to deploy their troops outside the home territory, thereby reformulating the image of a purely colonial military establishment.[7] Three months after Sierra Leone joined the world organization, the government in Freetown announced that a company-sized contingent of troops would see duty in the Congo under the command of a British major accompanied by a Sierra Leonean deputy commander and two African platoon leaders. The contingent left for Leopoldville on January 23, 1962 and was replaced in July of that same year by a second contingent of 120 men which served in the Congo until March 1963. Both contingents were attached to the fifth battalion of the Queen's Own Nigerian Regiment.

One Sierra Leonean reporter, writing for *West Africa,* viewed the dispatching of a Sierra Leone army unit to the Congo in heroic terms: "Although our army may well face great ordeals, perhaps even death, the Congo exercise will give them first-class training on what war is like in a far-off country."[8] Sir Milton for his part regarded the Sierra Leone military contribution as a useful means of asserting the country's independence as an actor in international affairs. Upon learning that the first duty of the contingent would require mounting a guard at Leopoldville Airport, he explained how "keen" the soldiers must feel to "show the new flag of Sierra Leone to the outside world" and added that the "first sight visitors and officials from many countries to the Congo will have of the UN Military Forces will be of you, the Sierra Leone contingent."[9]

In substantive, as opposed to purely symbolic, terms, it is doubtful that the Sierra Leone experience in the Congo did much to break the monotonous pattern of military life in an army which had historically preoccupied itself with the mundane duties of guarding the barracks, trooping the colors, and occasionally suppressing the Freetown mobs. The decision by the United Nations command to attach the Sierra Leone contingent to the fifth Nigerian battalion meant that the Sierra Leone troops would merely shift their place of operation without a concomitant shift in the mode of operation. According to one official report, the Sierra Leone company engaged in virtually no ''special supportive or non-supportive actions'' requiring patrols or combat.[10] This fact alone ensured that the soldiers involved could not possibly acquire those kinds of experiences—combatant or otherwise—that might be expected to boost the army's sense of mission or purpose.[11] Guard duties at Lovanium University, ceremonial parades at Leopoldville airport interspersed with some military training and opportunities for recreation at the Kitona military base—this was the sum total of the Sierra Leonean army experience in the Congo for the six African officers as well as the 240 African NCOs and enlisted men. Command opportunities for Africans never really materialized given the presence of two British majors, K. W. B. Sutton and A. E. Carter. Clearly little transpired during the Congolese experience that could be construed as precipitating role expansion.

On the home front, the public and the press displayed little interest in the entire operation—in marked contrast to Nigeria, where the ''exploits of the Army in the Congo received wide publicity and gave considerable boost to the army's prestige.''[12] The Freetown press rarely reported any details of Sierra Leone's participation in the Congo exercise and only occasionally mentioned the names of those Sierra Leonean officers servicing there. At one point the British commander of the first contingent complained about the lack of mail from the soldiers' relatives in Sierra Leone and made a direct appeal for more ''letters from home.''[13] A Sierra Leone Congo Contingent ''Comfort Fund'' designed to stir public interest netted some unusual but trifling contributions like the 5,000 cigarettes donated by Chief Justice S. Benka-Coker.[14]

In Sierra Leone, the army under the first SLPP government was largely a ceremonial mechanism—trotted out on occasion to greet the prime minister returning from trips abroad or to troop the colors for some visiting African head of state. Only sporadic forays into the Kono area to assist the police in rounding up criminals or the annual bush camps held in the provinces for instruction purposes served to break the daily routine. In 1965, the Governor-General, Sir Henry Lightfoot-Boston, in his annual address to the Sierra Leone House of Representatives called attention to what he termed the ''significant role played by Members of the Force during the Currency change-over and the funeral ceremonies of the late Sir Milton Margai.''[15] During the change-over to a decimal-system currency on August 4, 1964, a Bank of Sierra Leone report noted that ''the Royal Sierra Leone Military Forces also deserve special commendation for the vital part they played in distributing the currency prior to D-Day.''[16] A special train escorted by a military guard along with a number of army trucks was used to distribute the new currency and to retrieve the old West African Currency Board notes. In relative terms, 1964 represented an "active" year for the Sierra Leone military forces.

Apart from the continued relegation of the basic military function in Sierra Leone to glorified guard duties—albeit at one point requiring a shift in locale from Wilberforce Barracks to Leopoldville Airport and the Kitona base in the Congo—the army throughout the early years of SLPP tutelage experienced virtually no changes in its physical dimensions or technical structure, in short, no changes in its strictly military capacity. At the time of its founding in 1901 as the Sierra Leone Regiment, WAFF, the army consisted of a handful of rifle companies with only rudimentary supporting units. Sixty years later at independence, Sierra Leone still possessed a single battalion army of 1,400 men including approximately fifty officers. Except for a rifle company housed at Moa Barracks in Daru near the Liberian border to facilitate the rapid deployment of military force in the event of disturbances in Kono, all of the Sierra Leone troops occupied dilapidated housing at Wilberforce and Juba Barracks near Freetown. A headquarters company, staff offices, and related administrative services were to be found at Murraytown just north of Wilberforce on the Freetown peninsula. A tiny signals squadron typified the nature of the army's supporting services.

Military expenditures remained constant from 1961 to 1964 at approximately £ 800,000 per annum—the bulk of these funds being utilized for personal emoluments. Slight fluctuations in yearly defense expenditures could be traced in large part to rising tuition costs for Sierra Leoneans training at military academies in the UK. Troop levels were also unchanged so that the annual or biannual recruiting safaris usually conducted under the aegis of a British major working in conjunction with the district commissioners were tailored to maintain existing battalion strength. Defense estimates for those years did call for a number of improvements to the physical plant. African other ranks' married quarters, for example, were finally wired for electricity in 1962; and the Government embarked upon a five-year rebuilding program to ease crowded conditions at Wilberforce. In the process, however, the army acquired no heavy armaments such as tanks or armored cars that might have strengthened its combatant capacity and therefore its self-esteem as a military unit.

## INSTITUTIONAL MODIFICATIONS

The perpetuation of a minimal-visibility or low-profile military establishment in Sierra Leone during the reign of the first SLPP government did not preclude the occurrence of formal institutional changes within the army even though these changes did not lead to qualitative role expansion or the physical enlargement of the organization. This Africanization of the army officer corps developed initially through a greatly expanded intake of Sierra Leone cadets with a commensurate decline in the number of British officers on secondment to the Regiment and, much later on, by the promotion of Sierra Leoneans to senior staff and command positions.

On Independence Day, April 27, 1961, the Royal Sierra Leone Military Forces officer establishment of fifty-seven included but nine Africans, and of these only three at the rank of captain. As yet no African held the substantive rank of major, although David Lansana became a temporary or acting major in October 1960. By 1962, however, the percentage of African officers in a fifty-two-man establishment had risen to thirty while, at the time of Sir Milton's death in 1964, African officers now numbering thirty-four constituted 68 percent of the total officer establishment.

David Lansana became a colonel on April 24, 1964 with the official title of deputy force commander. This meant that in the absence of the British force commander, Brigadier R. D. Blackie, from June through August of that same year, Lansana assumed nominal control of the army. Furthermore, Major John Bangura, Sierra Leone's first Sandhurst graduate, received his promotion to lieutenant colonel on May 30, 1964 and subsequently assumed command of the first battalion at Wilberforce Barracks. Africanization of the army's noncommissioned officer establishment also proceeded at a steady pace during the years 1961 through 1964. By the end of 1963, expatriates held only twenty of 132 noncommissioned positions; it was intended that by January 1965 only five expatriate NCOs would remain, and these would perform certain noncombatant technical duties such as "radio artificer, medical laboratory technician, and bandmaster."[17]

Africanization of the Sierra Leone army officer corps—and, in particular, the vastly increased rate of Africanization in the immediate postindependence period—was facilitated by a number of policy changes within the military itself. Under plans drawn up at the time Great Britain agreed to underwrite the army on a diminishing basis through 1964; provision was also made for a stepped-up number of Sierra Leone cadets to attend military training academies in the UK. As in the past, a cadet could gain entry to the highly valued officer status either by attending an eighteen-month course at the Royal Military Academy at Sandhurst or, in the case of candidates for the "short-service" commission, a sixteen-week course at the Mons Officer Cadet School in Aldershot. It should be noted that in 1960 the Nigerian government made provisions for Sierra Leonean cadets to undertake their pre-Sandhurst and pre-Mons training at the Officer Training Wing of the Nigerian Military Training College (NMTC), Kaduna. Previously, the Teshie Officer Cadet School in Ghana had performed this service.

The decision to accelerate the rate of Africanization in the military's officer corps necessitated changes in the cultivation of a "proper" African officer. Since the Sandhurst course which led to the granting of the Queen's Regular Commission was both time-consuming and costly, the commissioning of short-service combatant officers had to increase even if, from the point of view of some British military authorities, it meant abandoning efforts to mold an elite African officer corps. Furthermore, only an average of two vacancies per year at Sandhurst were allotted to Sierra Leone in the early 1960s, so that reliance upon direct regular commissions could no longer be contemplated realistically if that country were to acquire an army truly her own. Thus of the twenty-three Sierra Leoneans who received their commissions (combatant) between 1959 and 1964, only seven passed out at Sandhurst, while the remainder completed the shorter and less expensive Mons course.[18] Most of the officers in the Mons category saw their short-service commissions converted into regular commissions within a matter of two years.

Having assumed full responsibility for the army in January 1959 the Sierra Leone government decided to revamp a number of procedures, in order to entice young Sierra Leoneans into what was still regarded, particularly in the Freetown area, as a low-status occupation. It was no longer sufficient to evoke visions of an army career as a builder of comradeship, decency, and honesty or as the best possible opportunity to serve one's Queen and Country. In a speech before students at the Albert Academy in 1959, Captain David Lansana paid deference to the "leadership-building" aspects of life in the military. In the same breath, however, he noted that potential short-service officers needed only four School Certificate passes (including English) in order to qualify. Furthermore Lansana stressed that military service as an officer would provide valuable experience for a future civilian career.[19]

In 1960 the government offered further enticements for those contemplating a military career by negotiating a general salary increase. The peculiar result was that a second lieutenant upon appointment to the Royal Sierra Leone Military Forces could now expect to earn more than a university honor's graduate entering the civil service, £ 720 as opposed to £ 684. Advertisements in the local newspapers spelled out the military salary range in considerable detail. Candidates for a commission learned that following a year's service as a second lieutenant and a subsequent promotion to the rank of lieutenant, they could easily gross over £ 900 per annum, including qualification pay, a tidy sum in a country with an annual per capita income of approximately $100.[20] Finally, the age requirement for entering short-service officers was raised to 25, thus accomodating those who, upon completion of several years of secondary education, had embarked upon civilian careers usually as minor clerks or primary school teachers and were now highly susceptible to the promise of greater earning power and the opportunity to travel abroad.

One final policy change deserves mention here. In June 1961, the government approved the opening of a Royal Sierra Leone Military Forces Secondary School for the coming fall term. According to an official announcement, the School "would produce Warrant Officers and NCOs for the Army," but it was expected that a number who did "particularly well" would be considered for officer training. The school planned for an eventual enrollment by 1965 of sixty-four boys. The army paid for their tuition plus room and board, although the parents or guardians of entering students were required to sign an agreement committing their sons to serve a minimum of three years with the army upon completion of their education. Graduates of the school who intended to become candidates for a commission would thus be expected to compete with their peers from civilian secondary schools. The hoped-for result of this competition was an increase in the quality of entrants into the commissioned ranks.[21]

Accelerated recruitment efforts in the Sierra Leone military tended to alter the source from which the cadets were drawn, particularly in the case of candidates for short-service commissions. During the 1950s those few Sierra Leoneans who received short-service commissions usually did so on the basis of their performance as enlisted men either as NCOs or as warrant officers in the army's technical and education branches. Lansana, as we have noted, toiled for over four years in the ranks before being permitted to attend the Eaton Hall course. Ambrose Genda, one of the most senior African officers in the army, enlisted in 1947 following the completion of primary school and served at one point as an "education instructor" (presumably teaching illiterates how to read and write). He did not receive his commission until February 1956. It was only in late 1958 that the first short-service commissions were granted to secondary school graduates who had been selected for training upon completion of their studies.

The government's commitment to Africanization changed this picture entirely. More and more the prospect of lucrative pay (in the context, at least, of a developing society), travel possibilities, and other assorted benefits attracted a number of secondary school graduates, even though a military career as yet conferred little of the prestige enjoyed by a civil servant with a university degree. This was particularly so in the Freetown area where Creole attitudes toward a military career were often assimilated by "up-country boys" who attended Fourah Bay College. However, lacking sufficient qualifications to warrant acceptance at a university, the young Sierra Leonean holding a General Certificate of Education could now earn a very respectable salary with little effort apart from some preliminary training at the NMTC, Kaduna, followed by four months at Mons.

Colonial recruiting practices during the middle and late fifties helped foster a considerable gap (even if this was not always reflected in terms of seniority) between the privileged few who qualified for Sandhurst and those officers with usually only a primary education who had often spent years in the ranks. Now for the first time, the bulk of the young army cadets with commissions had obtained a considerable level of education and had passed directly into the army. Between 1961 and 1964, except for a small number of NCOs granted administrative commissions in the Army Medical, Headquarters, and Transport Branches, the bulk of the short-service commissions fell to direct-entry secondary school graduates who probably anticipated a meteoric rise to the top even if this meant incurring the resentment of their colleagues who had struggled to gain recognition by their service in the ranks.

## THE POLITICAL ENVIRONMENT

Any observer of Sierra Leone politics in the early 1960s can hardly be criticized for neglecting to view the tiny Sierra Leone army as a potentially disequilibrating factor in Sierra Leone politics. To be sure, after Togo's President Sylvanus Olympio was assassinated in January 1963 by a group of rebellious veterans who had been recently discharged from the French army but had refused absorption into the Togolese army because of budgetary constraints, one needed few other reminders that any body of soldiers in sub-Saharan Africa could now operate as political adventurers. And yet in the Sierra Leone experience of the early 1960s, there seemed little reason for the army to exchange barrack duties for the more strenuous game of political intrigue. In short, Sierra Leone society manifested few of those early warning indicators of future military praetorianism, such as burgeoning ethnic divisions, elite corruption, flirtation with foreign ideologies, and single-party systems with reduced tolerance for the rights of minorities. On the contrary, both the ruling SLPP and the opposition All Peoples Congress (APC) displayed a rather notable regard for the democratic processes and a willingness to avoid simplistic or militant solutions to the problems of nation-building.

From its inception in 1951, the SLPP remained the party of the Sierra Leone bourgeoisie for whom ideology, party organization, and endeavors to mobilize the rural peasantry held little fascination. Thomas Hodgkin, in his pioneering study of African politics, juxtaposed "parties of personality" and "mass parties." Although some of Hodgkin's formulations have in recent years come under criticism from the revisionist school of Africanists, his description of the patron party does justice to the kind of political vehicle that was the SLPP.

Parties of the former type are dominated by "personalities", who enjoy superior social status either as traditional rulers or members of ruling fami-

lies, or as belonging to the higher ranks of the urban, professional elite (lawyers, doctors, etc.), or on both grounds. Their political machinery, central
and local, is of a rudimentary kind, consisting of those individuals, *chefs du
canton*, notables, men of property who naturally gravitate towards the party,
and function, intermittently and principally at election times, as a party
committee . . . They have little, if anything, in the way of a secretariat or
full-time officials: the work of running the party is regarded as a leisure-time
occupation of the party leaders.[22]

From the analysis of the SLPP—both during its formative years and later as
the government of an independent Sierra Leone—contained in studies of
Sierra Leone politics by Kilson and Cartwright, the party emerges as the
classic "patron" type described by Hodgkin.

As noted in an earlier chapter, the SLPP leadership was drawn almost
exclusively from the ranks of the professional classes and the traditional
ruling families in the provinces. In confirmation of Hodgkin, Kilson documents the "multiple office-holding" attributes of the SLPP "big men"—
lawyers and doctors who, besides serving as members of parliament, moon-
lighted as district councillors, city councillors, and members of Native Administrations.[23] The SLPP never worked to construct real party machinery,
manipulated traditional deference to chiefly office as a substitute for the
direct political mobilization of the peasantry, and most of all, never bothered to cultivate a nationalistic outlook. The SLPP became a party in the
western sense only at election time, as in the 1962 General Elections when a
manifesto was issued, membership drives initiated, and loudspeaker vans
toured Freetown and the provinces. In this loose association of elites which
called itself the SLPP, Sierra Leone found a reasonably effective guarantor of
pluralistic, competitive politics. Party strategy dictated the cooption of the
opposition through patronage and soothing appeals to national unity, rather
than seeking its outright elimination by whatever means possible including
detentions and formation of a single-party regime. This strategy was no
doubt at least partially influenced by the Creole value system that stressed
the efficacy of British legal institutions, free elections, and the peaceful
resolution of political differences. The 1962 general election, for example,
which saw a reduction in the SLPP plurality in the House of Representatives,
remains perhaps the fairest, most orderly election of its kind ever held in
sub-Saharan Africa. Of course, much of the high rate of tolerance for heterogeneity and personal liberties in the Sierra Leone political system during
the early 1960s reflected Sir Milton Margai's own cautious political style.

Lacking an ideology or even an interest in the precise formulation of party
policies, the SLPP leadership adopted an ad hoc approach to problem-solv-
ing—usually allowing the chiefs to deal with local issues and relying on
face-to-face contacts among the tiny elite in Freetown to work out the

running of government. Rarely did the SLPP enumerate a carefully considered party position on the so-called national issues. In short it would have been hard to determine with any degree of precision SLPP policy on such issues as economic development or Pan-Africanism. Government ministers rarely conducted their business in light of "what the *party* is thinking or would think" under such circumstances.

Given its patron-party style and, in particular, its lack of concern with policy formation, it would have been inconceivable for the SLPP to have adopted a clearly delineated stance on the subject of the Sierra Leone army. Elite distate for soldiers together with the absence of an overall ideological vision of the future Sierra Leone meant that the SLPP leadership inevitably displayed a negative bias toward military affairs. None of the few manifestos ever issued by the party mentioned the army or related SLPP plans for that organization. Parliamentary debates for the years 1961 through 1964 are almost devoid of any discussions of the military forces apart from an annual perfunctory question on the rate of Africanization, the tribal composition, and the size of the rank and file and officer establishments. No demands were ever forthcoming during this period for the purchase of new sophisticated weaponry, for new ceremonial uniforms, or for greater press coverage of the emerging African officer corps. Most important of all, the SLPP never seriously entertained any demands for the expansion of the overall military sector.

All of this contrasts sharply with the situation in Ghana where Nkrumah and the CPP leadership sought to integrate the military into Ghana's foreign policy. The expansion of the Ghanaian armed forces and the increased reliance upon military aid from the socialist countries was regarded by Nkrumah and by many of his more radical advisers as an inevitable concomitant to Ghana's "outer-directed," interventionist policies abroad. The more ideologically oriented, revolutionary-centralizing CPP dreamed of converting the former Gold Coast Colony into the fountainhead of African socialism and naturally regarded the army as one of the most visible symbols of that political transformation.

The SLPP did manage to construct a formal system of civil-military relations, albeit in a very rudimentary form. Following independence in April 1961, an embryonic Ministry of Defense was established, and the minister of external affairs concurrently assumed the Defense portfolio. Later that year, Sir Milton became his own minister of defense. The ministry itself consisted of a permanent secretary, who also served as secretary to the cabinet, as well as a handful of clerks and typists. The Royal Sierra Leone Military Forces Act also made provision for a Forces Council consisting of the force commander, the prime minister and the permanent secretary in the Ministry of Defense. The "operational use" of the army, however, remained the sole responsibil-

ity of the British commander, Brigadier Blackie; and Sir Milton is said to
have left military affairs almost entirely to the British officers at the army
headquarters in Murraytown. The fact that the permanent secretary of defense also acted as secretary to the Cabinet and that "few countries could
have as economical a Ministry of Defense as Sierra Leone"[24] gives us an idea
of the priority attached to such matters by the SLPP.

Two issues of national prominence in some African states—Africanization
and the question of ethnic balance (or lack thereof) in the military— under
certain conditions have introduced strains into the fabric of civil-military
relations particularly during the initial years following independence. In
Ghana, the first issue was dramatized by the rise of the militant wing of the
CPP. It exerted pressure on Nkrumah to expel the British chief of staff,
Major General H. T. Alexander, since his continued presence in the army
could not be reconciled with Ghana's "move to the left." In Nigeria, the
problem of achieving ethnic equilibrium in the army's officer corps assumed
vast political importance in 1961 when it became known that, as a result of
the superior educational facilities prevalent in the Eastern region and "an
only incipient military interest among the Northern elite,"[25] Ibos held over
75 percent of the commissions in the army. As Donald Horowitz notes, "the
proportions of various ethnic groups admitted to the bureaucracy are believed to be amenable to some form of political intervention," with the
result that "there is hardly an ethnically-divided country without its 'civil
service issue' and often those companions, the 'police issue' and the 'armed
services issue.' "[26] In Nigeria, the "armed forces issue" with its overtones of
"Ibo domination" of the officer corps aroused heated controversy, particularly in the north, and led to the imposition of regional quotas for entering
officers and made civil-military relations a key issue in Nigerian politics.

In Sierra Leone neither the Africanization nor the "tribal composition"
issue seriously affected the relations between the civilian and military sectors. Lacking any real ideology, the SLPP as a party never openly espoused
rapid Africanization. On those rare occasions when the subject reached the
level of parliamentary debate, SLPP MPs urged the necessity of Africanization of the army in rather cautious terms. For example, in December 1962,
an SLPP backbencher asked the prime minister about efforts being made
"to speed up effectively Africanization of the Royal Sierra Leone Military
Forces without in any way impairing the efficiency of our fighting forces."
Sir Milton's explanation, quite in keeping with his gradualist approach to
questions of institutional transfer, was that the "schemes in hand [were] the
speediest that [could] be effected without a serious loss of efficiency."[27]

Africanization did become a source of friction within the SLPP, as revealed in interviews with several of Sir Milton's cabinet ministers. Doyle
Sumner, Sir Milton's education minister, once stated that whenever Sir

Milton cautioned against over-zealous Africanization of the military, the majority of the cabinet ministers "got very angry with him." Gideon Dickson-Thomas, the former UPP member who held the Social Welfare portfolio in the United Front government, explained that the prime minister issued warnings against Africanization of the military although he "eventually deferred to the wishes of his cabinet" on this score.[28]

By 1964, the Sierra Leone army contained a number of officers—particularly those who belonged to the Mende tribe—who enjoyed family affiliations with members of the ruling party. Although the nature and political ramifications of these linkages between civilian and military will be explored more fully in our next chapter, we may conjecture here that, at least initially, such linkages served to hasten the Africanization process if only because a number of leading politicians may have expected "army jobs" for their less gifted brothers. Considerable attention, for example, was focused on the army career of David Lansana. After the 1962 General Elections, Lansana's sister-in-law, Madam Ella Koblo Gulama, a Mende paramount chief from the Moyamba District, became a minister without portfolio in the SLPP cabinet. Her rise into the party hierarchy received the blessing of the somewhat younger, more progressive members, especially Albert Margai who served as Sir Milton's finance minister. This group objected strenuously, although without any special persistence, to the prime minister's views on the so-called "expatriate question," among others.

Ella Gulama and Albert worked ceaselessly behind the scenes on behalf of David Lansana's military career.[29] They had expected Lansana to assume full command of the armed forces as soon as possible after independence even it it meant incurring the displeasure of Sir Milton who regarded Lansana as an ill-educated incompetent. Sir Milton's views were shared by a number of expatriate officers apparently including the last British battalion commander, who is said to have argued that Lansana "could not do the job," no doubt because of the latter's deficient education and his apparent inability to gain the confidence of the rank and file troops.[30] The prime minister, however, successfully neutralized the pressures brought to bear by the younger elements of the SLPP, and Lansana did not assume full command of the army until seven months after the prime minister's death. Once Albert succeeded his elder brother as prime minister in April 1964, the Margai-Gulama-Lansana axis acquired new importance and, in the process, radically altered the conduct of civil-military relations in Sierra Leone.

Just as the Africanization issue never engendered the kind of public attention that it received in places like Ghana, so the question of the tribal composition of the army officer corps remained a non-issue during the years of the first SLPP government. For the question of ethnicity in the military forces to achieve political consequence, there must exist two essential preconditions. First. the statistics ought to reveal a disproportionate number of representatives from a single tribe in the officer corps; and second, this imbalance must attract the concern either of government members who regard themselves as "underrepresented" in the army or of the opposition's members who believe that the ruling group is "over-represented."

An analysis of the tribal composition of the Sierra Leone officer corps in the years 1961 through 1964 reveals none of the glaring imbalances that so often characterized similar establishments in other African states. Before we examine the tribal structure of the military, it is necessary to offer a brief comment on the various ethnic groups which together form the people of Sierra Leone.

According to data derived from the 1963 census, two tribes, the Mende, who inhabit primarily the southern half of the country, and the Temne, who spread inland from the coast to an area north of Mendeland, constitute respectively 30.9 and 29.8 percent of a population of approximately 2.4 million. The Limba group which accounts for 8.4 percent inhabits primarily the Northwestern quadrant of the country. Fifteen minority tribes (including the Creoles) make up the remainder of the population. Finally it should be noted that some ethnic groups, on the basis of their geographical proximity to the Mende or the Temne (for instance in the "south" or the "north"), tend to identify with the two larger groups, so that tribal division in the country is often described in terms of the "southerners" versus the "northerners."

Let us postulate that the question of ethnicity in an African army, especially in the officer corps, will assume political overtones to the extent that tribal groupings are seriously out of line with the population as a whole and that this fact receives the attention of the politicians. Then we can perhaps explain the absence of an armed forces issue in Sierra Leone during Sir Milton's premiership by the fact that none of the aforementioned conditions had become relevant in the army. In April 1961, the Sierra Leone officer corps with an establishment of only nine Africans contained four Mendes, two Temnes, and three with mixed tribal ancestry. Temnes and Mendes together thus accounted for 66 percent of the tiny sample, with the Temnes somewhat underrepresented and the number of Mende officers exceeding the overall Mende population by 14 percent. In a sample of this size, however, a single "excess" Mende or Temne officer hardly could be considered statistically significant. Furthermore, marginal Mende overrepresentation in the army at this time could be interpreted simply as a legacy of colonial military policy. During the 1950s the three Sierra Leonean noncommissioned and warrant officers receiving commissions—David Lansana, Ambrose Genda, and John Kuyeembeh (who later retired)—were all Mendes. Mendes as a group enjoyed greater educational advantages as a result of the concentration of missionary and government-supported schools in the south and thus tended to predominate among the NCOs and warrant officers of the RWAFF.

By October 1962 in a sample of fifteen, the Mendes and Temnes accounted for 40 and 13 percent of the total, respectively. The Temnes thus continued to be technically underrepresented; however, if one includes two Koranko officers who came from the far north and who probably identified with the Temnes, the north as a whole was not suffering unduly. The most significant data available to us is that for 1964 (April) where there is a larger sample. Mende officers now constituted only 26 percent and Temnes 12 percent of a total sample of thirty-four Africans. Temne representation in the officer corps remained well below that of the Temne proportion of the total population, but so now did the Mende proportion. Minority tribes—most of them Muslims from the more sparsely settled regions of northern Sierra Leone—accounted for 62 percent of the officer establishment.[31]

If one averages the tribal percentages over a three-year period, 1961-1964, none of the gross imbalances that developed in sub-Saharan states like Nigeria and Kenya reveal themselves in the Sierra Leone officer corps. It would seem that at least as long as recruitment practices still fell under the primary jurisdiction of British officers, no single tribe in Sierra Leone acquired a favored position in the army. On the contrary, the steady increase in minority group representation throughout Sir Milton's time offers reasonable proof that tribalism had yet to infect the military subsystem. Suitability for an officer career based on achievement characteristics rather than ethnic or family background appears in general to have determined the level and quality of entering cadets, although admittedly there were exceptions. The absence of intra-army "parapolitics" at this time implied at least the tentative implementation of a professional military ethic while simultaneously ruling out future praetorianism of the kind initiated by tribal polarities within the officer corps.

Throughout the early 1960s, politics based on the assertion of primordial ethnic loyalties rarely surfaced in Sierra Leone, a fact that no doubt contributed to the lack of attention given the ethnicity issue in the military. Historically, the most conscious ethnic division in Sierra Leone has arisen between the peoples of the hinterland and the Creoles of the Freetown peninsula. The Creoles, because of their earlier access to higher education and their exposure to Christian norms, have long tended to deride those countrymen who, however well-educated, came from the provinces. Following the introduction of a limited "one-man-one-vote" constitution in 1951, the Creoles, although greatly outnumbered by those who came from the protectorate, did manage to perpetuate their monopoly over other key foci of power, notably the higher echelons of the civil service and the judiciary. However, traditional Creole distaste for things military forestalled the extension of the

Creole bureaucratic monopoly into the Sierra Leone army's officer corps. Furthermore, while a handful of Creole officers could always be found in the army, these officers rarely belonged to Creole families of any particular note. For this reason, there seems to have been almost complete alienation between the Freetown Creole elite and the officer corps, although opportunities for the formation of tactical alliances between Creoles and officers belonging to northern tribes always presented themselves. Except in very rare instances, however, the Creole-provincial division did not encompass the army.

Relations between the two major provincial tribes—the Mende and the Temne—though not wholly without friction (particularly when the two groups competed for employment opportunities)—were not as yet seriously strained in an overtly political sense. It is true that following the general elections of 1962, the SLPP began to acquire the label of the "party of the south" while the opposition APC, which picked up sixteen seats in the election, was generally associated with the north, especially with the Temnes. In actuality, the strong showing of the APC in 1962 could be traced more properly, as Cartwright states, not so much to a north versus south division as to a populist revulsion against the chief's abuses with which the SLPP was inextricably linked. The SLPP, after all, "had its own northern leaders such as Dr. Karefa-Smart, Y. D. Sesay, I. B. Taylor-Kamara, and Kandeh Bureh and all of its candidates were as much 'sons of the soil' as those put up by the APC."[32]

The slight Temne underrepresentation in the army might have provoked political discussion but for the fact, as we have already noted, that military affairs per se attracted little attention among the elites. Furthermore, for the APC to have raised in any serious way the question of ethnic imbalance in the officer corps would have been an open admission of a loss of faith in the efficacy and fairness of the two-party system. The APC, not as yet regarding the army as a political arm of the SLPP, had no reason to believe that, as an opposition party, it should be concerned that the proportion of Temnes in the officer corps was "insufficient." As it turned out, Stevens and his followers were generally well-treated by Sir Milton. The harassment and threats of extinction which accompanied life in the opposition during Sir Albert Margai's premiership, especially in the thirteen months preceding the military take-over of March 1967, were as yet inconceivable. In August 1961, following his release from detention, the APC leader declared that: "Independence having become an accomplished fact and the Government having given the assurance of General Elections in 1962, the APC calls upon all its members to maintain the Party policy line of (a) full respect for law and order (b) constitutional and lawful procedure in all matters. The APC has never stood, and will never stand, for violence, sabotage or unconstitutional action . . ."[33]

# 4

# *CIVILIAN CONTROL OF THE SIERRA LEONE MILITARY*

In June of 1964, the SLPP, under the guidance of a dynamic new leader, Albert Margai (who in January 1965 became Sir Albert Margai upon publication of the New Year's Honors List), held its annual conference in Makeni, the capital of Sierra Leone's northern province. Public attention focused on Sir Albert's vociferous, although largely ineffectual, plea for greater devotion to party discipline at the grass roots level and for the "speedy establishment of a national headquarters and party press." All of these proposals coincided with the new prime minister's endeavor to portray himself as a "mobilizer" or "man of the people" in opposition to the more conservative tendencies of his late brother, Sir Milton.

For our purposes, it was not so much the political substance of the convention itself, as some of the more behind-the-scenes developments that ushered in new directions for existing patterns of civil-military relations in Sierra Leone. Apart from the appearance of the prime minister and key SLPP officials, the convention was also graced by the presence of senior civil servants and by the army's David Lansana (then, the acting force commander) in addition to the newly appointed commissioner of police, William Leigh. Lansana was listed also as one of several prominent guests who attended the SLPP convention ball held on June 22, 1964.[1]

While the government would allege later that "security precautions" had warranted Lansana and Leigh's participation in the convention, the leading opposition newspaper, *We Yone,* drew a somewhat different lesson from the acting force commander's actions, as innocent as they might have appeared at the time:

So Colonel Lansana of the Army and Police Commissioner William Leigh were at the S.L.P.P. convention. . . .

One wonders what business the bosses of the police and the army especially, have in political party deliberations. Or, perhaps, they have a "soft spot" in their hearts for the new Prime Minister or for the S.L.P.P?

When top-ranking officials, in whose hands is vested such responsibilities as the maintenance of Law and Order and the preservation of the State begin to associate themselves with Party political activities, one is tempted to ask, Where are we . . . What are we heading for?

It is baffling enough to literate citizens and more so to the illiterate citizens in the Provinces who under such circumstances cannot but associate these officials with the S.L.P.P..[2]

Thus began Lansana's intimate association with Sir Albert Margai and the SLPP, an association, which, as we have seen, was initially forged in the latter half of the 1950s, and later strengthened but not culminated during the premiership of Sir Milton Margai.

Apart from the rather astute observations of *We Yone* on the matter, it seems unlikely that at first many people attached much importance to the presence of an army "representative" at an SLPP party convention. However, the cementing of a Lansana/Margai alliance in mid-1964—with Ella Koblo Gulama performing a useful mediating function—was merely the most blatant example of the new modes of interaction between the civilian and military sectors. These new methods of interaction grew out of Sir Albert's attempts to experiment with "home-grown" methods of civilian control of the military, which, when combined with the increasing incidence of organizational tensions within the army, brought about fundamental changes in the colonial pattern of civil-military relations.

There are a number of important theoretical issues useful for documenting these changes, considering them in light of the eventual military takeover in March 1967, and relating them to existing explanations of army intervention in sub-Saharan Africa. First is an examination of the methods of civilian control favored by a "patron-type" party operating—to borrow from David Apter—in a "reconciliation" political system under conditions of an Africanized, military force.

Second, since civilian control in Sierra Leone required a close linking together of the civilian and military elites, is the examination of those features of the political system that served to facilitate and reinforce such linkages. In so doing something must be said about certain socioeconomic characteristics that both groups of elites held in common. Such linkages apparently tended to prevent the development of precise boundaries of "competence" for the military and civilian sectors. Boundary diffusion in turn seemed to rule out a sustained process of institutionalization in the army, a process, which, if we call upon Huntington's description of political organizations in developing societies, takes into account the level of "adaptability, complexity, autonomy, and coherence."[3] Only in a perverse way, through its political intervention in 1967, did the Sierra Leone army become more "adaptable" as a result of the breakdown in boundaries between the military subsystem and the political subsystem. The development of civilian-military linkages hindered the ability of the army to remain politically neutral in the manner of the British and American armed forces.

A study of the flow of communications between civilian and military elites will broaden our understanding of the means by which intra-army disputes, once aided and abetted by cliquism in the political arena, can extend beyond the confines of the military establishment to be manifested as coups and countercoups. A final issue concerns the effects of nonmilitary praetorianism upon the coups of 1967. The kind of political decay, characterized by rural and urban violence, which has so often preceded military intervention in other African states (Nigeria from October 1965 to January 1966 and Ethiopia from late 1973 to September 1974 are important examples of this phenomenon.) arrived rather late during the postindependence era in Sierra Leone. Even when this variety of political disintegration did appear, it was muted and did little more than play a last-minute supportive role leading to the complete breakdown of ordered, civil-military relations. The origins of that breakdown must be looked for in the context of civilian-military linkages that were in the process of formation long before the Sierra Leone army decided to leave the barracks.

## CIVILIAN-MILITARY LINKAGES

The introduction of new forms of civil-military relations in Sierra Leone following the accession of Sir Albert Margai to the premiership was initially motivated by the changing political requirements of the time, and, in particular, by the need for the regime in power to safeguard its political destiny. Once he had succeeded his brother as prime minister following a bitterly contested struggle for the leadership of the SLPP, Sir Albert sought, on the one hand, to centralize the party's organization and, on the other, to move in the direction of a single-party regime in imitation of another West African leader, Kwame Nkrumah. Sir Albert's actions—the precise details of which need not concern us here—could not be regarded ostensibly as a by-product of any great ideological restructuring of the prime minister's views on government. It is true that he appeared inclined to flirt with foreign ideologies, and he went out of his way to cultivate the friendship of Sékou Touré and Nkrumah. None of these courtships, however, precipitated any drastic changes in the political system of Sierra Leone. Thus even though Sir Albert eventually sought to impose a single-party regime on the country, this only succeeded in raising the popularity of the APC which joined with opposition elements from within the SLPP to frustrate the prime minister's designs and to have him ejected from office following a general election.

The very elitist nature of the Sierra Leone ruling group—Sir Albert was a prominent lawyer and a successful poultry farmer in addition to his official duties—augured poorly for the substantive application of a leftist or revolutionary-centralizing ideology to Sierra Leone conditions. Even Sir Albert's sympathy with a single-party regime, especially after October 1965, reflected not a commitment by certain members of the ruling party to an abstract concept but rather the desire of the SLPP leaders and chiefs to protect their special class and personal interests against subversion by the more populist APC. The one-party state also appealed to the incumbent members of the SLPP who sought to entrench themselves against rivals in the SLPP elite. This emphasis on the safeguarding of ruling group privileges ultimately compelled the prime minister, perhaps unconsciously at least in the initial stages, to experiment with a special method of civilian control over the military, aimed particularly at connecting members of the SLPP executive to senior army officers. The SLPP method of civilian control envisaged, often with considerable modification in terms of its intensity or depth, the consolidation of civilian and military elites, with a pivotal role being reserved for the force commander. To this end, Sir Albert apparently solicited and received the support of his closest SLPP followers. However, before we can consider in detail just how this approach to civilian control of Sierra Leone's single-battalion army was implemented, we must consider the organizational changes wrought by the new government in the Royal Sierra Leone Military Forces.

The conversion of an established pattern of civil-military relations in Sierra Leone from one characterized by "objective" expatriate control to one involving control by the SLPP executive could not have been possible without a significant acceleration of the government's Africanization program in the army. The possibility for sociopolitical intercourse between the civilian and the military elites required the promotion of a number of Africans to positions of responsibility in the military and the commensurate reduction of British personnel. Since coups d'état in other sub-Saharan African states generally have followed the departure of expatriate officers, it is reasonable to assume that the latter may perform a useful "buffer" role—perhaps through their special intelligence networks—thereby restricting any possible avenues of significant penetration by outside political influences.

In Sierra Leone, British officers such as Brigadier Blackie had enjoyed a cordial working relationship with Sir Milton and probably did little more than exchange pleasantries with the prime minister at social occasions in Freetown. These officers exercized a de facto monopoly over control of the army, and contacts that may have arisen between a few Sierra Leonean officers such as David Lansana and the younger supporters of Sir Albert Margai in the SLPP could merely set the stage for future intrigue once the locals had assumed command. For it was not until Sir Albert's time that Sierra Leoneans in any significant numbers replaced expatriates in the key staff and command positions, although a number undertook staff training at British defence colleges in the early 1960s.

Between May 1964 and March 1967, the years of Sir Albert Margai's premiership, a truly Sierra Leonean military force became a distinct reality. We have noted previously that at the time of Sir Milton's death, some sixteen British officers on secondment continued to hold staff and command positions in a fifty-man officer establishment. By June 1967, at the time of the first passing-out parade held at the newly established Benguema Military Academy, the Sierra Leone army could claim an establishment of eighty-eight officers of which only three were British. On January 1, 1965 David Lansana became force commander,[4] and by early 1966 Africans also held the positions of deputy force commander and battalion commander, as well as all the company and platoon commands. The two general staff positions usually held by officers with the rank of major were also Africanized, and Sierra Leoneans for the first time commanded such "specialized" units as the military training company at Juba barracks, the officer academy at Benguema, and the Ordinance Depot at Murraytown. The few remaining British officers held such relatively innocuous positions as Army bandmaster or force paymaster so that their influence in matters of civil-military relations was negligible. In March 1967 at the time of the military intervention, the Sierra Leone officer corps contained one brigadier, a colonel, a lieutenant-colonel, four majors, and ten captains.

The introduction of indigenous civilian control over the Sierra Leone army in the years 1964 through 1967 presents a number of difficulties for the researcher trying to decipher its effects on civil-military relations in that state. The major difficulty arises from the fact that the process, at least until its later stages, remained largely ad hoc and almost wholly unpublicized, especially in proportion to the attention devoted to the more central issues of political development. Even when it paid at least lip service to the formulation of policy as in the case of the single-party regime proposals, the SLPP under Sir Albert never sought to politicize the military in the manner attempted by Kwame Nkrumah with the Ghanaian armed forces. No institutions were established where army officers might learn the "ideology" of the SLPP, nor were officers required to become card-carrying members of the party. The very attempt to create a fusion of loyalties between the upper levels of the military hierarchy and the central figures of the political ruling group seems not to have merited a high priority in Sir Albert's mind if indeed he ever thought about the whole problem in a truly conscious way. At least up until early 1966, particularly before Ghana's February coup, the linking up of civilian and military influentials began to acquire its own essential momentum not as a result of any specific action taken by that group of elites calling itself the SLPP but rather as a result of a not unsurprising convergence of interests between certain army officers and members of the party in power. The implementation of a more conscious pattern of civilian control would probably only come when the SLPP felt a clear and immediate threat to its very survival as a party.

The most, if not the only, conspicuous feature of the civilian control "mechanism" during SLPP rule under Sir Albert was the special emphasis attached to the placement of the force commander in a network of elite relationships. Under this system, David Lansana, who assumed command of the Regiment in January 1965, became an intimate associate of the Sir Albert clique within the SLPP. This clique was often referred to as the "Moyamba group" since a number of its members came from the Moyamba district of western Mendeland. It included, apart from Sir Albert himself, such prominent individuals as Lansana's sister-in-law, Madam Gulama, and a number of senior civil servants all of whom never lost an opportunity to show their loyalty to the prime minister.

Beginning with his appearance at the SLPP party convention and convention ball held in June 1964, it would seem that at least when it came to army matters, Lansana's courtship of the politicians and Sir Albert's favorable response could scarcely remain a secret. Even after his official appointment as officer commanding the regiment, Lansana continued to appear at a number of party functions including rallies held in the far distant reaches of the provinces.[5] In Freetown the heads of the army and the civilian government were often photographed together at social affairs. Several of Sir Albert's most trusted associates in the civil service made speeches extolling the virtues of the first Sierra Leonean force commander. For example, George Panda, secretary to the prime minister and head of the Civil Service, wrote a letter to the *Daily Mail* in January 1965 in which he suggested that all the senior officers of the army cooperate with and give full support to Lansana for, as he expressed it, "any failure in the army would not be that of Brigadier Lansana but the [other] officers of the army."[6]

The prime minister himself went out of his way to express support for his trusted representative in the military forces. In March 1965, Siaka Stevens, leader of the opposition APC, delivered a speech on the floor of the House of Representatives in which he noted the increasing "feeling of insecurity of tenure in some quarters of the armed forces." According to Stevens, Lansana had just dismissed an enlisted man from the army without showing due cause.[7] Sir Albert responded to Stevens's comments as follows:

On the question of the dismissal of a man from the army I would like to say that I have implicit confidence in the Force Commander and in his conduct and in his judgment, and any decision he takes without looking into it I can say 99 out of 100 chances he has taken it on good grounds.[8]

Sir Albert clearly could impune no wrongdoing to his military commander, a fact which undoubtedly did much to reinforce Lansana's self image.

In his willingness to become "one of the boys," to court the favor of the politicians, particularly Sir Albert, and to do their bidding when the occasion required, Lansana reaped a number of side benefits. As force commander he earned a salary almost equivalent to that of a government minister. He enjoyed the luxury of a lodge at Hill Station, an official car, and perhaps as a result of his close association with senior SLPP officials the opportunity to share in the fruits of corruption. Furthermore, Lansana acquired at least the trappings of prestige that derive from extensive foreign travel. Apart from frequent trips abroad on strictly military duties, Lansana served as Sierra Leone's official representative at a United Nations peace-keeping conference held in Ottawa in November 1964 and attended Israel's Independence Day celebrations in Tel Aviv in May 1965. The force commander also played a prominent role in arranging for the holding of the second Ordinary Session of the OAU Defense Commission in Freetown in February 1965. In September of that same year, Lansana presided over a Military Commission of Enquiry (consisting also of representatives of Mauritania and the Cameroon) which visited the interior of what was then Portuguese Guinea at the request of the African Liberation Committee of the OAU to determine which of the nationalist movements operating in that territory was most deserving of OAU assistance. The commission eventually determined that Amilcar Cabral's African Independence Party of Guinea and the Cape Verde Islands (PAIGC) was engaged in actual military action while the Liberation Front for the National Independence of Guinea (FLING), supported by Senegal, was shown to be totally ineffective in this regard.[9]

The emphasis on the importance of Lansana in the government's civil-military relations schemes elicited comment on a number of occasions from the opposition APC. *We Yone,* as already observed, had chronicled the emergence of Lansana as the "protector" of the SLPP and especially of Sir Albert Margai. Following the holding of District Council elections in June 1966, the prime minister visited a number of districts in the southern and eastern provinces where the SLPP had managed to win most of the council seats. Another opposition newspaper, *Think*, asked why "it was necessary for the army commander to accompany Sir Albert and his SLPP supporters from chiefdom to chiefdom during his round of visits?"[10] One opposition member of parliament also took note of the excessive attention being lavished upon the career of the force commander to the exclusion of other officers:

Africanisation. Government has been talking about Africanisation. In 1964, what did the speech of the Governor-General say about Africanisation? Lieutenant-Colonel David Lansana has recently been promoted. In 1965 here it says again Colonel David Lansana has been promoted. In 1966 it will be Brigadier David Lansana who will be promoted. That is the Africanisation policy of the government.[11]

While this may have somewhat overstated the case, Lansana's career and particularly his association with a number of high-ranking politicians did seem to have received an inordinate amount of publicity. We do not mean to imply that Lansana's position as force commander did not entitle him to a certain measure of social interaction with the civilian ruling group. It is just that in Sierra Leone, where role categories have not been defined adequately, the lack of clear-cut and proper areas of "competence" for Lansana and for the politicians could in fact encourage greater penetration of the society by the army and perhaps vice versa.

The Lansana-Margai axis represented a mutually profitable exchange for both parties and may have been indicative of similar exchanges between other politicians and military officers. For Sir Albert, Ella Koblo Gulama, and other members of the inner circle, the Lansana tie seemed to bring the army into the SLPP camp without the kind of effort often expended by more ideologically oriented mobilization parties. Lansana was made to believe that he belonged to the elite so that he might become a useful, if often unwitting, instrument of civilian control of the army organization. Margai and company knew full well that by entrusting a "small boy" with the trappings of a "big man," they could count on Lansana's enduring loyalty even in a period of declining government legitimacy as in late 1966 and early 1967— in such times a friend like Lansana for politicians and senior civil servants might be a prerequisite to their very physical survival. For Lansana, in a society where, particularly in the urban areas, a military career alone did not confer a great deal of prestige, the chance to be seen with the political and professional elites in Freetown gave him, the son of a petty trader, a great deal to be thankful for.

While the kind of "cross-boundary" linkages that developed between the army commander, Lansana, and the SLPP politicians successfully garnered most of the literate public's attention and are therefore easiest to document, they were by no means unique. The SLPP method of civilian control apparently penetrated considerably deeper than the top level of the military hierarchy. Mass party leaders have long recognized the necessity of politicizing the entire officer corps toward support for the regime in power. For example, officers of Guinea's army refer to each other as "comrades" and are considered part and parcel of the ruling PDG.[12] In Sierra Leone, the SLPP leaders may have been cognizant of the potential for a breakdown in cohesion among senior army officers and thereby sought to bring as many officers as possible into the SLPP fold. This was accomplished, as we have seen in the case of the force commander, through the ad hoc fusion of military and civilian elites. Cross-sectoral alliances for the SLPP became a kind of built-in life insurance policy. Were the ruling group to find its political future in jeopardy, it could call upon the army to help ward off the more zealous members of the opposition.

During Sir Albert Margai's period of rule a fusion of senior army officers and leading members of the civilian elite became the order of the day. Thus of the nine most senior officers in the army, seven belonged to "extended families" whose members played a prominent role in Sierra Leone political life. In some instances, the civilian relatives held political office directly, either as an ordinary member of parliament but more usually as a minister in the government. In others, the civilian "member" of the civil-military alliance exercized political power in a more indirect manner, generally as a trusted associate or adviser to the prime minister himself. Since all these ties would eventually determine the form of military intervention in March 1967, it is now necessary to consider the origins and structure of the coalition between Sierra Leone's civilian and military elites.

On the most elementary level, a common ethnic identity helped forge bonds between military officers and civilian "big men." Lansana and Sir Albert, of course, both belonged to the Mende tribe and as Gershon Collier expressed it, "the Force Commander, Brigadier Lansana, was completely loyal to Sir Albert Margai, his *tribesman.*"[13] Several other officers in the "group of seven" referred to above were also Mendes, notably Major Ambrose Genda, Captain Bockarie Kai-Samba, and Captain Sandi Jumu. To the extent that Sir Albert endeavored to ensure Mende hegemony in his government and in the senior civil service, largely through the careful weeding-out of such non-Mendes as Dr. John Karefa-Smart and through the promotion of a number of Mendes to the rank of permanent secretary, this tribal factor assumed some importance, particularly during the waning days of SLPP rule. In Sierra Leone, however, extensive intermarriage among provincials and the generally widespread emphasis on flexibility, heterogeneity, and pluralism in political behavior has tended to mute the kind of virulent tribal antagonism found in places such as Nigeria, except perhaps during periods of hectic political campaigning. For this reason, a Sierra Leonean army officer might not be expected to identify with his civilian "brother" *solely* on the basis of ethnicity to the extent that an Ibo officer would identify with an Ibo civilian influential in January 1966.

A common identification with one's home region also provides a clue to an understanding of civilian-military linkages. In Mendeland considerable primordial sentiments are directed toward an individual's district of origin. Thus among Mendes in the SLPP government, those MPs who represent the Kenema District in the east generally regard themselves as somehow "different" from those MPs whose constituencies are to be found within the Moyamba District some 125 miles to the west. For this reason, a Mende officer such as Captain Kai-Samba, who was born in the Kenema area, could be expected to identify more readily with the "eastern wing" of the SLPP rather than with Sir Albert's Moyamba clique. Although David Lansana spent his childhood in the Kailahun District on the Liberian border, his marriage to the sister of one of the leading stalwarts of the Moyamba group no doubt fostered an identification with that particular faction of the SLPP.

Along with shared ethnic and regional identities, secondary school affiliations commonly known in West Africa as the "old boy" network, facilitated linkages between the military and civilian elites. This factor assumed a special prominence once the Sierra Leone army decided to eschew the commissioning of former NCOs and warrant officers in favor of direct-entry school certificate holders. Since Sierra Leone is such a small state, it contains only a limited number of what, for want of a better term, can be described as "prestige" schools. These include the government-sponsored Bo Secondary School in Bo, and the Prince of Wales, St. Edwards, and the Albert Academy secondary schools located in Freetown. The Bo School old boy linkage traditionally has played a significant role in fostering "subgroup identities" within Sierra Leone's political parties.[14] Cartwright notes that of the forty-two members of parliament in 1962 who claimed to be affiliated with the SLPP 40 percent had attended the Bo School.[15] On the military side, all four Sierra Leonean officers commissioned between April 1959 and January 1961 and thus well toward the top of the military command matriculated at the Bo School. At the time of the coup d'état in March 1967 this group would demonstrate clearly their loyalties to the "anti-Albert," Bo School group within the SLPP, a problem with which we shall deal in some detail in the next chapter.

Extended family relationships rather than vague consociational identities based on shared ethnicity or other such general affiliations seem to have formed the real stuff of civilian-military linkages in Sierra Leone. In a society where loyalty to one's family, whether in the nuclear or extended unit, molds the entire range of sociopolitical behavior, it is not at all surprising that most senior Sierra Leone officers, particularly those of the Mende tribe, could claim a direct relation in high places.

Interpersonal linkages between army officers and high officials in the government and the civil service were formed initially by two distinct processes. In one instance, an officer might belong to a family already enjoying status in the community based on the achievements of its nonmilitary members. As was more often the case, however, an officer from a somewhat proletarian background who initially lacked ruling family connections could "rectify" the situation by marrying into a ruling family. A detailed examination of the family ties of several key officers who would later initiate military intervention in Sierra Leone can be used to substantiate this thesis. Since accurate data is generally difficult to obtain except for those officers who have achieved a measure of public notoriety, one can only hazard a guess that a number of interpersonal linkages of this type may have escaped detection.

The extended family relationships of Captains Charles Blake, Bockarie Kai-Samba, and Sandi B. Jumu—the three who, as majors, would stage a pro-SLPP coup in March 1967—can be traced readily. By far the most senior of this group was Charles Blake who, as a native of the town of Bonthe on Sherbro Island, belonged to the tiny Sherbro tribe which constitutes only 3.4 percent of Sierra Leone's total population. His father was a minor functionary in an expatriate-owned commercial firm, and an uncle, an SLPP backbencher, represented a Sherbro constituency in parliament. Blake married the daughter of a prominent Creole civil servant with connections to Sir Albert's minister of finance, R.G.O. King. Thus even though Blake was not a Mende, he did attach himself to members of the civilian elite with ties to the SLPP.

Captains Kai-Samba and Jumu were also involved in a close-knit system of elite relationships. Kai-Samba's father, an admirer of Sir Milton, was perhaps the most enlightened of the Mende chiefs until his death in 1956. Kai-Samba's eldest brother who served in the RWAFF during World War II, then succeeded his father as paramount chief of Nongowa chiefdom until he was later declared mentally unstable and suspended by Sir Albert in February 1966. Captain Kai-Samba's other brother, Kutubu Kai-Samba, a prominent Mende lawyer from Kenema, was returned to parliament in 1963 and eventually became minister of agriculture. The army captain was brought into the Margai extended family following his marriage to one of Sir Albert's nieces.

In the same manner as his army colleague Kai-Samba, Captain Jumu could claim traditional authorities as his relations. Both his mother and father came from ruling houses in the Tikonko and Nongowa chiefdoms, respectively; and Jumu married the daughter of Amadu Wurie, Sir Albert's minister of education, also the son of a chief. Wurie had a relative, Captain Seray-Wurie, who ranked among the top fifteen officers on the basis of seniority.

A number of other officers were linked indirectly to the SLPP. The *Daily Mail* noted in April 1966 that Sir Albert's minister of external affairs, Maigore Kallon, was at the Mons Cadet School in England to witness the passing-out of a younger brother. Kallon's brother was admittedly not senior enough to become a full-fledged member of the civilian-military coalition; but if we are to include Ella Gulama's ties with Lansana, no less than four of the most influential SLPP ministers of government could count a senior officer as a close member of the family. A number of other senior officers were linked indirectly to the SLPP. A more senior officer, Captain Turay, a Temne and Bo School graduate, was related by marriage to a prominent businessman from the town of Makeni, who was closely identified with the prime minister. Lieutenant Mark Koroma, as in the case of Turay, an important figure during the period of military rule in Sierra Leone, was a nephew of A. B. Magba-Kamara, secretary-general of the Sierra Leone Ex-Servicemen's Association and an SLPP activist.

In the final analysis, the very physical dimensions of Sierra Leone's capital city probably encouraged frequent and substantive associations between army officers and members of the civilian elite, even if the particular individuals involved were not directly related. Compared with other West African capitals, Freetown is quite small in population and compact in area. Most of the country's tiny elite—particularly the high-ranking politicians and civil servants—live in the hills that overlook the city. By far the largest gathering of these elites is at Hill Station, and not more than a quarter mile away from Hill Station are the army officer quarters near Wilberforce Barracks. According to one informant, most senior officers spent more time sleeping in ministerial quarters when the SLPP was in power than in their own barracks.[16] A former deputy minister explained that, as a consequence of Africanization in the army, Sierra Leone officers decided to "leave the barracks and to circulate with the politicians" in the nightclubs of Freetown.[17] Berthan Macauley, attorney-general under the SLPP and later tried for treason on charges stemming from his alleged involvement in the 1967 military coup, explains how his relationship with David Lansana developed:

I have known Brigadier Lansana since 1955 about when he was a young army officer training in England and I was a young barrister practicing in London.

Whenever he came down to London he would call me to see me and my wife in my flat and I used to take him for drives in my car in London. When I came to Sierra Leone in late 1956 we continued being friendly. When I moved to Bo in 1960, I lived there and he would drop in at my house to see me whenever he passed through Bo. When I took the office of Attorney-General I moved into Hill Station and he dropped in to see me. When he moved to Flagstaff House we were not far from each other.[18]

The absence of artificial constraints upon day-to-day contacts between officers, politicians, and other influentials was certainly a key factor in the formation of civilian-military alliances.

P. C. Lloyd has described the modus vivendi of elite interaction in an African capital city:

A close-knit network of friendships is further fostered by the small size of the elite and the concentration of its members in the national or regional capitals. Even where they are not congregated in affluent suburbs, the possession of a car and its free use makes interaction among them easy . . . . very large parties to celebrate marriages or christenings are common and call for elaborate arrangements. Many of the marriages are, in fact, between persons from families with a number of educated members, and these new ties provide fresh relationships among the elite.[19]

Throughout the colonial period and well into the early 1960s, an accurate portrayal of the urban African elite would not have been required to mention the role of army officers. As the degree of Africanization in the military sphere became equivalent to that in the civilian sphere, however, the urban elite now encompassed a wider variety of members. Few scholars have yet to ponder the nature of relationships between the civilian elite and the first generation of military elites particularly as such relationships became viable in a precoup setting. Although, to be sure, the kind of data necessary to produce "scientific" judgments on such matters is still lacking, we can venture a number of initial conclusions that require further research by political sociologists.

The close identification of senior army officers in Sierra Leone with members of the civilian ruling group beginning around mid-1964 cannot be attributed simply to chance. We have already suggested that in Sierra Leone, until perhaps very recently, the army had been regarded especially by the Creoles as a haven for men who, while possessing a fair amount of formal education, could not successfully cope with civilian society. Even when a member of a prestigious family found himself in an army uniform, he was usually considered something of an "oddity" or "black sheep"; certainly not to be regarded with the same esteem as his lawyer brother. It is quite possible that these attitudes were readily internalized by at least the first generation of African officers. Four months after the Sierra Leone army had seized power in March 1967, the Chairman of the National Reformation Council, Lieutenant-Colonel Andrew T. Juxon-Smith, vocalized at least one army man's special feeling of status deprivation: "There was a time in this country when a man would ask his children who was passing in his compound. The children would reply that it is not a person, it is a soldier."[20] If an army officer was in fact regarded as "something less than human," he would quickly perceive an incongruity between the formal attributes of his professional role—crisp uniforms, a respectable salary, opportunities for European travel—and the low level of status attached to his position by civilian outsiders.

One response to this status incongruence might involve efforts to acquire at least a modicum of acceptance in the community; in short, to take certain steps that could encourage a civilian's perception of an officer as something more than a "glorified soldier." Perhaps the easiest method of dealing with the problem is the acquisition of a civilian patron through intermarriage. Not only does association with a leading member of the civilian elite result in certain material benefits in the form of car loans and faster promotions, but it also up-grades civilian perceptions of the officer's status.[21] Intermarriages then between senior army officers and the civilian elites seem to have fulfilled the officer's upwardly mobile expectations, on the one hand, and on the other, to have facilitated civilian control of the military.

The notion of a shared community of interests between the civilian and military elites in a precoup milieu does not conform especially to a certain shibboleth which so often appears in the literature on civil-military relations in developing countries. It has been argued generally that there is somehow an inherent antagonism between the ascetic, puritanical officer of humble origins who comes to the "big city" and eventually views with the disgust the goings-on of the corrupt politicians who guide the nation's destiny. Janowitz writes that "as a result of social background, education and career experiences, the military of the new nations become interested in politics, but they continue to distrust organized politics and civilian political leaders."[22] While this statement conceivably could account for the hostilities generated between Nzeogwu and Balewa in Nigeria, it does not necessarily account for patterns of civil-military relations in Sierra Leone except, as we shall see, in the case of those officers who lacked extensive ruling group connections or who enjoyed ties with the civilian elites in only the most marginal sense. In fact, the fusion of civilian and military elites in the years 1964 through 1967 bears some resemblance to a similar alliance between politicians and army officers in nineteenth century Great Britain—an alliance based on a perceived congruence of "class interests."[23] The major difference between the two patterns stems from the fact that in a number of cases, Sierra Leonean army officers did not join the elite until rather late, often through intermarriage. In the final analysis, therefore, we cannot rely on theories that predicate the appearance of military coups d'état on the basis of an underlying dissonance in the interests of civilian and military leadership. We must instead probe for other causal factors.

## NEW DIRECTIONS IN SIERRA LEONE POLITICS AND CHANGING PATTERNS OF CIVILIAN CONTROL

In December 1965 a paramount chief member of the Sierra Leone House of Representatives called upon the SLPP leadership to ". . . give serious consideration to the introduction of a unitary (one party) system of Government in this country."[24] For a period of months, Sir Albert and a number of SLPP stalwarts, including Lansana's sister-in-law Madam Ella Koblo Gulama, had notified the people of Sierra Leone of the government's intention to seek the elimination of political opposition, if only, at least in the initial stages, through the adoption of de facto measures. Sir Albert and Kwame Nkrumah exchanged official visits in October 1965 and apparently discussed the "technical" prerequisites of a single-party state including the sacking of "meddlesome" judges.

Between fall 1965 and the May 1966 District Council elections, Sir Albert and his clique of supporters lobbied continuously on behalf of a one-party system but only succeeded in rousing a substantial block of opposition throughout Sierra Leone. The APC challenged the ruling party on this particular issue not so much on ideological grounds—the APC, after all, claimed to be left-of-center in its inspiration—but rather because of objections to the "speed with which the Prime Minister was trying to rush the matter and on the grounds that the SLPP lacked sufficiently wide popular support."[25] In this belief, they had the support of the "young turks" within the SLPP, led by Kutubu Kai-Samba, who were not prepared to accept the one-party proposal as long as Sir Albert remained leader of the SLPP and Sierra Leone's head of government. These groups in turn exploited the sympathies of the Creole intelligentsia in Freetown who took issue with the "anti-libertarian" spirit of the SLPP proposals. A personal dislike of the prime minister and his blustering political mannerisms also served to unite the various groups in opposition to the ruling party. A vigorous national debate on the subject developed in late 1965 and early 1966, causing Sir Albert to entertain doubts as to the wisdom of his proposals. In the final analysis, as Cartwright notes, "Sir Albert was not prepared to go to any lengths to get his one-party state."[26] While he was willing to harass the APC by raising a number of logistical impediments to the opposition party's efforts to acquire support in the provinces, he was decidedly unwilling to ban the party outright.

Faced with a rising tide of well-organized opposition particularly among educated Creoles in Freetown, Sir Albert decided to abandon his plans for the introduction of a single-party system.[27] Nevertheless, believing that the time had come to sever the umbilical chord still binding his country to the Queen of England, the prime minister began to lobby for a new republican constitution to replace the independence constitution. As he was still very much a legalist, Sir Albert realized that, for his government to change Sierra Leone's constitutional status it was necessary to follow certain well-defined procedures. Specifically the SLPP found itself at the mercy of Article 51, Sections 4 and 5 of the 1961 Constitution which stipulated that any bill enacting a new constitution could not become law before passing by a two-thirds majority in two successive sessions of the House of Representatives. Furthermore, following passage of the bill at the first session, there had to be a dissolution of parliament and then a general election. Thus, for the SLPP to preside over a republican Sierra Leone it first had to receive an entirely new mandate from the voters. The 1961 constitution also required the holding of general elections at least every five years; and as the last ones were held in May 1962, Sir Albert knew that his party would have to face the Sierra Leone electorate some time in mid-1967.

Although there had been some talk in the latter half of 1966 that the SLPP intended to introduce a bill calling for an executive presidency with unbridled powers of the Nkrumist variety, the draft Republican Constitution, gazetted on December 22, 1966, instead provided for a ceremonial presidency (which would replace the office of the governor-general) and considerably enhanced powers for the prime minister. The president, for example, would be appointed by the Cabinet and ''hold office during the pleasure of the Cabinet.'' The Judiciary was also directly affected by the new constitution since the chief justice could be appointed—and was subject to removal—by the president acting in accordance with the advice of the prime minister. The proposed constitutional arrangements also permitted the prime minister to appoint three ministers and three deputy ministers to his cabinet who were not members of parliament.[28] Since the SLPP enjoyed a very comfortable majority in the House of Representatives, passage of the bill was easily secured on January 25, 1967 after only a perfunctory debate; and Sierra Leoneans began preparing themselves for the announcement of the second general election since independence.

Sir Albert's political strategies, having as their principle objective the consolidation of SLPP rule, appear to have been paralleled by a more conscious approach to the question of civilian manipulation of the armed forces. The coups d'état of early 1966 in Nigeria and Ghana helped to identify the dangers that the conspiratorial groups within the army might pose to the SLPP elite's instinct for self-preservation. On the most general level, the overthrow of Nkrumah and the CPP must have alerted Sir Albert to the inherent fragility of any regime, whether single-party or otherwise, that was unable to develop an effective method of civilian control over its armed forces. There is ample evidence to suggest that the events in Accra, when considered together with the virulent opposition the prime minister's policies aroused at home, compelled Sir Albert to take a very hard look at his own army. In so doing, it appears clear that he began to move toward strengthening the linkages between his party and the officer corps. The process of binding together civilian and military elites within a specific subgroup or subnational identity continued as before but with a new-found emphasis on tribal affiliation as the sole basis for one's recruitment as an officer.

A number of changes in military policy during Albert's premiership rendered possible a more explicitly tribal approach in the SLPP's endeavors to coopt the army. The decision to push ahead with the all-out Africanization of the officer corps accompanied by the relegation of British officers to perfunctory roles in military affairs greatly increased Sir Albert's capacity to "infiltrate" the army organization. During Sir Milton's time, British majors performed recruitment duties and acted as the final judges for those Sierra Leoneans seeking a short-service or regular commission after a course at either Mons or Sandhurst or both. Once these recruiters no longer wielded any influence either over commissions or promotions, Sir Albert, through his loyal client, David Lansana, gained a virtual monopoly in deciding who would become an army officer and who might be passed up at promotion time. Such an arrangement certainly could not be expected to further the development of a professionally recruited armed force. Now any SLPP "big man" who favored a position for his fellow tribesman in the army would find no constraints placed on the realization of this objective. Even the so-called "Forces Council" which was originally designed to check any perceived excesses on the part of the force commander never became fully operational during Sir Albert's premiership with the result that a man like Lansana, who possessed only a most limited nationalist vision, could ensure the recruitment of government loyalists.

The decision in late 1965 to carry the localization of military control in Sierra Leone to its logical conclusion through creation of a locally based military academy in turn had a positive effect on Sir Albert's ability to exercise rigid controls over the army. Presumably with his own military academy, Sir Albert could more readily "bend the rules" governing the intake of new officers if the individuals in question were viewed as loyal supporters. The vacancies created at such an academy would assist indirectly the prime minister in discharging his patronage function in addition to furthering the government's efforts to create an SLPP-oriented army. In any case, by 1965, both Mons and Sandhurst had begun to accept a larger and larger proportion of cadets from Eastern Africa; for this reason, if for no other, it behooved Sierra Leone to develop a capability to train its officers locally. Sir Albert also sought to reduce Sierra Leone's dependence on Great Britain as the sole supplier of military hardware. Israel, as so often the case in sub-Saharan Africa, stepped in to assist the cause of "multidependency" through the Ministry for Foreign Affairs' Department of International Cooperation and presumably to gain an additional pro-Israeli vote at the United Nations. Both David Lansana and Sir Albert were on very close terms with the Israeli ambassador in Freetown; and, according to Abel Jacob, Sierra Leone requested Israeli assistance for the establishment of a local officer training school in view of the limitations on the number of Sierra Leonean entrants at Sandhurst.[29]

In November 1965, Sierra Leone announced the Israeli decision to assist in the training of Sierra Leonean army officers and NCOs. Several months later, a team of high-ranking officers from the Israeli Defense Force arrived to help establish a military academy at Benguema, just outside Freetown. The Benguema Academy which opened on March 15, 1966 was placed under the control of five Israeli and four Sierra Leonean officers including Major A. R. Turay who served as chief instructor and deputy to the Israeli commandant. The initial intake consisted of twenty-six Sierra Leoneans and one Nigerian in the Officer Training Wing who were required to undergo a twelve-month course in order to obtain their short-service commissions. The Academy also provided for the instruction of twenty-five Sierra Leonean NCOs and a number of "youth leadership" trainees.

The combination of a wholly Africanized recruiting section in the army together with the establishment of a Sierra Leone military academy opened the way for Sir Albert Margai together with his force commander to stack the army with their own tribesmen, and, by so doing, to seemingly guarantee SLPP control of the army well into the future. In July 1968, following the overthrow of the National Reformation Council, Sarif Easmon, a Freetown physician and vociferous critic of the Margai regime, recalled Sir Albert's military policies in a *Daily Mail* article:

The number of Mendes in the higher echelons of the officer corps was all out of proportion to the percentages of Mendes in the country as a whole. Moreover, in the training school run for him by the Israelis, Sir Albert was training such large numbers of Mende cadet-officers that *there can be little doubt that his intention must have been to hold this country down by the armed force of a largely Mende army.*[30]

The statistics certainly do not belie Dr. Easmon's claims. They show that, largely as a response to fears of possible anti-government sentiments within certain sections of the army—fears which Sir Albert unquestionably linked to the rising tide of open opposition to his domestic programs—the prime minister decided upon creation of a Mende-controlled army.

Between mid-1964 and mid-1967—Sir Albert Margai's period of tenure—the African contingent of the Sierra Leone officer corps more than doubled in size from an establishment of thirty-four men to one of seventy-nine. Whereas Mendes represented some 26 percent of the total at the time of Sir Milton's death, by mid-1967 their proportion of the entire officer corps had reached approximately 52 percent, well over the Mende proportion of the population as a whole. Furthermore, of the forty-five officers commissioned in that three-year period, some twenty-nine or 64 percent were Mendes. If one includes in this calculation representatives of those minority tribes who, because of their physical proximity to Mendeland, can be expected to empathize with that tribe, then the proportion by 1967 of "southerners" and "easterners" in the officer corps came to exceed 70 percent. This was in sharp contrast to the "other ranks" which remained rather mixed.

The tribalization of the Sierra Leone army under Sir Albert Margai was not a chance occurrence. To be fair to the prime minister, a number of special circumstances favored Mendes over northerners in bids by both groups to obtain the coveted commission. We have noted that secondary schools of relatively high quality are far more numerous in the south than in the north; and, if for this reason alone, Mende officers under a system of direct-entry commissioning will be more numerous than Temnes. Also, the rise in the percentage of Mende army officers reflected to some degree the promotion of a large number of NCOs in 1965 and 1966 who received noncombatant or administrative commissions in the army's special branches. Since Mendes have historically predominated among both the skilled NCOs, and the warrant officers it is not surprising that eight of the ten Sierra Leoneans NCOs who reached officer status at that time belonged to the Mende tribe. These factors, however, can account only partially for the spectacular increase in Mende army officers in Sierra Leone.

The most significant evidence available to us of a direct effort by the SLPP government to create a Mende-controlled army comes, as Dr. Easmon pointed out, from an analysis of the entering class of cadets at Benguema. A total of twenty-six Sierra Leoneans embarked upon the twelve-month course in March 1966, and, of this group, seventeen were graduated in April 1967, one month after the military takeover. Of the seventeen who passed out of Benguema, some thirteen, or 80 percent, were Mendes. The deck was now apparently stacked against any non-Mende in Sierra Leone who anticipated service as an officer in that country's armed forces.

Sir Albert's efforts to manipulate the ethnic composition of the army for clearly political ends was no more than an extension into the military sphere of more tribally based politics in Sierra Leone during the later period of his leadership. With the entrenchment of the Sir Albert clique as the source of real power in the country, the SLPP became more and more sectional in its appeal; and most Sierra Leoneans came to identify the party with the Mendes. The APC in turn acquired an image as the "party of the north." The dismissal of SLPP cabinet members with northern backgrounds, the very succession of one Mende, Sir Milton, by yet another, Sir Albert, and the replacement of some expatriate and Creole permanent secretaries with Mendes—however well-qualified the successors—furthered the notion of a Mende-dominated SLPP. For example, in the District Council elections of May 1966, the SLPP won only twenty-three of ninety-five contested seats in those areas of the north inhabited by Temnes and other minority tribes. This tribal factor then began to spill over into the army; and for the first time the game of "ethnic arithmetic" was introduced into Sierra Leones' civil-military relations with, it might be added, unfortunate consequences for the political development of that state. The establishment of Benguema and the induction of a high percentage of young Mendes helped reinforce "from the bottom" the tribal and family linkages that existed between civilian big men and officers in the upper echelons of the military organization. Civilian control of the army now appeared assured for a long time to come.

$P$rofessor Huntington has often drawn a precise distinction between what he terms "objective" as opposed to "subjective" civilian control of the military. Thus, the "essence of objective civilian control is the recognition of an autonomous military professionalism; the essence of subjective civilian control is the denial of an independent military sphere."[31] According to the former method, governments render the military politically impotent by professionalizing the officer corps. Objective civilian control, however, has only been realized occasionally, if at all, in sub-Saharan Africa generally because of the often precipitous departure of British and French army personnel and the concomitant absence of a fully internalized professional disposition in the African officer establishments. In endeavoring to cultivate a common identity of interests—and thus an atmosphere of mutual trust—between civilian and military elites followed by the rather last minute build-up of tribal homogeneity in the army, Sir Albert Margai clearly favored a form of subjective civilian control. Lansana's connections with Sir Albert and the SLPP symbolized civilian control of this type in its most obvious dimension; but such connections, as we have shown, were scarcely unique. For a patron-style party such as the SLPP, subjective civilian control simply assisted the Sierra Leone elite to rationalize and consolidate its position for purposes of maintaining political supremacy.

Subjective civilian control as formulated under Sir Albert's direction contained a rather acute irony—the system never envisaged the outright prohibition of military intervention. On the contrary, Lansana and his fellow officers were molded into allies of the regime to defend that same regime from its domestic and possibly, its foreign, enemies. This does not seem unusual considering the fact that the colonial experience, as we have shown, encouraged the role for the embryonic RWAFF organization of "coming to the aid of the civil power." Lansana and the other senior officers who experienced British tutelage probably would have had little difficulty in substituting the notion of "aid to the SLPP" for "aid to the civil power." In this way, the use of supportive as opposed to evictive military intervention—as if the distinction between the two were all that clear—was apparently contemplated by both civilians and army officers alike, even if it meant, as Dr. Easmon so astutely observed on one occasion, "using Sir Albert Margai's 'government' as a facade and catspaw" for outright military dominance.[32] Subjective civilian control of the Sierra Leone military therefore actually held out the distinct possibility of military control of civilians, perhaps with the politicians remaining on as figureheads.

Civilian control of the army in Sierra Leone also failed to meet its stated objectives because of a lack of comprehensiveness in scope. Not only was the system theoretically programmed to accomodate a coup d'état in support of the civilian group, but it also could not control those officers who lacked ties with the SLPP elite and who, for whatever reason, contemplated actions aimed at harassing or displacing the civilian-military coalition. No doubt as a result of the non-discriminatory nature of colonial recruitment policies that sought to check possible Mende dominance of an increasingly Africanized officer corps, there were a number of high-ranking officers who were not Mende and who could not be expected to act as a unified block of SLPP loyalists.

The second and fourth most senior Sierra Leonean officers presented a special problem because neither was Mende and neither enjoyed ties with any leading members of the ruling group. The first of these, John Bangura, was of mixed Temne-Loko ancestry and came from the village of Kalangba in the northern province. The other, Andrew T. Juxon-Smith, came from a Creole-Sherbro background with some infusions of Mende blood. His father had at one point been an official with the Railway Department and later served as one of three SLPP nominees on the Freetown City Council although in March 1965 he crossed over to the APC.[33] Both attended well-known secondary schools—Bangura, the Bo School and Juxon Smith, the Methodist Boys High School and the Prince of Wales Academy—and both had passed out of Sandhurst by the mid-1950s. The placement of two such officers in the military command structure would at some point endanger subjective civilian control in Sierra Leone.

One reason that the middle level of the officer corps—that is those officers who by the end of 1966 held the rank of captain—also threatened to undermine Sir Albert's efforts to control the army was because this group contained but four Mendes of the thirteen men holding combatant commissions. Luckham has noted that civilian control of the Nigerian military was only institutionalized at the level of the "highest military commanders and civilian government leadership; but not necessarily at the level of the officer corps and other elite groups or at the level of the military order as a whole and the society as a whole."[34] He also suggests that the pattern of civilian control established in Nigeria "did not correspond to some of the organisational realities of the military, in particular its lack of cohesion, and the lack of support amongst junior officers either for the authority of their commanders or for the kind of political role the latter played."[35] In Sierra Leone, the prime minister, through the unification of the civilian leadership (including some senior civil servants) and the military leadership, succeeded to some degree in institutionalizing civilian control at the level of the force commander, among a number of Lansana's colleagues, and with the establishment of Benguema, among the very junior ranks. But there were those in the army—even some Mendes and northerners with SLPP connections—who were not willing to play the game exactly according to the rules.

As in Nigeria, a number of Sierra Leone army officers became enmeshed in the internal tensions or "quasi-politics" of the military organization and simply would not submit to the "authority of their commanders" or support "the kind of political role the latter played." Once army disintegration had become a reality of civil-military relations, the only course remaining to the civilians was to give the SLPP loyalists virtually all the top posts in the army and to have unreliable officers either spied upon, cashiered, or arrested. The breakdown of authority patterns in the Sierra Leone army ultimately coalesced with increased praetorianism in politics generally. All of these developments eventually helped to initiate a military-in-politics syndrome in Sierra Leone.

# 5
# DISINTEGRATION OF THE ARMY OFFICER CORPS

For a Force Commander like you, all . . . things . . . are possible. . . . We all know you and your administration too well. . . . You have always demonstrated [an] arbitrary approach to military situations. . . . You [have] also created for yourself a mystique in the army—where you thought that it was not important to consult your officers because they were all small boys, and I can recall events . . . which brought this type of situation to a head.[1]

Between January 1966 and February 1967, the officer corps of the Royal Sierra Leone Military Forces experienced a breakdown of those disciplinary and command patterns that the British had long hoped would be established in the fabric of African armies. During that fourteen-month period, an unrelenting spate of bickering among members of the senior command became the order of the day. This turning of soldier against soldier itself formed an apt prelude to the turning of soldier against the state, although the former weakness would continue to haunt the Sierra Leone military even during the period of rule by junta.

None of the fissures that appeared in the Sierra Leone officer corps during 1966 and early 1967 can be attributed properly to the impact of ideological or other substantively political issues. In armies with a "North African tradition," divisions among officers are often—although not always—exacerbated by differences of political conviction. In the fall of 1971 in the Sudan, for example, a split developed between those officers who sympathized with the Sudanese Communist Party (and thus with the Soviet Union) and those who favored closer ties with Cairo. In Nigeria, there surely existed in January 1966 a conflict between the aspirations of the young radicals like Nzeogwu and the views of older, more conservative officers such as General Ironsi, apart from all the other primordial sentiments that eventually led to intra-officer fratricide in the Nigerian army. In Ghana, the pro-British and anti-Communist views of Afrifa and Ocran contrasted sharply with the leftist posturing of Nkrumah and the CPP.

In the Sierra Leone case where the politics of the "big man" and of the family determine loyalties, it is fruitless attempting to explain the lack of cohesion in the officer corps in terms of a clash of political views. When politics did impinge upon the army, it was primarily the politics of ethnicity or sectionalism and of the family and home district sentiments that cut across civilian-military boundaries. At no time, however, did disputes of an overtly political nature—disputes inspired by events taking place outside the army itself—ever wholly supplant those disagreements within the officer corps resulting from a struggle for leadership roles within the Sierra Leone military organization. There seems to be a distinct path by which organizational stress, personality differences, and praetorian politics made a shambles of subjective civilian control in Sierra Leone.

On a most general level, a number of environmental conditions, perhaps inherent to any small army in a sub-Saharan African state with limited economic resources, contributed to a spread of disaffection among the Sierra Leone military elites. For one thing, living arragements at Wilberforce, both for enlisted men and for officers, bordered on the "worst in West Africa."[2] Substandard living conditions must have offered additional incentives for officers to spend a great deal of time in the residences of government ministers, apart from the reasons given in our chapter on civilian control. In a number of instances, the army failed to provide any accommodation for both enlisted men and officers, requiring many of them to live with friends or relatives in Freetown. For some, living in Freetown implied the paying of rent often without the assurance of prompt and adequate compensation from the force paymaster. Sir Albert apparently never felt the need to "buy off" the military since subjective civilian control was believed sufficient to keep the officers in line.[3]

To be sure, the SLPP and Lansana introduced a number of reform measures for the rank and file. Lansana raised the allowance paid to those who could not be accommodated at Wilberforce or Juba Barracks, inaugurated a bush allowance for enlisted men who traveled up-country while on leave, and constructed new quarters for members of the enlisted ranks with wives and children. In 1966, however, the government appropriated some £ 50,000 for barracks construction, but due to the budgetary squeeze of that year actually spent less than a third of the sum.[4] Furthermore, the force commander generally would not grant car allowances except to officers high on the seniority list (and presumably in his good graces); even then a number of high-ranking officers found it necessary to request financial assistance from their civilian patron if they wished to purchase an automobile.[5] Following the arrest of Brigadier Lansana on March 23, 1967 just prior to the formation of the National Reformation Council, Blake addressed both the officers and the enlisted men of the army, promising the assistance of the NRC in the soldiers' efforts to obtain better housing, hospital facilities, and new uniforms.[6]

Dilapidated barrack conditions and difficulties in buying a private car were probably not by themselves sufficient to reduce morale in the officer corps. Assuming that all officers suffered equally under the system, then the fact of inferior living arrangements might actually boost the morale of the officers as a unit and provoke them to seize political power in the hopes of alleviating such conditions. More important in creating an atmosphere of boredom and malaise in the officer corps must have been the continued relegation of the army to a minor or peripheral role in Sierra Leonean society. The last army bush camp was held in March 1965; and for the two years preceding the coup d'état of March 1967, the Regiment, as in the past, did little of an operational nature apart from mounting a guard over its own barracks.

This was in sharp contrast to Nigeria and other states where internal security operations became the raison d'etre for many armies. In Nigeria between November 1964 and June 1965, almost the entire Third Battalion of the Nigerian army was deployed to maintain law and order in the Tiv Division of what was then the Benue Province.[7] Such internal security operations along with frontier patrols and civic action programs (almost unknown in sub-Saharan Africa) may act to preoccupy armies with the performance of specific tasks as well as to help keep alive the illusion of an activist army with a definitive function in society.[8] In Sierra Leone, however, it was not really possible to sustain the myth of a tiny, ill-equipped army acting as a defender of the state against external aggressors while, at the same time, there was little need for internal security operations. True, if personally insulted by a recalcitrant paramount chief, Sir Albert was not adverse to despatching soldiers to the chiefdom in question as a show of force. However, this type of activity never involved more than a platoon of troops and was a relatively infrequent occurrence.[9]

The very basic lack of duties and the continuing absence of efforts by the

SLPP to inject the military career with a sense of meaning, or even to provide busy work for the Sierra Leone army, rendered a spirit of cooperation and brotherhood extremely difficult especially with the departure of the British officers. With so few officers of senior rank, daily face-to-face contacts between staff and command personnel were commonplace and contributed to frequent dissension. Officers devoted the bulk of their time and attention toward personal relationships with their fellow officers, a process which only succeeded in rousing petty jealousies and mistrust, although not of the blatantly murderous variety found in Nigeria in 1966. We must now document what Gershon Collier terms the "many instances of serious insubordination and disloyalty among junior officers . . . during the year preceding the military take-over."[10] Having done this we can then proceed to consider in a theoretical vein the common threads that linked all such instances of insubordination.

In mid-February 1966, a government notice in the Sierra Leone *Gazette* curtly announced the termination of the army commission held by Ambrose Genda who at the time was an acting lieutenant-colonel. For Genda, dismissal brought only the dubious honor of being the first Sierra Leonean officer to find himself summarily discharged from military service. Initially the decision to cashier a lone army officer did not rate front-page headlines—the government-owned *Daily Mail* ignored the story altogether—but the long-term repercussions of that decision were another story. Although Genda's departure from the Sierra Leone army did not result in immediate "coup talk," dissension among senior officers soon began in earnest.

A week after Genda's dismissal from the army, the SLPP's official propaganda organ, *Unity,* pointed with obvious glee to the fact that Genda was not a northerner. This apparently was meant to signal members of the opposition APC, which by this time had become identified increasingly with the north, that the decision to sack Genda was not based on tribal considerations.[11] In fact, given his origins, he could hardly be portrayed as some sort of rebel against the SLPP establishment. Mende by tribe (from Gerihun in the Southern Province), an ex-warrant officer, and a close associate of David Lansana throughout the 1950s, Genda had at one point been married to a relative of Lansana and therefore, at least in an indirect sense, belonged to the SLPP inner circle.

In June 1965, John Bangura, the commander of the first and only Sierra Leone battalion, departed for England to attend the Joint Services Staff College at Latimer; and Genda, upon receipt of his appointment as an acting lieutenant-colonel, assumed the position vacated by Bangura. On the basis of his ethnicity, his earlier association with the force commander, and his recent promotion to the second command spot in the army, Genda's eventual break with Lansana cannot be ascribed to differing tribal backgrounds, to the so-called generation gap between ex-NCOs and warrant officers and the younger direct-entry school certificate holders, to disgruntlement over promotion prospects, or to any of the other factors that are often listed as impediments to intraofficer cohesion. Rather it appears that the falling out of Lansana and Genda mirrored a clash over differences in personal life-styles and professional "minutiae."

It was rumored that relations between the two officers took a turn for the worse upon the death of Genda's first wife. The force commander is said to have resented Genda's subsequent decision to marry an Englishwoman whom he had met while on a training course. What was most critical was that Genda had become a popular figure in his own right and preferred to carve out an independent image for himself. According to Ibrahim Taqi who reported the internal power struggles of the officer corps for *We Yone,* Genda "had always felt that the army should not become a political vehicle; he was outspoken in his views and thus suspect."[12] Genda was also known to have compiled an excellent record when he served as deputy commander of the second Sierra Leone contingent in the Congo; and later on, he appeared on his own television program, "Uncle Ambrose," in which he showed off the animals collected for his private zoo. For David Lansana, however, notoriety was little more than a function of his connections with key political figures, most notably, Madam Ella Koblo Gulama and Sir Albert Margai.

In early January 1966, the Organization of African Unity's Committee of Five on Rhodesia (also known as the OAU Defense Committee) met in Accra to formulate an African "military position" in response to Rhodesia's Unilateral Declaration of Independence. Lansana attended the meeting; and, during his absence from Freetown, he appointed the expatriate force paymaster, Major Frank West, to serve as acting commander. This action incensed Genda who as battalion commander would have normally acted for the brigadier under such circumstances. Genda's promotion to the rank of acting lieutenant-colonel had also made him senior to the British officer.[13] Genda is said to have addressed a meeting of the troops at Wilberforce Barracks and to have harangued the absent Brigadier Lansana for having appointed West. While the exact reason for Lansana's decision to appoint an expatriate as acting force commander is not clear, the break between the two Sierra Leonean officers became a clean one.

According to a senior Sierra Leonean officer, Sir Albert believed that Genda wanted to "overthrow the government."[14] It is improbable, however, that Genda entertained political ambitions; and even if this were so, he would have found few Mende officers prepared to join him in any effort to topple the Margai/Lansana coalition. In any case, the prime minister had Genda cashiered as of January 15 and transferred to the Ministry of External Affairs as an assistant secretary.[15] Soon afterwards, Genda was dispatched to

New York as the second secretary in the Sierra Leone mission to the United Nations. If "diplomatic exile" has proved useful in ridding countries of opposition politicians, then this same technique could no doubt be used to preserve civilian control of the military.

The dismissal of a highly respected lieutenant-colonel from the Sierra Leone army scarcely improved chances for the development of cohesion within the officer corps. Genda's willingness to flout the authority of his commanding officer merely offered a pretext for any other officers who might harbor a grudge against David Lansana. Within a few weeks after the incident involving the appointment of Major West as acting commander, discontent with the Lansana administration surfaced again. While the Lansana-Genda controversy had only involved a power struggle between two senior officers, the new challengers were five in number and most certainly could count on the sympathies of a large number of their colleagues, particularly those belonging to northern-based ethnic groups.

The new cohort of "anti-Lansanites" included John Bangura, then a lieutenant-colonel, Major Andrew T. Juxon-Smith, Major Abdul Turay, and two lieutenants, S. Tarawallie and A.A.K.Seray-Wurie. Sometime in late February these officers began holding secret meetings in order to articulate their longstanding grievances against the brigadier. They apparently chose Juxon-Smith as their spokesman and drew up a list of charges subsequently presented to the governor-general in the form of a petition. The governor-general, Sir Henry Lightfoot-Boston, refused to deal with the matter and suggested instead that Juxon-Smith and his fellow petitioners deal directly with the prime minister. Sir Albert then ordered his personal secretary, Peter Tucker, to investigate all the charges. Tucker compiled a long memorandum, and a committee of senior cabinet ministers and civil servants was recruited to help solve the dispute.[16] Juxon-Smith and the other officers pushed ahead with what was essentially a demand for Lansana's resignation and became particularly incensed when Lansana lectured them "about suspicion in government circles that they were contemplating a coup."[17] Sir Albert hoped to prosecute the officers concerned on charges of mutiny or treason, but the attorney-general, Berthan Macauley would not accede to such tactics.[18]

What convergence of interests solidified this "quasi-conspiratorial" group and what was the specific nature of their grievances? The very ability of officers of sharply differing rank, seniority, and military training to formulate a common objective would seem to indicate that peer group identities—given extensive treatment by Luckham in his study of the Nigerian military—could not have linked the entire group together. Obviously, the union of a Sandhurst-educated lieutenant-colonel who had risen through the ranks with a direct-entry lieutenant from Mons required the forging of common objectives that cut across such differences in career patterns. This does not rule out the possibility, however, that peer group loyalties served to strengthen bonds on a supramicro or subgroup level. Bangura and Juxon-Smith certainly could evoke their pioneering Sandhurst experience during the early 1950s, although their actual terms at the military academy did not precisely overlap. If Brigadier Afrifa of Ghana is to be believed, the Sand-hurst "old boy" network colored much of the West African army officer's psyche (or world view). Tarawallie and Wurie passed out together at Kaduna and Mons on precisely the same date and were thus of equal seniority and rank.[19] However, this still does not explain the alliance of Wurie and Bangura in a common cause.

Regional ties seem to have played an extremely important role in this affair. Most of the officers involved came from northern tribes at a time when the SLPP could no longer claim much legitimacy outside of Mende-land. In addition to Bangura and Turay whose northern credentials were impeccable, Tarawallie belonged to the minority Koranko tribe which inhabits the Koinadugu District in the far north, and Seray-Wurie came from a prominent Fula family, with Temne connections. Juxon-Smith, as we have already had occasion to note, came from a Freetown family in which a distant Mende tie counted for very little. The involvement of both Turay and Wurie is of special interest because of their indirect ties with the Sierra Leone Peoples Party. However, it will be remembered that in Genda's case, Lansana's seeming disregard for the niceties of command arrangements helped sever ties between two officers sharing a common tribal and extended family heritage. For Turay and Wurie, a vague identification with the north and a more particularistic concern with Lansana's weakness as an army commander overshadowed those factors which under other circumstances would have cemented their allegiance to Lansana and the ruling group.

In calling for the resignation of their force commander, Juxon-Smith and his fellow petitioners charged Lansana with "nepotism, tribalism, immorality, drunkenness and the inability to administer."[20] The reference to "tribalism" and "nepotism" contained decidedly political overtones if only because Juxon-Smith and the others had begun to perceive the emerging interrelationship between events in the civilian sector and those in the military organization. One reason that the whole Sir Albert-ruling party-Lansana "arrangement" came under particular criticism was because Lansana appeared unable to stand on his own as a professional army officer. Furthermore, to charge that Lansana sought an exclusive position for his Mende brothers in the army was to vocalize a latent discontent among non-Mende as to their prospects for a fair shake at promotion time. Bangura, Juxon-Smith, and Turay must have feared the consequences of any SLPP attempt to establish a Mende hegemony at the very highest level of the officer corps.

The younger officers who petitioned Lansana probably experienced considerable unease at the increasing entrenchment of Mende officers at the top and the rising intake of second lieutenants at the bottom purely on the basis of their tribal affiliations. Certainly the army could not be expected to expand forever, and the senior posts must have seemed decidedly off-limits to all non-Mende aspirants as long as Lansana remained in charge of promotions.

Young Mende officers such as Sandi Jumu and Bockarie Kai-Samba with their close ties to the SLPP naturally attracted Lansana's attention. Jumu, in particular, posed a special threat to the northern officers. With Genda's dismissal from the army, Jumu, only recently promoted to captain, became an acting major and commander of the first battalion, a post heretofore reserved by military tradition for substantive lieutenant-colonels. Soon afterwards, Bangura, himself a lieutenant-colonel and still the second most senior officer in the army, returned from his Latimer course to find himself deprived of a command. The situation was further aggravated when Lansana promoted Kai-Samba and Blake to serve as his staff officers—grades one and two, respectively—while the Sandhurst-educated Juxon-Smith who was senior to both still worked in the army pay and records office. Both Bangura and Juxon-Smith, then, clearly had reason to feel slighted by Lansana's promotional strategy.[21]

The remaining catalogue of charges against the force commander were indicative of a prevailing disgust with his personal deportment and his more general failings as a military man. Lansana's handling of the Genda affair unquestionably prompted a direct reference to the brigadier's "inability to administer" and, according to the former SLPP secretary-general, Genda "got the northern officers to resent Lansana's decision."[22] The allusions to the force commander's "immorality" and "drunkenness" demonstrate that sophisticated generalizations about such things as promotional frustrations as a source of cleavage among army officers may not solely suffice to explain such rivalries. Thus while ethnicity, promotional anxieties, and other sociopolitical factors were at the heart of the challenge to Lansana's authority, these issues were reinforced by bickering over perceived grievances of a highly personal nature. On the subject of immorality, for example, one officer allegedly accused Lansana of attempting to rape his wife. On the subject of drunkenness, it is a well-known fact that the brigadier enjoyed his liquor as, of course, did many other officers in the Royal Sierra Leone Military Forces. According to one informant, Lansana himself parted ways with Bangura because of Bangura's apparent addiction to alcohol. On such issues were command patterns in the Sierra Leone army often subverted.

Efforts to reduce tensions between Lansana and his fellow officers inevitably ended in failure. Sir Albert apparently told Lansana to "cool it," and the Forces Council theoretically regained its control over promotions. It was patently naive, however, for Bangura and the others to expect a redress of grievances at the hands of the prime minister. Sir Albert certainly was not prepared to cashier his force commander, for the latter's presence, more than that of any senior officer, was absolutely necessary if subjective civilian control in Sierra Leone was to remain a viable policy. The only courses of action remaining to the SLPP leaders and the army commander were either to eliminate the dissident faction with as little embarrassment as possible to the government and to Lansana, or at least to reduce it in size. Probably fearing "victimization," Major Juxon-Smith and Major Turay requested a leave of absence—Juxon-Smith to attend the Senior Military Officers All Arms Battle Group Course at Latimer and Turay to read for a degree at Cambridge University. In an apparent act of appeasement, Bangura was promoted to the rank of colonel with the title of Deputy Force Commander, a position largely symbolic in value since effective command of the army rested with Lansana and his younger Mende and Mende/Sherbro subordinates. Possibly as a result of the intervention of the cabinet committee, the other officers connected with this incident managed to avoid punishment; they nevertheless remained exceedingly suspect as events would later demonstrate.

The elimination of Genda, Juxon-Smith, and Turay from interofficer competition did not and could not in the long run solve the problem of cohesion in the officer corps and, by the same token, ensure continuing subjective civilian control of the military organization. For one thing, the most bitter rivalry of all—that between Lansana and Bangura—became even more bitter. For another, it simply was not possible to keep discharging officers supposedly constituting a threat to the SLPP and their military counterparts. Lansana, perhaps sensing this, turned to more subtle but just as divisive methods of control. Charles Blake, in testimony delivered at his trial for treason in 1969, claims that in mid-1966 the army dismissed a group of northern enlisted men who were attending APC meetings. According to Blake, Lansana, using Israeli assistance, immediately thereafter organized a special intelligence branch in the army, the sole aim of which was to "penetrate the army as much as possible and to *ascertain the political inclinations of officers and men.*"[23] At this time only officers with northern backgrounds would have been targets of such investigations; but by late 1966 and early 1967, Lansana could no longer trust even some of his Mende officers, no matter how close these were to the SLPP.

Within several months after the unsuccessful drive to oust Brigadier David Lansana, relations between the army commander and Colonel John Bangura reached a breaking point. Bangura's promotion to deputy force commander had effectively removed him from any participation in staff or command decision-making. Increasingly, Lansana chose to rely on his junior officers, particularly Blake, Jumu, and Kai-Samba, during consultations over military, and presumably, political affairs. Bangura, whose academic and officer training far out-distanced that of his commander, became a mere figurehead and a perfect candidate for any future "pogrom" against anti-Lansana elements in the army. At the same time, Bangura, once his relationship with Lansana had deteriorated past the point of no return, would serve as a highly visible rallying point for any claimants to Lansana's post, including those willing to use violent tactics if necessary.

Frustrated expectations of a highly particularistic nature rather than those reflecting tribal antagonism or political cleavage continued to mold the nature and form of officer conflict. On a very basic level, to be sure, Lansana was Mende and Bangura was of mixed Temne-Loko ancestry; Lansana orchestrated the SLPP sphere of influence in the officer corps, while Bangura's political sympathies lay with the opposition APC. But at least until late 1966 and early 1967, the rivalry between the two was less a manifestation of differing ethnic and political allegiances than of perceived inequities in their respective military roles. The rag-sheet, *Think,* which claimed to speak for the Creole dissidents in Freetown, noted that "for some considerable time now, there has been bad blood between the Brigadier and his Deputy based on the jealousy of the former for the latter—Colonel Bangura is a soldier in every sense of the word and was Sandhurst educated—not so the Brigadier."[24] One SLPP politician explained that the dissension between Bangura and Lansana was accentuated by Lansana's use of an official car and chauffeur; a privilege denied Bangura. This apparently "made both Bangura and his wife jealous."[25] Ibrahim Taqi discussed the origins of the dispute in an editorial written for *We Yone.* Beginning with a reference to the events of the previous February, Taqi wrote:

It would appear that the Force Commander has learnt no lesson from those happenings. Or else how does he explain the non-provision of a state car for his deputy? Lansana himself had such a car when he was deputy to Brigadier Blackie or has he forgotten so soon? Early in the week I found [the Deputy Force Commander] stranded on the road in far away Bombali District when the rickety landrover in which he travels suffered a breakdown. Then mid-week I came across him on foot along Hill Station as the landrover was still unserviceable. Why should a deputy commander be treated in such a way while *Lansana and his family travel the length and breadth of the country in a chauffer-driven Mercedes and quite often on matters that have not the remotest connection with the army.*[26]

Calculations of status based on the provision of an official car and other such trappings of elite standing within the army clearly shaped conflict patterns among senior officers and together with disputes over such things as bedroom activities or resentment over possession or nonpossession of an automobile made a shambles of officer cohesion.

The extent to which the Lansana-Bangura dispute became the subject of political controversy was largely due to the entry of both SLPP and APC "sympathiques" on the side of the major protagonists. *We Yone* and *Think* continuously monitored developments in the senior ranks of the army and brought nearly all the details to the public's attention. In October 1966 Sarif Easmon, a critic of Sir Albert's one-party state proposals and the SLPP's management of the country's finances, suggested that "maybe the wisest thing to do in the circumstances would be to suspend the constitution [and] ask the army to take over. . . ."[27] While this did not constitute overt support for Bangura and the other northern officers, Easmon's words were clearly not meant for Lansana. For their part, the *Daily Mail* and *Unity* refused to discuss any matters relating to the disintegration of the Sierra Leone army; however, since Sierra Leone remained a fairly open, competitive society, precoup, civil-military relations were not easily concealed by official government silence. In those states without a vigorous opposition or opposition press—and this includes most of Africa—public knowledge of civil-military relations and, in particular, of intra-army tensions can be based only on hearsay.

According to one newspaper account, several weeks before the Commonwealth Prime Ministers Conference of September 1966, Brigadier Lansana accompanied by two junior officers (possibly Jumu and Kai-Samba) called upon the prime minister to inform him that "Colonel Bangura [was] no longer 'with [them]', that he must be considered to be A.P.C., and that he was planning a coup d'état."[28] Talk of a Bangura coup was certainly guaranteed to upset the prime minister. Following the events in Ghana, Sir Albert must have known only too well the fate which could easily befall his government if ever he ventured abroad. Thus he decided to draft Bangura as his military aide-de-camp, a position normally reserved for promising young lieutenants. Bangura then left for London on September 5, 1966 as part of Sir Albert's delegation to the conference. Ibrahim Taqi of *We Yone* sought to explain the strategy behind this decision:

I therefore started wondering what really prompted Sir Albert bringing the Deputy Force Commander to dance conga around him. I find this humiliating for a second-in-command of a national army. Was a comparatively junior officer not available? I would not want to believe the rumour that . . . John had been brought because Sir Albert had been informed he would probably be the gravitating point for an attempted coup while he is away and the only foundation for such malicious and slanderous information is that John is a northerner.[29]

Had the SLPP government been able to gather enough solid evidence to implicate Bangura in a coup plot, then he would no doubt have been formally arrested. Upon their return from London, Lansana called for Bangura's court-martial, but Sir Albert was not yet willing to drive the deputy commander out of the army altogether. Since Bangura was known to have solid support among northern officers and enlisted men, any government action to effect his removal might have easily backfired. Only at that time when the SLPP was clearly prepared to abandon the north altogether to the APC would such a step have been seriously contemplated.

By December 1966, the officer corps of the Sierra Leone army remained a "corps" in name only. Tiny cliques of officers, some of them consisting of no more than one or two majors, vied for those few positions which carried prestige. Lines of command were almost entirely disrupted and security of job tenure rendered somewhat farcical by the frequent dismissal or exile of senior officers. Rather than focusing on the tasks of their profession, most Sierra Leonean officers preferred to indulge in scrambles for the top of the heap.

Conflicting political ideologies—for example, one-party versus multiparty systems—did not intrude upon the officer corps and destroy its cohesion, even if such issues were discussed often in Sierra Leone. Ethnic identities, although becoming more pervasive both within and without the army, could not as yet undermine the viability of the military organization. The bitter hatreds that by 1965 divided Hausa and Ibo or Yoruba and Ibo in Nigeria were not to be found in Sierra Leone although some senior officers often seized upon ethnic differences as a convenient means of dramatizing and rendering their own highly personal grievances more credible.

Since so much of the army infighting involved primarily David Lansana versus the other senior officers, this latter view gains considerable credence. Lansana was a Mende, to be sure, but this apparently counted for less than his glaring inability to command the respect of his men. The force commander's relationship with the civilian elite—a relationship which he made no effort to conceal—transformed him into the tool of Sir Albert Margai and, in the process, destroyed his credibility as the head of an independent military organization. The force commander also won few converts with his personal bearing. One Sierra Leonean officer explained that "Lansana was a very uninspiring human being who felt inferior because he lacked a good education and therefore had to bluff." Lansana, the boy with the eighth-grade education who made good, thus became a convenient target for all those relatively new entries into the promotion race who coveted the number one spot. So complete was the eventual isolation of Lansana from his subordinates that by March 1967 even his trusted battalion commander and staff officers were prepared to effect the arrest of their commanding officer. Lansana was eventually eliminated, therefore, not by his northern or anti-SLPP subordinates but by officers who, because of their tribal and family affiliations, belonged to the same ruling circle.

This view of the disruption of authority patterns in the Sierra Leone officer corps is at least partially supported by Morris Janowitz:

> Military organizations seem particularly vulnerable to rivalries generated by the clash of personalities, which in turn may develop into political rivalries. . . . Men of strong ambition recognize that the top leadership post can be occupied by only one man and that opportunities for even sub-leadership are limited. As a result, cliques develop that represent no more than personal followings and personal ambitions but that subsequently assume political significance.[30]

Janowitz neglects to mention, however, that tiny military organizations, particularly those of the single-battalion type, are especially susceptible to disputes over leadership since only the top two or three posts carry with them real status. Furthermore, Janowitz does not adequately account for the process by which intra-army cliques develop political ambitions and extra-army goals. By early 1967, cliques in the Royal Sierra Leone Military Forces were no longer especially interested in petitioning for the dismissal of David Lansana. For now the overtly political aspects of intra-organization feuding could hold their own against the more purely localized aspects of those disputes. It was largely because of politics that the coup d'état and not the petition became the generally accepted form of dealing with the "Lansana/Margai problem."

# 6

# COUP PLOTS AND CORRUPTION: THE WANING INFLUENCE OF THE SIERRA LEONE PEOPLES PARTY

On the evening of February 8, 1967, Sir Albert Margai appeared on the national radio and announced in somber tones the discovery of an army plot to overthrow his government. According to the prime minister, "the plot by Army Officers was timed in the first instance at murdering the Force Commander, myself . . . and a certain number of Ministers and Civil Servants, taking over the Government and appointing a Committee of Advisers, about seven in number." Sir Albert laid full blame for the coup plot on the All Peoples Congress and mentioned what he termed "the blatant incitements to military personnel to overthrow the government by force."[1] On that same day, Brigadier Lansana had ordered the arrest of eight army officers including his deputy, Colonel John Bangura. Lansana also ordered the arrest and detention of some five NCOs thought to be indirectly linked to the coup plot.

The discovery of a conspiratorial group in the Sierra Leone army with political objectives forestalled the possibility—assuming that any still existed—that intramilitary dissension might remain strictly an organizational question with only minimal extraorganization implications. Sir Albert's claim that the plotters sought the death of their force commander, of their prime minister, as well as the deaths of prominent SLPP leaders, heightened the process by which struggles among officers' cliques were joined with struggles among politicians' cliques. More particularly, the identification of Sir Albert and David Lansana as objects of a possible assassination attempt emphasized the extent to which the anti-Lansana forces in the army regarded their commander and the civilian leadership as essentially the same enemy.

Within the two-month period between January 24 (when Colonel Bangura and his followers were apparently planning to stage their coup) and the formation of the National Reformation Council on March 23, Sierra Leone experienced an almost total vacuum in its national leadership as groups of military men and civilians contested that leadership. Military praetorianism finally came to Sierra Leone although admittedly without the kind of endemic violence that has so often characterized praetorian behavior in other African states. Following the prime minister's unveiling of a coup plot, both the continued interaction of civilian and military elites as well as the issues that persisted in dividing the military elites themselves were intensified; and the diffusion of boundaries between civilian and military became almost complete, at least until just prior to the introduction of direct army rule.

In a number of other West African states civilian-military alliance formation has also been observed. In 1963 for example, trade unionists, threatened with substantial wage cuts as a result of a government austerity drive, called upon the Dahomean army to remove the politicians. In 1972, it was said that Ghanaian civil servants with the informal backing of the urban workers had urged the military overthrow of Kofi Busia and the Progress Party. In Sierra Leone, however, the army and the politicians were never really working at cross purposes. Rather it was the ruling civilian elite—including a substantial representation of politicians—which joined with the military to impede the transfer of power to an opposition party.

THE SLPP TURNS CORRUPT

By the end of 1966 that loose coalition of traditional rulers, educated elites from the provinces, and Freetown professionals, known as the Sierra Leone Peoples Party, found its future political prospects increasingly jeopardized. As in other black African states where civilian leadership in the immediate postindependence period has almost inevitably experienced setbacks in its wider pursuit of legitimacy, so Sir Albert and his followers confronted a growing gap between the expectations of the Sierra Leone masses and their own political record while holding office. Before we discuss the nature of political opposition to the SLPP and the role of this opposition in disrupting traditional patterns of civil-military relations, let us first consider just how the ruling group became vulnerable to widespread criticism.

Undoubtedly the most notable feature of Sierra Leone society in the years preceding the military take-over was the extent to which that society more than any other in sub-Saharan Africa still clung to at least a reasonable facsimile of Westminister parliamentarianism. W. Arthur Lewis writing in 1965 described Sierra Leone and Nigeria as the only West African states with "at least two substantial parties."[2] However, by the time of the western regional elections of October 1965, few observers still believed that Nigeria could manage political conflict in a peaceful and democratic fashion; their assessment was soon to be proved correct. In Sierra Leone, a different situation prevailed. Government and opposition only occasionally traded blows of a physical nature, and that violence that existed rarely moved beyond the level of the chiefdom palaver. And perhaps most important, the relatively open and competitive nature of the Sierra Leone polity placed definite constraints on the ability of the ruling group to conceal its less praiseworthy activities. In Freetown especially, newspapers—usually no more than cyclostyled throwaways—appeared in scores; and no subject, however delicate, fell beyond their purview. Several of these bulletins spearheaded the attack on Sir Albert's plans to introduce a one-party state and were instrumental in virtually destroying the prime minister's constituency particularly in Freetown and its immediate environs where there was a fairly high literacy rate.

By the latter half of 1966, the single-party issue no longer preoccupied the attention of the opposition newspapers; instead, sharp-witted columnists like Ibrahim Taqi and Sarif Easmon focused their writings on the more sordid aspects of SLPP rule. The public soon learned of Sir Albert's blatant acquisition of extensive financial assets including overseas property. The Forster Commission of Inquiry established during the rule of the National Reformation Council would later reveal that by March 23, 1967 Sir Albert possessed assets worth £250,000, based on an annual salary amounting to £4,000. Other ministers and permanent secretaries also indulged in the unlawful acquisition of wealth whether through illicit trafficking in diamonds or through kickbacks on prefinanced contractor schemes. The prime minister and his SLPP loyalists were also not opposed to diverting funds collected at SLPP rallies directly into their own pockets.

The opposition newspapers also called attention to the perilous state of the economy which was suffering partially as a result of administrative incompetence and partially because of the magnitude of corruption. Between 1961 and the end of 1966 Sierra Leone's net foreign exchange reserves declined from Le 29 million to a level of Le 11.4 million, a figure that was slightly less than two months' worth of imports.[3] According to Brian Quinn, the IMF's resident representative in Sierra Leone from 1966 to 1968, this decline in external reserves could be attributed directly to the diversion of funds belonging to the Sierra Leone Produce Marketing Board (SLPMB) into a number of oil palm and coffee plantations with few controls over how the money was actually spent.[4] Contractor finance schemes in the form of a luxury hotel, a cement factory, and an oil refinery were undertaken also with virtually no checks on expenditure. According to an IMF staff study:

The SLPMB, which had committed its liquid assets to long-term projects, was unable to meet current liabilities to the buying agents of approximately Le 3.0 million and did not have the financial resources needed to purchase produce for export. At the same time, large repayments were falling due on external supplier's credits, and it was anticipated that the balance of payments would deteriorate further.[5]

Faced with a sharply rising balance of payments deficit as well as a chronic budgetary deficit, the SLPP in August 1966 turned to the International Monetary Fund for relief. Under the terms of a stand-by arrangement which took effect on November 1, 1966, the government received some Le5.4 million and agreed to freeze all vacancies in the civil service, to tighten up revenue-collecting procedures, and most important of all, to avoid incurring any new short-term debt that the government could not realistically expect to retire. It was hoped that within three years Sierra Leone could achieve a balance of payments equilibrium on both the current and capital accounts.

Even had Sir Albert adhered rigidly to the terms of the IMF agreement—which he did not—the ruling clique probably could not have saved itself. Opposition to the prime minister's political tactics, especially those clearly designed to enrich SLPP leaders monetarily, was not easily pacified by half-hearted economic stabilization schemes. As head of government and leader of the SLPP, Sir Albert was forced to contend not only with the formal opposition of the APC but with growing unrest from within his own party. The Dove-Edwin Commission of Inquiry which examined the conduct of the 1967 General Elections concluded that "even staunch SLPP members had themselves got fed-up with their leader and turned against him and the Party."[6]

The ostensible leader of the SLPP "radicals" was Sir Albert's minister of agriculture, Kutubu Kai-Samba, whose brother, Major Bockarie Kai-Samba, served as David Lansana's senior general staff officer. K. I. Kai-Samba articulated the sentiments of the younger, more professionally enlightened members of the SLPP who objected to the prime minister's blustering political leadership, his penchant for channeling public money into private hands, and his oft-expressed wish to reshape prevailing political habits in Sierra Leone in the direction of a single-party regime. Other members of this group included L.A.M. Brewah, an SLPP backbencher from Bo, and Salia Jusu-Sheriff, the minister of education.[7] All three graduated from the Bo Secondary School, and all three had led successful careers as lawyers and businessmen prior to entering politics. Kai-Samba and Jusu-Sheriff, both

Kenema products, epitomized the "Kenema wing" of the SLPP as opposed to the Moyamba group and its Creole allies in Freetown. They felt threatened by Sir Albert's continuous meddling in their regional politics, especially when the prime minister, in a direct attempt to undermine Kai-Samba, sought to impose his own loyalist candidate as paramount chief in Nongowa Chiefdom, one of the largest and most progressive chiefdoms in Kenema District. By early 1967 none of these men—and there were others—could be expected to support the SLPP; at least two of them would refuse to accept the party symbol and would run as independents in the 1967 general election. Furthermore, as we shall see, their involvement in an anti-Albert political clique influenced those within the army seeking to terminate the special arrangement between Sir Albert and his force commander which protected the inner circle of the SLPP leadership.

In addition to the feud among different claimants to the leadership of the SLPP, there was the long-standing struggle between the ruling party and the opposition All Peoples Congress. The rise of the APC has been amply documented in its early stages by Kilson, while Cartwright and others have described the forces that led to the eventual overthrow of the SLPP at the polling booth. Kilson attributes the birth of the APC in 1960 to the presence of young clerks and skilled workers who "were ideologically uncomfortable in alliance with the SLPP," in addition to a "motley category of urban and town-dwelling poor who, though normally backing the SLPP, were open to alternative political outlets."[8] While the APC never articulated an extreme socialist approach, it could easily present itself as a populist alternative to the elitist and prochief policies of the SLPP. To this class appeal was later added a definite regional appeal aimed at welding together a coalition of northerners, including those living in Freetown, against "Mende domination." By the time of the 1962 general elections, the APC managed to win sixteen seats in the Sierra Leone House of Representatives and in the process, garnered 17.2 percent of the total vote.

Once in power Sir Albert Margai did not take lightly to the prospects of a dynamic opposition movement that sought his ouster. He refused to bring into his cabinet such prominent northerners as Dr. Karefa-Smart (who had served under Sir Milton) because of their meeting to oppose Albert the night after his appointment as prime minister was announced. He utilized his clients among the ruling families in the provincial chiefdoms to cajole the opposition and often charged the editors of *We Yone* with sedition and defamatory libel, although the courts usually ruled in favor of the defendants.[9] By 1966, however, revelations of widespread corruption in the SLPP helped reinforce the notion of the party as the monopoly of the "big men" and not of the common peasant or urban worker. This was particularly so in the north which did not receive as much development assistance as the

Mende south and where memories of past excesses by the chiefs in alliance with the SLPP had not yet dimmed.

The one-party state proposals helped exacerbate tensions between the Mende and a considerable number of Creoles who, for tactical reasons and perhaps out of a class bias, had supported the SLPP in the past. As a result, the Creoles began to desert the party in large numbers. They also perceived a threat to their long-standing control over the middle and upper levels of the civil service when Sir Albert elevated a number of educated southerners to key positions. Particularly suspect were the appointments in early 1966 of Peter Tucker, a Sherbro, as the prime minister's personal secretary and of John Kallon, a Mende, as the establishment secretary. From the Creole point of view, the promotion of "country boys," no matter how well qualified in terms of their educational achievement, appeared tantamount to a conspiracy by southerners loyal to the SLPP to seize control of the bureaucratic machinery. The Creoles thus found a natural ally among the less-educated northerners of the APC who, in the event of an APC electoral victory, would definitely require Creole managerial and bureaucratic skills.

On February 16, 1967 Sir Albert announced plans to hold general elections in mid-March of that year. Balloting for "ordinary" members in the House of Representatives would take place on March 17 and for paramount chief members on March 21. This announcement followed the discovery a week earlier of a plot to overthrow the government. Taken together, these two events stood as an ominous portent of the future if only because, in an atmosphere of seemingly irresolvable political differences within the SLPP and between the two parties, there seemed little prospect of the army remaining on the sidelines as a neutral bystander. In short, the stage was now set for the final disintegration of civilian-military boundaries and the total diffusion of political power between the civilian and military authorities.

## THE JANUARY COUP PLOT

When Sir Albert announced the discovery of an apparent coup plot in a radio broadcast on February 8, 1967—an announcement preceded by the arrest of eight army officers including David Lansana's deputy commander —the various problems of military and political disintegration in Sierra Leone became one. For the past year, senior military officers had quarreled with each other on an almost round-the-clock basis so that by early January 1967 the officer corps lay in shambles. Most of the participants in these altercations sought to dramatize accumulated frustrations over perceived nepotism and over the glaring incompetence of the military command. David Lansana personally bore the brunt of this discontent, and by the end of 1966, there existed a considerable number of officers who wished to effect his removal.

Sir Albert and his trusted army associate were well aware of the names of those officers who, they believed, wanted the force commander either arrested or killed. These were the officers who were seized and placed in Pademba Road Prison on the morning of February 8. They included Colonel John Bangura, Captain Sheku Tarawallie, Captain F.L.M. Jawara, Captain A.A.K. Seray-Wurie, Lieutenant A. B. Noah, Lieutenant E.G.O. Caulker, Lieutenant A. O. Kamara, and Lieutenant F. S. Josiah. Clearly the prime minister felt threatened by the continued presence of disgruntled officers and sought to eliminate any remaining obstacles to his complete mastery of the army, particularly on the eve of a general election. Against a background of increasing polarization between the SLPP and the opposition APC, we must consider the credibility of the so-called "coup plot" and ponder its impact on civilian-military alignments.

Reconstructing a coup plot as opposed to a coup attempt calls for a good deal of guesswork on the part of the researcher. A coup plot, after all, exists only in the mind of the plotter and, if foiled in its early stages, never becomes observable behavior. The evidence, however, suggests that there probably was a coup of some sort intended; but that internal quarreling among the plotters hindered coordination; and civilian-military boundaries had become so fragmented that it was impossible for the conspirators to maintain secrecy.

There exists prima facie evidence of a plot designed, at the very least, to rid the army of David Lansana. First, by February 1967, the split between the force commander and his deputy, Colonel John Bangura, could no longer be papered over. Bangura was by this time clearly an aggrieved party who had begun to consider violent tactics as a means of restoring his floundering military career. In pursuing this end, it must have been a relatively simple matter to recruit other officers who shared Bangura's loathing of Lansana and who believed that only drastic action could salvage their wounded pride. One might begin with Captain Tarawallie, the officer commanding the battalion's headquarters company and Captain Seray-Wurie, who at the time of the coup plot was in charge of the ordinance depot. Tarawallie, (a Koranko from northern Sierra Leone) and Seray-Wurie, (the only Fula tribe member in the officer corps and a northerner who, however, had lived a good portion of his life in Freetown) together with Bangura, had petitioned the governor-general and Sir Albert about a year earlier to demand dismissal of the force commander. The fact of their arrest in February suggests continuity with past actions and a renewed willingness on their part to foresake democratic methods of protest in favor of more radical methods. As northerners, both officers were probably extremely conscious of the extent to which southerners, especially Mendes, had begun to acquire most of the prestigious command and staff posts in the army. Thus resentments over perceived southern subjugation now overshadowed the more particularistic grievances of the past and helped to solidify anti-Lansana cliques.

An adequate explanation for the involvement of the five additional officers in "l'affaire Bangura" is not easily obtained. Most of this group were only lieutenants with differing seniority dates, and all held relatively minor positions in the army. About the only apparent link was a regional cum ethnic one, which really accounted for only two of the five remaining officers. Lieutenant Kamara, the quartermaster in the 1st Battalion and Captain Jawara, the governor-general's aide-de-camp, were Temne and Koranko, respectively—they shared, therefore, a common regional outlook. Lieutenant Noah, the adjutant at Benguema, while a Creole, was known to be zealously sympathetic to the northern cause; and, according to some interpretations of the relevant events, it was he and Jawara who originally introduced the idea of a coup in conversation with Bangura. Caulker, a platoon commander, belonged to the Sherbro tribe. Lieutenant Josiah, a transport officer, was of mixed Sherbro-Mende blood and thus, like Caulker, something of an ethnic outsider. However, at the time of his arrest, he was apparently serving as Bangura's personal driver; and for this reason, if for no other, he probably was seen as a Bangura loyalist. Once again each of these newer recruits to the pro-Bangura cohort may have belonged to a much larger group of officers who could no longer countenance Lansana's lack of discretion in his dealings with the prime minister.[10] Most of the younger officers who lined up behind Bangura probably banked on faster promotions once the coup was successful. Lacking more sufficient data the expansion of the pro-Bangura clique may be ascribed only to the ever widening belief at most levels of the officer corps that the preservation of some semblance of professionalism in the Sierra Leone army required, at the very least, the removal of Brigadier Lansana.

Fairly detailed accounts of the January plot leaked out during the treason trials of David Lansana and Andrew T. Juxon-Smith in 1969 and 1970. Since the APC government, then in power, made no effort to suppress these accounts even though some officers mentioned in them held senior army positions, one must presume that the testimony delivered at the trials contained a considerable element of truth. Other sources of evidence included a number of ex-SLPP partisans and a senior army officer who told me what they believed actually transpired. Even a prominent APC minister admitted in an interview that there was, in fact, a plan to topple Lansana if not Sir Albert and the SLPP.

Sometime in early January, according to these reports, Bangura and the other officers implicated with the deputy force commander began holding secret meetings where they discussed the possibility of dealing with Lansana and his intimate acquaintances in the SLPP. At one point, at least one conspirator suggested expanding the clique to include another newly emergent group of anti-Lansanites—Majors Blake, Jumu, and Kai-Samba. This proposal was rejected apparently on the grounds that one could not accurately enough gauge the depth of opposition to Lansana among his Mende subordinates. However, that anyone even entertained the possibility of including Mendes in the coup plot supports the view that relatively simplistic concepts like tribalism cannot by themselves explain the formation of military cliques in Sierra Leone.

However instrumental was the Lansana-Margai alliance in stimulating further clique formation within the Sierra Leone army, there still remained the problem of sustaining the momentum of these rebellious cliques over time, especially as the situation now seemed to demand more drastic measures than in the past. Throughout the latter half of January, the plotters quarreled continuously over the precise goals of the coup. Some wanted simply to concentrate on Lansana while others expected to strike at the civilian leadership as well. Some apparently favored a bloodless coup while others favored a "Nigerian solution" with all that that entailed. The officers also failed to agree on who should assume full responsibility for the coup itself. Bangura's movements were now exceedingly circumscribed so that the leadership question devolved mainly upon the more junior participants in the conspiracy. Testimony given during the treason trial of Juxon-Smith during the summer of 1970 affords us insights into the leadership crisis:

Lieutenant Noah then said that he [Tarawallie] had been made leader but Tarawallie said that he [Tarawallie] would prefer Captain Seray-Wurie to be leader; this suggestion was turned down and he [Tarawallie] became the leader.[11]

The plotters did agree that the coup should take place sometime during the last week of January, possibly at the Myohaung Day Ball on January 24 where all senior officers would be in attendance. By that date, however, dissension over the leadership issue had reached such extremes that it was no longer possible to hold the plotters together in a cohesive unit.

At least two members of this conspiratorial group, although non-Mendes, were related to an SLPP minister and a deputy minister. These links made it difficult for either officer to contemplate political assassination no matter how much they may have disliked David Lansana, Sir Albert, and the SLPP; it was not long, therefore, before a number of SLPP leaders acquired detailed knowledge of the developments within the army. While the Myohaung Ball passed without incident, several of the coup plotters approached Major Jumu and Brigadier Lansana with confessions. On January 30, another officer, Captain Seray-Wurie contacted a senior government official who in turn informed the prime minister's personal secretary, Peter Tucker, of the unrest in the officer corps.[12] As a relative of Sir Albert's minister of education, Wurie apparently did not have the heart to kill anyone within the SLPP. By the following day most of the details of the "coup that never was" became known to the ruling circle. This very frequency of social intercourse across civilian-military boundaries and the accompanying lack of secrecy allowed the prime minister sufficient time to mobilize a counteroffensive including calling on foreign assistance.[13]

The bickering that characterized participation in the Sierra Leone army's first attempt at coupmaking does not seem unusual in light of the precedents set in 1966. Throughout that year, a number of cliques, inspired by the examples of Ambrose Genda and John Bangura, challenged the prevailing military pecking order. Most of these cliques never consisted of more than a handful of men who came together on special occasions to call attention to deficiencies in military standards of service. Allegiances were formed on the most tenuous grounds, since few Sierra Leonean officers possessed a vision of things that extended beyond their own special milieu. In the absence of a shared notion of politics, of ideology, or even of peer-group solidarity, it was inconceivable that such a hastily formed group of Bangura supporters could have maintained the cohesion necessary to plan and execute a coup d'état. Even in the relatively formless arena of sub-Saharan Africa, at least a modicum of order and rationality must be brought to bear on the conduct of a drastic political action. Yet such an underlying sense of purpose totally escaped the kind of cliques that sprang up on any pretext to support some army big man. Efforts to enlarge these cohorts only succeeded in aggravating the situation.

One aspect of the January coup plot needs some clarification—the extent of an outside political input. Sir Albert in his broadcast referred to opposition press reports as "blatant incitements to military personnel to overthrow the Government by force." He also listed the names of APC leaders and Creole sympathizers such as Sarif Easmon who apparently would have been picked to serve on a future Committee of Advisers under an army junta chaired by John Bangura. Testimony in the treason trials during 1970 also linked the APC with the anti-Lansana faction, and some believed that money and "legal advice" was to pass from the APC to the plotters. At the time of the coup plot announcement, both *We Yone* and *Think* thoroughly denied opposition party involvement and charged Sir Albert with "an obvious attempt to discredit his political opponents."[14] *Think* asked "what military personnel wanting to stage a coup would take civilians into their confidence to the point where they would be told in advance of their plans?"[15]

Whether or not the plotters did read *Think* or engaged in direct negotiations with APC leaders probably matters very little. The officers were fully cognizant of Bangura's popularity with the APC and rightly expected APC support for any coup attempt in exchange for a quick return to civilian rule. The APC, after all, stood for the rights of northerners; and by February 1967 this ethnic aspect of heightened political competition in Sierra Leone counted for more than ever before. Sir Albert, moreover, had every reason to be disturbed by Sarif Easmon's only slightly veiled call for military intervention four months earlier. From another perspective, however, there was little indication that the APC had yet to abandon the existing rules of the game as long as there remained the possibility of overthrowing the SLPP at the ballot box. It was not until November 1967, during the period of the National Reformation Council, that Siaka Stevens would become convinced of the need to employ violence in the pursuit of political aims.

As an immediate consequence of the February arrests, the Republic of Guinea decided to enter the fray. Sékou Touré's involvement in Sierra Leone's increasingly fluid political scene is understandable in terms of his fear of possible domino effects resulting from military takeovers in neighboring states. Sir Albert himself already had been visited by two Guinean army officers during the last week in January as rumors of unrest in the Sierra Leone officer corps began to elicit the attention of the SLPP government. Two days following the meeting between Captain Seray-Wurie and Peter Tucker, Tucker and another senior civil servant departed for Conakry. The purpose of their mission was to inform President Touré of the trouble brewing in the Sierra Leone army and to discuss the possibility of Guinea rendering assistance to their beleaguered leader. Apparently Touré immediately endorsed the need for an arrangement whereby the Guinean military would be used to back the authority of Sir Albert.

On February 2, the attorney-general, Berthan Macauley, also visited Touré for discussions concerning the international legal implications of the agreement. Then on February 4, Radio Conakry announced the conclusion of a pact between the two countries "to help each other to deal firmly with internal subversion aimed at toppling legitimate and democratic governments of either party."[16] Macauley, the Guinean army commander, the Guinean police commissioner, and Touré's legal adviser then flew by helicopter to Kono in Sierra Leone's eastern province to inform Sir Albert directly of the signed agreement. Sir Albert stayed in Kono, but the remainder of the group went on to Hastings Airport outside Freetown and met with Sierra Leone Police Commissioner William Leigh and an official from the Ministry of Defense.[17] At that time the Guineans were probably informed of the prime minister's intention to arrest the suspected plotters in the army. In any case, official acknowledgement of the agreement with Guinea was not forthcoming in Freetown until Margai's radio broadcast of February 8. Sir Albert seems to have delayed deliberately the arrest of Bangura and his coconspirators until after all the Guinean troops had positioned themselves on the border. He must have feared a general uprising of the northern rank and file if he made any move to arrest the popular Bangura without first taking certain external precautions.

Apart from their combined effects on the rapidly declining legitimacy of the SLPP, the Bangura arrests and the subsequent mutual defense pact with Guinea revealed the declining power of subjective civilian control of the Sierra Leone military. Thereupon, contacts between senior army officers ostensibly loyal to the regime and SLPP leaders increased both in their intensity and in their frequency. As a result, the military elite and especially Force Commander David Lansana assumed an importance in shaping the nation's political future previously denied them. Members of the SLPP who had for so long associated themselves with Sir Albert Margai and who for this reason feared displacement by competing civilian elites turned more and more to Lansana for physical protection. He willingly accommodated them, now perhaps in his new role as a patron rather than as a client. And yet what both Lansana and his new band of SLPP followers neglected to consider was the extreme narrowness of the army leader's constituency within his own organization. In the final analysis, the elimination of Bangura and his supporters could solve very little as long as Majors Jumu, Kai-Samba, and Blake waited in the wings. No system of subjective civilian control could possibly account for that myriad of bickering cliques and subcliques which now constituted the Sierra Leone military.

## THE ARMY AND THE GENERAL ELECTIONS

The holding of a national election in any developing country inevitably raises the prospect of violence, whether of the random, anomic variety favored by the mob or the swift precise kind favored by coupmakers. General elections in western societies theoretically afford the electorate an opportunity to hold their government leaders publicly accountable for past actions. If found wanting, the existing leaders may be replaced by still others who are expected to improve upon their predecessors' record. In developing states, however, particularly in sub-Saharan Africa, the notion of a peaceful transfer of power or of general parliamentary modes of behavior never constituted part of the precolonial heritage and was in most cases a rather last minute innovation of imperial rule. In the absence of institutionalized democratic processes, the majority of black African states have abandoned the holding of general elections in favor of creating parabureaucratic or single-party regimes. Those few attempts at conducting fair and free elections in the post-independence era generally have ended in chaos as in Nigeria's Western Region election of October 1965. The military coup has in fact become the most frequent method of changing leaders and regimes.

It was with this spotty record in mind that Sierra Leone endeavored to effect a peaceful changing of the guard in March 1967. Many observers, both foreign and domestic, held to the belief that in light of Sierra Leone's impressive handling of the 1957 and 1962 elections, the country just might become the first in black Africa to rid itself of patently corrupt government through the ballot box. Arnold Payne has noted, however, in his study of the Peruvian coup d'état of 1962 that ''. . . a characteristic common to many golpes, including the 1962 coup, is their prevalence during an electoral or post-electoral period.''[18] Electoral campaigns usually help uncover all the praetorian tendencies—ethnic conflict, cliquism, increased reliance on brute force—that have previously remained latent in the political culture. The old order simply may not want to ''changeth'' but instead turns to subterfuge as a means of staying in power. This proved the outcome of the general election in Sierra Leone as evidenced by the military takeover of March 21, four days after the balloting for ordinary members in the House of Representatives. It is to the general election and, in particular, to the steadily expanding political involvement of the military in the weeks prior to the actual intervention that we now turn.

So as not to duplicate the numerous treatments of the general background and conduct of the 1967 General Election,[19] we shall emphasize the special position of the army during the process of clique formation, bargaining, and campaigning which followed nomination day on February 27. In this way, the relationship between what Barrows terms with respect to Sierra Leone ''la politique extra-militaire'' and ''la politique intra-militaire'' can be better explained.[20] The general election and the campaign which preceded it brought the relationship between these two forms of military praetorianism into sharper focus.

The issues that divided the SLPP and the APC in addition to those that turned members of the ruling party against one another have been summarized in previous sections. The APC challenged the ruling party on the grounds that government members partook in self-enrichment, seriously mismanaged the country's fragile economy, and favored Mendes over northern tribes in the dispensation of political rewards or development revenues.[21] As election day approached Sir Albert piled blunder upon blunder. In particular, his threat to unleash, as it were, the Guinean army compounded the gravity of past errors and sharply reduced his base of support especially in the Freetown area. The prime minister also manipulated ethnic imagery with a new-found vehemence, ''charging that a 'Temne-Creole axis' which constituted the APC would 'cut the Mende man's throat' if it came to power.''[22] Furthermore, by early February the SLPMB—its reserves squandered on ill-conceived agricultural plantations and political patronage—could no longer pay off its buying agents in the provinces. This threatened Sierra Leone's cash crop producers with bankruptcy, Mende and Temne alike. When on February 27 six seats were declared unopposed for the SLPP, including the Bonthe-South seat held by Sir Albert's brother, Samuel Margai, the ruling party demonstrated exactly how endangered was its security of tenure. Faced with the prospect of imminent electoral defeat and yet unwilling to hold a totally fraudulent general election, Sir Albert turned more and more to the army as his only remaining trump. That eleventh-hour decision to call upon military assistance—a decision somewhat reminiscent of the reliance on the RWAFF to protect the SLPP and its colonial partners from the Freetown mobs in 1955—was facilitated by favorable tribal and family alignments in the army's officer corps.

The arrest of John Bangura and seven of his followers reduced Lansana's vulnerability to an APC-inspired coup attempt as the political campaign began. Command and staff billets were also organized along sectional lines. Southerners and easterners whose loyalty to the government seemed reasonably assured monopolized all the company commands and presumably most of the platoon commands. The only remaining nonsouthern officer with the rank of major or above was Mark Koroma, who served under Major Jumu as second in command of the army's only battalion. Lansana, however, apparently did not regard Koroma—a nephew of SLESA's A. B. Magba-Kamara who ran on the SLPP ticket in Koinadugu North—as a significant threat to his position. Northern troops supposedly loyal to Bangura were carefully watched and in some instances, only Mende rank and file received arms.[23]

The increased military praetorianism of March culminating in a direct army takeover assumed several forms. In the first place, the army experienced significant role expansion in the weeks prior to the election. For the first time in postindependence history, soldiers of the RSLMF found themselves engaged in domestic internal security duties on a fairly widespread if sporadic scale. Though none of this activity could rival the experience of the third Nigerian battalion in suppressing Tiv unrest between November 1964 and June 1965; at least in Sierra Leone terms, the deployment of troops outside Wilberforce Barracks symbolized a break with past procedures.

The utilization of soldiers to back up the police both in Freetown and the provinces became commonplace after rioting in Kono on nomination day between APC and SLPP partisans led to a declaration of a State of Emergency in that district. Beginning in early March, platoons of soldiers from Daru and Wilberforce took up positions near those urban centers in the provinces inhabited both by Mendes as well as Temnes. Towns that acquired significant concentrations of troops included Makeni, Bo, Blama, Kenema, and Kono.[24] On March 3, following the declaration of a State of Emergency in the Western Area, demonstrators protesting the unopposed return of four

SLPP candidates clashed with police and soldiers outside the office of the Electoral Commissioner in Freetown. Near Blama on March 13, crowds sympathetic to the local SLPP candidate, George Panda, mistakenly fired on an army landrover which happened to have been painted red, the color of the APC's rising sun. One soldier was wounded in the melee, but the contingent under the command of a Kono officer, Lieutenant S. E. Momoh, refused to return the fire once it recognized the attackers as pro-SLPP. Peter Tucker then wrote Lieutenant Momoh to congratulate him and his men for exercising dignity and restraint.[25] On the whole, however, there were no major clashes between the army and the civilian population until just prior to and during the course of Lansana's forty-six-hour reign.

More significant from the perspective of a future civilian-inspired coup d'état was the increasing use of soldiers to protect leading SLPP candidates and civil servants who favored Sir Albert's reelection. The Dove-Edwin Commission noted that the prime minister himself "seemed to have full use of the Army from the 9th of March 1967 when he went to Loko Masama to address Paramount Chiefs, Section Chiefs, Presidents of Courts, Mammy Queens, and others."[26] On this particular trip, according to a returning officer who testified before the commission, "many soldiers" accompanied Sir Albert; and indeed, throughout the campaign the SLPP leader never traveled outside of Freetown without an entourage of security police and armed troops. In his own compound at Lumley Beach he maintained an armed bodyguard which included soldiers of the Sierra Leone Regiment.

Other SLPP stalwarts who felt threatened by APC supporters in their respective constituencies called upon the military for protection. During the treason trial, George Panda, the SLPP candidate for Kenema West, explained how Lieutenant Momoh, who commanded the army platoon stationed in Blama, personally stayed at Panda's residence from March 13 until election day. Peter Tucker told the Dove-Edwin Commission on June 28, 1967 that following the arrests of Bangura and the other predominantly northern officers, soldiers began guarding his compound in Freetown—some five and one-half weeks before the election. Presumably other SLPP loyalists who profited from the Margai-Lansana "connection" could request similar protection, particularly in the days immediately preceding the army's intervention.

With the army now strategically implanted in the countryside and with most SLPP big men now ringed with soldiers as if to cushion them against the unpleasant realities to follow, there remained but one final touch to complete the precoup politicization of the Sierra Leone military. In testimony delivered at the treason trial, David Lansana explained how, during the preliminary investigation into the coup plot involving John Bangura, he decided to conduct all further military operations out of his personal residence at Flagstaff House. Lansana claimed that his decision to switch the army's operational headquarters from Murraytown Barracks to Flagstaff House was prompted by the wish not to confuse "documents in the [Bangura] case . . . with routine matters."[27] Subconsciously, however, Lansana probably viewed the move as a symbolic expression of his increased importance in Sierra Leone's political life. Flagstaff House after all was surrounded on all sides by ministerial quarters as well as by houses inhabited by senior civil servants with vested interests in the perpetuation of SLPP rule. In light of this fact, the move to Flagstaff House would no doubt facilitate easy intercommunication between Lansana and leading figures in the regime. Furthermore, fewer eyebrows might be raised if ministers, paramount chiefs, and other individuals close to Sir Albert shuffled in and out of Flagstaff House to consult with their army "friend" or just to seek refuge than if these same persons called upon the force commander at military headquarters. In the weeks that followed, Flagstaff House offered an ideal setting for civilian-military interaction; as a consequence, Lansana's purely military role assumed less and less importance.

The stationing of troops in the provinces, the formation of military bodyguards to protect leading members of the regime, and the transformation of Flagstaff House from the force commander's personal residence into a quasi-political headquarters—these things considered together seemed to bring the army and the ruling party into close harmony and to assure Sir Albert of the necessary backing in the event of a defeat at the polls. There is even some fragmentary evidence that the whole scenario had been in the planning stages for months. For example, during the treason trial proceedings, Paramount Chief Bai Koblo Pathbana, who had played a prominent role in Sir Milton Margai's administration but who later turned against Sir Albert, related the details of a meeting with George Panda some time in late January. At this meeting Panda apparently explained how he and "other stalwarts" had arranged for a Lansana rescue-operation should the APC prove victorious on March 21. At a "later stage," according to Panda, the army would hand power back to the SLPP—presumably still a political party with Sir Albert at the helm.[28] While a number of SLPP officials whom I interviewed denied Bai Koblo's allegations, three years of continuous social intercourse between members of the government and the armed forces made it probable that a number of such meetings took place. Furthermore, even if Lansana's eventual takeover was not planned on a step-by-step basis, no one in Freetown with an inside line on such matters doubted for one minute that the force commander and the rest of the senior officers of the Sierra Leone army would play some role in the forthcoming elections.

With the removal of Colonel Bangura followed by the strengthening of long standing civilian-military allegiances, Sir Albert's system of civilian control appeared ready to neutralize all claimants to the seat of power. The SLPP inner circle apparently failed to perceive, however, that the Lansana-Margai axis could not alone assure their leader's survival; for by March 1967, cliquism was so rampant in the upper echelons of the officer corps that it had begun to infect even supposed SLPP loyalists such as Majors Blake, Jumu, and Kai-Samba. As the election campaign progressed, these officers posed as much a threat to Sir Albert's position as had Colonel Bangura and the now-departed northern officers. Perhaps it was the less easily decipherable nature of an anti-Lansana but pro-SLPP clique which escaped the prime minister's attention. On the other hand, one wonders why Sir Albert should have failed to anticipate the formation of an anti-Lansana grouping to match the equivalent faction challenging the leadership of the SLPP.[29]

While the exact origins of an anti-Lansana but pro-southern army clique may never be known, the potential for a breakaway Mende-Sherbro sub-group within the Sierra Leone officer corps must have existed for months. Certainly between the discovery of a Bangura-inspired coup plot and Lansana's takeover on March 21, there appears to have been very little consultation between the force commander and his subordinates. The very election campaign, to the extent that it brought the struggle for the SLPP leadership into sharper focus, exacerbated tensions between the southern and eastern "section" of the officer corps.

Perhaps only in the case of Blake did blocked mobility and frustrated career expectations help to initiate anti-Lansana sentiments. Even though with the elimination of Bangura and Genda, Blake became the third most senior officer in the RSLMF (after Lansana and Andrew Juxon-Smith), he was only a GSO, Grade II and thus somewhat lower in status than Major Kai-Samba, the GSO Grade I, and Jumu, the battalion commander. He might have possibly felt slighted by the fact that although he had served on and off in the ranks for some eight years prior to being commissioned in September 1960, he had never received a command post. Jumu, on the other hand, although only passing out of Sandhurst in July 1961, had done very well under Lansana as had Kai-Samba, the senior general staff officer. Furthermore, both Kai-Samba and Jumu shared with Lansana a common ethnic as well as a common regional identity. The two officers enjoyed links with the SLPP either based on existing family connections or those acquired as a result of marriage. Even Blake's Sherbro background technically made him a southerner while his ties with an SLPP cabinet minister linked him to the ruling party and indirectly therefore to the force commander. None of these officers, possibly excepting Blake, appeared to have parted ways with David Lansana over the issue of perceived job discrimination based on nepotism.

As in the Lansana-Bangura controversy, resentment over the force commander's apparent disregard for professional or organizational etiquette helped to precipitate a split between the army leader and at least two of his immediate subordinates. Major Blake explained during the treason trial how, following the discovery of the February coup plot, Lansana ordered the distribution of arms on a purely sectional (read Mende) basis. Blake noted further that "this order to arm this particular section . . . originated from the Force Commander completely side-stepping me through whom the order as the general staff officer should have been relayed."[30] Along similar lines, Major Jumu explained how incensed he became when Lansana together with Sir Albert arranged for the possible deployment of Guinean troops.[31] In the course of arriving at this decision, Lansana failed to weigh the views of either his battalion commander, Jumu, or those of his staff officers. In fact Lansana seems to have avoided any contacts involving substantive staff or command matters with his subordinates after the move to Flagstaff House in mid-February. By the time of election day, the force commander no longer fully trusted the loyalties of anyone but himself, Sir Albert Margai, and those of the Margai diehards such as Peter Tucker, George Panda, and Berthan Macauley.

The decision of Kutubu Kai-Samba, Sir Albert's minister of agriculture, and other members of the SLPP's dissident wing to repudiate their party leadership and to run as independent candidates in the general election offered external justification for the formation of the intra-army cliques. The relationship between the politician Kai-Samba and the army officer Kai-Samba provides the most obvious link between the anti-Margais and the anti-Lansanites. While there is no evidence of extensive contacts between the two Kai-Sambas until just two days prior to Lansana's martial law declaration (when Kutubu Kai-Samba was staying in the major's Freetown house), the elder brother's disgust with SLPP corruption and with Sir Albert's ceaseless meddling in Kenema's "internal affairs" must have long since caught the attention of the army officer.[32]

Sandi Jumu also turned a sympathetic ear toward anti-Margai elements within the SLPP. His paternal uncle, F. Vangahun, belonged to a ruling house family that was contesting the paramount chieftaincy of Nongowa Chiefdom in Kenema District. In June 1966, Vangahun gained a thirty-vote plurality over his nearest rival, a candidate who had received the backing of the prime minister. However, the administrative officer who was supervising the election refused to recognize Vangahun's victory and ruled that the latter needed at least 55 percent of the vote rather than a simple majority. Another attempt was made to hold the election in early 1967 although once again Vangahun failed to gain the 55 percent majority. These decisions seem to have angered both Jumu and the Kai-Sambas who were supporting Vangahun. Furthermore, Jumu's father-in-law, A. D. Wurie, did not belong to the Moyamba group and no longer enjoyed a particularly close relationship with the prime minister. As the struggle over the SLPP leadership intensified during the months prior to the general election, Jumu's loyalty to Lansana and Margai became more and more questionable.

In other ways, a Jumu-Kai-Samba alliance was a logical development. The two officers were born within three months of each other in 1937 and, in light of their ties to ruling houses in Nongowa Chiefdom, were actually distant cousins. Both received their education at the Bo Secondary School and both enlisted as RWAFF cadets in 1958. Jumu's Sandhurst background afforded him a slight advantage at promotion time, but the two always remained close friends. In any dispute with Lansana, the two men could be expected to act in unison.

The changing political alignments that preceded the 1967 general elections also affected Charles Blake's relations with his force commander. Here it was the SLPP-APC struggle rather than the dispute over the SLPP's leadership which impinged upon internally generated army cliques. Although a Sherbro, Blake had attended secondary school in Freetown and apparently "lived with the Creoles." From the perspective of those who did not know him intimately, Blake's indirect links to a Creole minister in Sir Albert's cabinet seemingly counted for less over the long run than his identification with the larger Creole grouping in Freetown and the Western Area. It was the Creoles, after all, who had transferred their allegiances to Siaka Stevens and the APC; according to Blake, his purchase of a red-colored automobile triggered speculation that he favored the APC. Lansana himself subscribed to this view for in his cross-examination of Blake during the treason trial held in 1969, he accused Blake of having purchased the car "because you wanted it to appear that your sympathy lay with the All Peoples Congress."[33] It is highly improbable, however, that Blake leaned in any specific way towards the APC as did Colonel Bangura at the time of his arrest. At the same time, however, Blake lacked the kind of direct ties with the Mende element within the SLPP which were shared by Jumu and Kai-Samba. Nevertheless, Blake's southern origins in addition to his growing disaffection with Lansana rendered him suitable for eventual recruitment into the Jumu-Kai-Samba group. If only in terms of their ages alone—the three officers averaged only thirty-two—these men clearly stood apart from their boss who was almost forty-five.

By March 17th, 1967—election day in Sierra Leone—those actors who would participate in the forthcoming game of musical chairs assumed their respective positions on the stage. As a result, distinctions between the appropriate military sphere of influence as opposed to the appropriate civilian sphere blurred considerably. Civilian cliques came to be identified with army cliques and vice versa. Virtually none of these cliques, whether of the civilian or military variety, was motivated by absolutist political ideologies, but rather by elementary leader-follower relationships. Groups of people lined up behind certain big men who were expected to act as providers or patrons. Alliances of this nature, both within and without the army, were inherently fragile and unstable, capable of forming at one moment and dying the next.

As election day approached, the most noteworthy clique was that under the joint direction of Sir Albert Margai and David Lansana. Beginning around March 17, Lansana—the army commander—became the undisputed boss of this particular clique while Sir Albert barricaded himself in his own Lumley Beach residence. Large numbers of civilian leaders who persisted in associating themselves with a dying political regime came to Lansana rather than to Sir Albert in order to pay homage. But the civilian clique with an army commander at its helm was to prove very short-lived; for on March 23, yet another clique—this one almost entirely military in composition—stepped in to form Sierra Leone's first noncivilian government.

# 7

# *COUPS AND COUNTERCOUPS: THE FALL OF THE SLPP*

In most sub-Saharan African countries, so-called "national" politics remains largely the affair of the capital city. It is here, for example, that one finds the presidential palace, the broadcasting services, and all government offices. Moreover, under a system of civilian leadership, the ruling party—to the extent that it has not atrophied completely or become a parabureaucratic machine—conducts the bulk of its operations in the capital. The governing elites, whether of the political, military, or bureaucratic variety, spend most of their time in the capital and conduct their intrigues in fashionable suburbs nearby. It is this often top-heavy centralization of political and managerial power within a very small area which has afforded such a compelling target for ambitious young African army officers. By deploying a few troops here and arresting a few ministers there, almost any member of the armed forces, whether he be a private, an NCO, or brigadier-general, can assume control of the state on almost a moment's notice.

In Sierra Leone, the concentration of "things that matter" in the capital, Freetown, is perhaps more pronounced than in many other African states. From a coupmaker's perspective, the physical setting of the city leaves little to be desired. Sandwiched between a range of high mountains on one side and the ocean on the other, the city affords a neat, compact milieu for army takeovers. Except for one company of troops at far-off Daru, all members of the armed forces, both enlisted men and officers, live in barracks located only five to ten minutes from the heart of Freetown. From Wilberforce Barracks, which commands a sweeping view of the city's west end, a single road winds its way past the main studios of Radio Sierra Leone to the governor-general's and prime minister's offices. Furthermore, by a short jaunt from both Wilberforce and Murraytown, one can reach almost all the homes of government officials. The logistics of coupmaking in Sierra Leone present virtually no physical obstacles even to the most unsophisticated of strategists. Round up a few big men, mount a guard over several buildings of symbolic value, and you have your coup d'état.

One other factor—the obvious lack of significant countervailing forces or checking agents—made the execution of the 1967 series of coups a relatively mundane undertaking. In Ghana, Kwame Nkrumah established the President's Own Guard Regiment (POGR) as a defense against a possibly mutinous regular army or elements within that army. In Uganda, President Milton Obote organized an elite core called the "Special Forces" which "functioned primarily as a kind of special presidential unit, potentially performing a bodyguard role and deriving special status from its privileged position within the military."[1] Sir Albert Margai, however, never believed that the Sierra Leone army would turn against him and designed a system of civilian control that apparently ruled out military intervention except of the "protective" type. For this reason, Lansana faced virtually no impediments to his course of action. As far as Blake, Jumu, and Kai-Samba were concerned, nothing more was required for the execution of their counter-coup than to arrest the brigadier and Sir Albert. Furthermore, with Bangura, Tarawallie, and other northern officers detained in Pademba Road prison, countervailing forces within the army could not possibly rally themselves.

## THE LANSANA COUP

Military intervention in Sierra Leone can be said to have occurred over roughly a six-day period—that is from the morning of election day, March 17, until the early afternoon of March 23 when the National Reformation Council came into existence. That intervention did not take place in one bold stroke can be attributed to several factors. First, the whole process of coupmaking soon became rather ad hoc. Second, the progress of the election results determined so much of the intervention's timing, and third, army cliquism delayed the establishment of full-fledged military rule.

During the course of the takeover, no less than four individuals actually ruled Sierra Leone, although from March 17 onward de facto control of the country resided largely with the army. Theoretically, Sir Albert remained prime minister from March 17 to the morning of March 21. On the afternoon of that same day, Siaka P. Stevens was sworn in as prime minister by the governor-general, Sir Henry Lightfoot-Boston, in a brief ceremony at State House. About one hour after Stevens's appointment, the new prime minister along with several members of his cabinet were placed under house arrest by Lieutenant Samuel Norman, acting upon the advice emanating from Flagstaff House. Exactly two days later, Lansana was, in turn, the object of a countercoup engineered by his two general staff officers and by the commander of the 1st Battalion. On the evening of March 23, Major Charles Blake went on national radio to announce in matter-of-fact tones that he and his fellow officers had disassociated themselves from the brigadier's "line of action" and "had no alternative but to divest the brigadier of control of Sierra Leone."[2] Blake concluded by saying that the army and police were totally in control of the country and would establish a new government.

Any account of Sierra Leone's muddled civil-military relations during this period of political vacuum must begin with a brief account of the conduct of the 1967 general elections, particularly the handling of election returns. In spite of all the SLPP's efforts to manipulate the election results—efforts which ultimately floundered because they were implemented in such a half-hearted, inefficient way—it was clear by March 18, the day following polling for the ordinary members of parliament, that the APC would probably prove an eventual victor.[3] On Saturday morning, March 18, the SLBS began broadcasting the returns in pairs, always taking precautions to show the SLPP in the lead. By noon on Sunday the radio claimed a total of thirty-one seats for the SLPP, twenty-eight for the APC, and two seats going to the independents with five more seats yet to be declared. This breakdown in seats won by by both parties also appeared in the morning issue of the *Daily Mail* of March 20. Not until 8:00 PM on the evening of the 20th did the public receive another up-to-date election report, over the BBC, calling attention to an APC claim that the election had in fact resulted in a deadlock, 32:32, between the two parties. Finally, on the morning of March 21 at 11:30, SLBS broadcast the results of four of the remaining seats outstanding, noting APC victories in three of these. Most Sierra Leoneans never heard the results of Moyamba West since these were deliberately held back as an APC victory in that constituency grew imminent.[4] According to the SLBS figures, therefore, the SLPP had won thirty-two seats, the APC, thirty-one seats, and the independents, two seats.[5]

The election results as reported over the national radio were clearly fraudulent. In order to produce an electoral victory, the SLPP, and specifically the hand-picked chief elections officer, doctored the figures to include the six "unopposed" returns, even though in each instance slight technical errors in the nomination forms resulted in the initial disqualification of APC or independent candidates. Also, about ten days prior to the election for regular MPs, a number of independents were requested to sign documents stating that, in the event of their winning in their respective constituencies, they should be declared "independent SLPP candidates" by returning officers. This was done primarily to avoid further intimidation by followers of Sir Albert. During the broadcasting of the election results, the radio claimed that four of the six victorious independents—Messrs. Prince J. Williams, J. B. Francis, Frank S. Anthony, and Manna Kapaka—had declared for the SLPP. However, by noon of March 21, the governor-general, Sir Henry Lightfoot-Boston, was in receipt of a letter from Mr. Anthony in which the latter indicated that he had not in fact declared for the SLPP and that he was remaining an independent member of parliament. Sir Henry was also informed by four other independents—L.A.M. Brewah, K. I. Kai-Samba, as well as Francis and Williams—that all intended to take their seats in Parliament as "Independent Members" and they wanted "it to be known to the People of Sierra Leone that we shall at all appropriate times co-operate in whatever measure may be deemed necessary in the national interest with any of the two Political Parties which commands the majority of members in the House, provided that in the case of the Sierra Leone People's Party the present leader of that Party Sir Albert Margai, resigns the Premiership and his leadership of that Party."[6] In actual fact, the APC was the real winner with thirty-two seats (including Moyamba West), while the SLPP could only rightfully claim victories in twenty-two contested seats with six unopposed SLPP returns and six independents.

As the flow of election results—however doctored—continued to proclaim the demise of Sir Albert Margai, the power of the force commander, of his immediate subordinates, and of the Sierra Leone military as a political referee increased concomitantly. This precoup expansion of the army's importance in things political assumed two forms. On one level, soldiers of the Royal Sierra Leone Military Forces became exceedingly visible in the Freetown area, both in the streets and near public buildings. On another level, Flagstaff House became the real center of political power in Sierra Leone at least four days prior to Lansana's martial law declaration. It was at Flagstaff House that civilian and military elites prepared for what Cartwright terms their "last desperate fling."[7]

Beginning on the morning of March 18, scores of troops took up positions at strategic points throughout Freetown and its immediate environs. By March 21, the number of soldiers involved in duties associated with the general elections probably exceeded 200 or more in the Western Area alone. Almost a full company of troops armed with automatic weapons and commanded by a young Kissi officer, Captain S. J. Foyah, bivouacked at Tower Hill, just adjacent to the governor-general's residence. Members of this unit were later to participate in the house arrest of the governor-general, Siaka Stevens, and several newly appointed APC ministers.

On March 17, fifty to seventy-five troops mounted sentry duties at the studios of the Sierra Leone Broadcasting Service (SLBS) and at the Goderich Transmitting site, a few miles outside of Freetown. Theoretically these soldiers were sent to protect SLBS employees from APC harassment, but in fact their presence signified an outright army takeover of the nation's communications system, a takeover designed to influence the reporting of the election returns.[8] The troops also established a wireless network linking the broadcasting studio and the transmission site with Brigadier Lansana at Flagstaff House so as to keep the army commander fully informed of developments in the APC-SLPP electoral struggle. All of the contingents involved in these operations were commanded by Mende lieutenants who took orders directly from Lansana.

Since March 3, soldiers had guarded the Electoral Commission against APC supporters in Freetown who suspected an SLPP attempt to manipulate the election returns. On the morning of March 18, according to evidence given at the treason trial, Brigadier Lansana ordered two Mende warrant officers along with a number of soldiers to reinforce the already sizable contingent at the electoral commissioner's office. These officers were to keep Lansana posted on the election returns and apparently worked hand in hand with a senior member of the Electoral Commission office in falsifying the election returns announcements, particularly when it became evident that the independents would refuse to declare for the SLPP.[9]

The despatching of troops to State House, to the broadcasting and transmission sites, and to the office of the Electoral Commission in Freetown all seem to have formed part of a deliberate precoup strategy. The brigadier himself, with at least the tacit compliance of his battalion commander and staff officers, engineered the placement of soldiers at these locations in Freetown. Each unit of troops, as we have said, was commanded by a Mende officer or by an officer with minority group affiliations but loyal to the southern cause. This meant that when the time arrived to actually set the coup in motion and seize power, it would not be necessary to engage in large-scale troop movements or to conduct last-minute loyalty tests among the officers. Lansana, in his defense, claimed that on March 15, Sir Albert Margai, acting under the terms of the Royal Sierra Leone Military Forces Act, requested him to "deploy the army in aid of the Civil Authorities during the period of the General Elections in 1967." "Armed with that request," Lansana continued, "he gave orders for the deployment of troops at key points and other areas in the Western Area which included the State House, the SLBS Transmitting Station. . . ."[10] Having been a young lieutenant during the 1955 Freetown riots the brigadier no doubt recalled the historic role of the RWAFF as a mechanism for preserving internal security in times of disorder. Given his long period of tenure under a colonial army, it should not be surprising that Lansana easily confused the notion of "aid to the civil power" with that of "aid to the SLPP" even though this latter objective required the army to shore up a crumbling, discredited regime and, in the process, to exercise a discriminatory political judgment.

This is not to deny that there did exist some genuine internal security threats. *Unity,* a pro-SLPP newspaper, noted that on election day, "several returning and presiding officers had to seek army protection as APC supporters threatened to beat them up."[11] Along Kroo Town Road in Freetown clashes between Fulas and APC voters on March 18 and 19 resulted in scores of injuries and necessitated the deployment of troops along with police. But these were relatively isolated incidents, for most people in Freetown were waiting patiently for the appointment of their chosen leader, Siaka P. Stevens. At no time, did there exist a threat of real violence near State House or at the broadcasting stations. Lansana's decision to saturate these areas with troops seems in retrospect to have formed part of a calculated precoup alignment of forces, deployed under the guise of internal security duties.

As armed troops moved into key positions throughout Freetown, consultations between the force commander and leading SLPP enthusiasts—heretofore confined primarily to social events and to occasional party rallies—assumed an unprecedented urgency and explicitness. From the morning of March 17 onward, a number of officials closely associated with Sir Albert Margai visited Flagstaff House, some ostensibly to seek protection from APC "red shirts," others apparently to dispense advice on how best to cope with the rapidly declining fortunes of the ruling circle.[12] Included in this first group were Kandeh Bureh, an SLPP minister; S.B. Daramy, the financial secretary; and Peter Tucker, secretary to the prime minister. Bureh explained during the treason trial how, upon receiving news of his defeat at the hands of the APC's Ibrahim Taqi, he decided to "ask for refuge at Flagstaff House" where "Brigadier Lansana was happy to receive me." The brigadier also agreed to despatch a contingent of soldiers to Bureh's Freetown residence where "some people were molesting his supporters." Bureh claimed further that as of Sunday afternoon, March 19, his wives, his children, and most of his loyal followers were firmly under Lansana's personal protection at the now heavily guarded Flagstaff House compound.[13]

Other SLPP stalwarts sought help from their ally in the Sierra Leone army. S. B. Daramy saw the brigadier on the afternoon of March 20 and requested a military bodyguard. In his testimony, Daramy mentioned Peter Tucker as yet another individual who had literally moved in with the brigadier.

About 4 p.m. [March 20] some hooligans came up to his place stoning his house. So he went up to Flagstaff House to see [Lansana]. When he got there he told [Lansana] how he was being molested; that his life was in danger. Peter Tucker whom he found there also told him that as a matter of fact he was also molested and had gone to [Lansana] for refuge.[14]

Some informants reported that Tucker became a permanent resident at Flagstaff House as of the first of March.

By late in the afternoon of March 20, just twenty-four hours before Lansana's arrest of Siaka Stevens and declaration of martial law, Flagstaff House had become a "refugee camp" for virtually all those members of the ruling elite who could not permit the SLPP to die a natural death. Apart from Bureh, Daramy, and Tucker, this expanded civilian clique also included Gershon Collier, the chief justice; John Kallon, the establishment secretary; George Panda, who had lived under army protection for over a week; A. B. Paila, who lost to the independent L.A.M. Brewah in Moyamba North, as well as several more obscure figures. All members of this group were apparently united in their determination to salvage SLPP rule at any cost, if only to preserve their respective jobs. As the election results warned of impending disaster, Collier, Tucker, Daramy, and the rest shifted their immediate loyalties away from the formal head of government to the man who possessed the guns. In his willingness to receive these men and to provide security in their hour of need, Lansana was fulfilling his very special role as guardian of the civilian ruling group—a role bestowed upon him almost three years earlier at the SLPP convention in Makeni.

The physical presence of SLPP loyalists in the private residence of their army commander gives us at least prima facie evidence of a civilian-inspired military coup. The prosecution during the treason trial of Lansana and his supporters in 1969 and 1970 paid considerable attention to several incidents that it believed confirmed the existence of a premeditated conspiracy. According to the testimony of a number of prosecution witnesses, the decision whether or not to call upon the services of David Lansana hinged on the results of an SLPP campaign to win over those former party members who were returned as independents in the general election. For example, after it had been confirmed that L.A.M. Brewah had defeated the official SLPP candidate, A. B. Paila, in the Moyamba North constituency, an attempt was made to persuade Brewah to declare for the SLPP. One prosecution witness, a lecturer at the Njala University College, testified that late on the evening of March 19, Brewah met with Peter Tucker and other Margai supporters in Bo. When they were unable to convince Brewah to rejoin the party, Tucker announced that "I am going to Freetown and I believe that the Army will have to intervene."[15] In testimony delivered at the proceedings of the Dove-Edwin Commission, Brewah stated that "when it was realized that he and

Mr. Kai-Samba would not go over to the S.L.P.P. the Secretary to the Prime Minister was heard to say 'Let us go to Freetown and let Lansana take over.' ''[16]

According to other accounts, yet another group of Margai enthusiasts met with the force commander's sister-in-law, Madam Gulama, in Moyamba. Along with Gulama were to be found Sir Albert himself, George Panda, and the prime minister's brother, Samuel, who was returned unopposed in the Moyamba South constituency. At this meeting, Ella Koblo Gulama is alleged to have said "that as they had been unable to get the government again they all should go down to Freetown and meet Brigadier Lansana . . . with a big sum of money for him to take over the government."[17] She claimed that once in power Lansana would soon restore Sir Albert. This story, however, loses a certain degree of credibility by the reference to the "big sum of money." There were already an adequate number of nonmonetary incentives for Lansana to intervene without the uses of bribes.

Whether or not the Bo and Moyamba incidents occurred exactly as described matters little. What has never been disputed is that, beginning at least several days before the army actually assumed control of Sierra Leone, the force commander found himself surrounded by members of a doomed regime whose only hope of retaining power lay with a military take-over—disguised, as we shall see, as an attempt to "uphold" the constitution of Sierra Leone. Never mind that this group included a judge, an attorney-general, and other prominent civil servants who, under normal circumstances, were expected to act as impartial observers of political comings and goings. On the contrary, a number of these men owed their positions to governmental nepotism and feared possible victimization in the event of an SLPP defeat. Through a self-serving appeal to primordial loyalties, Tucker, Bureh, and the rest easily persuaded Lansana to reciprocate for favors previously received and to intervene in pursuit of a narrowly defined good. Even if we never know precisely what transpired at Bo, Moyamba, and most important, at Flagstaff House in the days prior to the Lansana coup; no one can challenge the view that a group of people who should have known better had lined up behind the commander of the Royal Sierra Leone Military Forces, and by so doing, made a mockery of orthodox patterns of civil-military relations.

The underlying approach to coupmaking in Sierra Leone hardly differed from practices observed in a number of black African states with a single urban center and with tiny, fragmented armies. In almost every instance of African army takeovers, the capital city has witnessed the bulk of the action. Moreover, it is almost exclusively the urban elites who conduct these affairs with the common man often no more than a helpless, if not necessarily an impassive onlooker. During the course of the coup d'état, formal political institutions—for example, political parties, legislative assemblies, and constitutions—are decreed out of existence. Overall command of real political resources will often pass from one group of civilians to a single army strong man to yet another clique of army officers. Since almost anyone with a gun may become supreme in the land simply by "arresting" his enemy, no one claimant to political power emerges as any more or any less legitimate than his fellow competitors. All of this accurately describes civil-military relations in Sierra Leone from March 21 until the return of Lieutenant-Colonel Andrew T. Juxon-Smith from England on March 28.

The events that touched off Brigadier David Lansana's intervention were set in motion on the afternoon of March 20. At that time, Sir Henry Lightfoot-Boston, acting on the belief that the SLPP and the APC had deadlocked at thirty-two seats apiece with two seats going to the independents, requested a meeting with Sir Albert Margai and Siaka P. Stevens. The governor-general suggested that the two political leaders consider forming a coalition government, and, if agreeing to do so, they should return to State House on the afternoon of March 22 to work out the necessary details. However, within a few hours after his meeting with Sir Albert and Sir Henry, Stevens decided to reject the governor-general's offer since no one in the APC would support such a plan. He then proceeded back to State House to inform Sir Henry of the APC's unwillingness to collaborate with the SLPP. Accompanying Mr. Stevens were Ibrahim Taqi and C. B. Rogers-Wright, two newly elected APC parliamentarians. One source claims that a substantial Creole delegation with obvious APC leanings also appeared with the soon-to-be-appointed prime minister. Included in this delegation were Sir Emil Fashole Luke, a supreme court justice; the Anglican bishop of Sierra Leone, M. O. Scott; and the Reverend S. M. Renner, an old associate of Sir Milton Margai.[18] By the time of their arrival at State House, large crowds of APC sympathizers had gathered. Major Kai-Samba told a treason trial jury that when Sir Henry's aide-de-camp, Lieutenant Samuel Hinga Norman, refused Stevens's request to see the governor-general, he [Kai-Samba] prevailed on Norman to arrange for an audience after Stevens agreed to disperse the scores of people who congregated around the State House gates.[19]

Once inside State House, Stevens delivered a formal note in which he listed his reasons for refusing to join with the SLPP in a coalition government. The APC leader noted that "the differences between the two parties, such as the differences between the One Party System and the proposed Republican Constitution, are so fundamental that the two Parties could not possibly work together."[20] He stated further that in terms of the popular vote alone, the APC, with "over 270,000 votes as opposed to the 240,000 gained by the SLPP and 120,000 for the independents" could and should be allowed to form a government.[21] Sir Henry told Siaka Stevens that he would be in touch with both leaders by the following morning and would "prepare an announcement."

Despite the SLPP's best efforts to manipulate the election returns, by the morning of March 21 the governor-general knew the true standing of the parties and was thus in a position to dismiss as false the SLPP claim of having persuaded four of the six independent victors to declare for Sir Albert's party. In Freetown itself, whose citizens cast 72 percent of their votes for the APC, a sophisticated rumor mill provided more accurate election results than those broadcast by the SLBS. By the morning of March 21, members of all those Freetown groups from Creole barristers to Temne taxi-drivers who supported the APC knew of their party's victory at the polls and gathered near State House to cheer the expected appointment of Siaka Probyn Stevens as prime minister of Sierra Leone.

According to Section 58(2) of the independence constitution, "whenever the Governor-General has occasion to appoint a Prime Minister he shall appoint a member of the House of Representatives who appears to him likely to command the support of the majority of the members of the House."[22] It was on the basis of this article that Sir Henry, when confronted with the facts of the 1967 general elections, decided not to reappoint Sir Albert Margai as head of government. Accordingly, Siaka Stevens and a number of his future ministers were summoned to State House and informed that a swearing-in ceremony was planned for 3:00 that afternoon. Sir Henry's decision to exercise his seemingly unfettered discretion in the appointment of a prime minister brought home the reality of the SLPP's defeat and the impossibility of a peaceful changing of the guard untainted by military praetorianism.

Faced with the impending appointment of a man who would no doubt call a halt to his military career, Brigadier David Lansana embarked upon a course of action that would sabotage Sir Milton's oft-repeated assertion that Sierra Leone would become "a model state." Around 10:00 AM on the 21st, Lansana visited State House and learned firsthand of the governor-general's intention to appoint Siaka Stevens. Accounts differ as to Lansana's reaction to this news. A number of prosecution witnesses such as Sir Henry's personal secretary, O.P.A. Macauley, testified that Lansana during the course of his conversation with the governor-general suddenly became extremely agitated and warned Sir Henry not to act precipitously. Lansana apparently pointed to a map of Sierra Leone and suggested that, since the electorate had divided along tribal lines, an appointment of a new prime minister would lead to a riot and to bloodshed.[23] Lansana in his defense claimed that Sir Henry agreed not to make an appointment until all the results of the paramount chief elections—being held on March 21—were tabulated. This was an obvious distortion of the facts, for not only was Siaka Stevens at State House at the very time of Lansana's interview but, in addition, Sir Henry no longer entertained any illusions as to who appeared "likely to command the support of the majority of the members of the House." Furthermore, apart from the relatively minor and isolated scuffles between Fulas and APC supporters along Kroo Town Road, Sierra Leone could hardly be depicted as on the verge of a tribal bloodbath requiring massive army intervention. On the contrary, the crowds that lined the streets of the capital were in a decidedly jubilant mood, waiting patiently if a bit anxiously for their place in the sun.

The "constitutionality" of Sir Henry's decision to appoint Siaka Stevens prime minister without waiting for the results of the paramount chief elections deserves brief mention here as this particular issue offered the brigadier a convenient pretext for declaring martial law. In early February, C. A. Kamara-Taylor, the APC secretary-general, wrote Attorney-General Berthan Macauley seeking clarification as to the role of the paramount chiefs in the forthcoming elections. Macauley in turn referred the letter to the governor-general on February 18. In expressing his own views on the subject, Macauley, apparently favoring the position eventually adopted by Sir Henry on March 21, noted as follows that " . . . the duty of the Governor-General is *not* to determine what person has the support of the majority of the members of the House. His duty is to determine what person is *likely* to command the support of the majority of the members of the House."[24] This was clearly not the same as saying that the governor-general must wait for the results of the paramount chief elections *prior* to exercising his judgment under the constitutional section. Custom, of course, dictated that the paramount chiefs support the government of the day if only to preserve their staffs.[25] They were most definitely not in a position, as Cartwright shows, to exercise freedom of choice in granting or withholding their confidence from an incumbent prime minister. No paramount chief ever ran on a party label and was thus qualitatively different from an ordinary member. Once Stevens had been appointed, only the most daring of paramount chiefs would attempt to defy the government in power for fear of being dethroned. In the final analysis, Sir Henry's decision was fundamentally cricket, so it was scarcely appropriate for the army commander to interpret key clauses of the Sierra Leone constitution.

Once it became known that Stevens would soon be sworn in as prime minister, the APC made preparations for the formal assumption of political office. Sembu Forna and Cyril Foray, later to become ministers, approached the Guinean ambassador in Freetown and were assured that Sékou Touré (who perhaps for the first time recognized the inevitable) would not intervene.[26] Stevens then met personally with the commissioner of police, Leslie William Leigh, at the office of *Shekpendeh,* an opposition newspaper. According to Leigh: "I asked Mr. Stevens whether he trusted me because I knew he was the third Prime Minister I was going to work for [the others being Sir Milton and Sir Albert]. Mr. Stevens said, yes 'I trust you' and that I should do all I could to assist him.''[27] Leigh then promised to accompany the new prime minister from the Shekpendeh press building to State House for the swearing-in ceremony that afternoon.

Leigh's readiness to support Mr. Stevens at this crucial moment can be easily explained. In the waning days of SLPP rule, Leigh was known to have fallen out of favor with both Sir Albert and the force commander. On several occasions, Leigh opposed what he considered an infringement of police prerogatives when Lansana stationed troops in the provinces as a show of force during chiefdom palavers. Of mixed Liberian and Susu ancestry, Leigh grew up in Freetown, attended the St. Edwards secondary school there, and probably regarded himself as a Creole. Like other Creoles, Leigh rallied to the flag of Great Britain during the war and served as an RAF fighter pilot. Upon his return to Sierra Leone, he joined the Colonial Police Force and, as a culmination to an outstanding career, became commissioner of police in July 1963. By March 1967, his loyalties had become suspect; and, had Sir Albert retained the premiership, Leigh might have been forcibly retired. Most SLPP leaders considered Leigh unreliable for not doing "enough to protect the Fulas and the government itself.''[28] Considering most of the senior gazetted officers in the police force were either Creoles or northerners, their loyalties to the SLPP regime could not be taken for granted, unlike those in the army.[29] As for the APC's relationship with the RSLMF, the departure of Bangura eliminated any possibility of elements within the army staging a pro-APC countercoup should Lansana attempt to intervene on behalf of Sir Albert. About all the APC could do was to proceed with its plans for the assumption of office and to hope for the best.

As Siaka Stevens and members of his future cabinet waited to be sworn-in by the governor-general, David Lansana and other SLPP loyalists made preparations of their own. The permanent secretary in the Ministry of Information, Mr. Thomas Decker—a close follower of Sir Albert—initiated the day's activities when he visited State House but a few hours after the force commander had departed in a rage. Decker was handed a script announcing Steven's appointment and, under normal procedures, should have headed directly for SLBS in order to broadcast this momentous news. Instead, Decker received a telephone call from the attorney-general, Berthan Macauley, who requested him to proceed immediately to the latter's Hill Station residence.

Upon his arrival at Hill Station #1, Decker came upon the attorney-general, the brigadier, and Peter Tucker all engaged in a spirited discussion of the Sierra Leone constitution. In Decker's own words:

I now say that, on my arrival at the A. G.'s house, and having been informed by the Brigadier that he had taken over the government of Sierra Leone, I told him that I had an announcement to make, received from the Governor-General about the appointment of Mr. Siaka Stevens as Prime Minister of Sierra Leone. The Brigadier then asked me, where is the announcement script. I took it off my coat pocket and he snatched it from my hand, and said "You make no announcement".[30]

Tucker, Decker, and Macauley then proceeded with Lansana to Flagstaff House where they met John Kallon, Kandeh Bureh, and other SLPP supporters. By this time, Majors Blake, Jumu, and Kai-Samba had also joined the throng as did Lieutenants Emile Gbassa and Humphrey Swarray, although civilian big men at Flagstaff House still outnumbered army officers by well over two to one.

It was in the early afternoon of March 21 that a civilian-military coalition which had come together out of enlightened self-interest, decided that the governor-general's "hasty" action required drastic measures. Armed with an apparent mandate from Berthan Macauley who expressed the "honestly held opinion" that Sir Henry's decision to appoint a new prime minister violated the constitution, Brigadier Lansana concluded that "the only measure left open was military intervention pending the resolution of the political crisis which had arisen by the appointment of a Prime Minister whilst elections were still going on."[31]

Whether or not Lansana was actually incited by Bureh, Tucker, and the rest is an academic issue. We already have shown that all these individuals had a very important stake in the preservation of SLPP rule, were on the whole intimately acquainted with the force commander, and would not under any circumstances have sought to thwart the brigadier's strategies. As for Blake, Jumu, and Kai-Samba, each shared with the brigadier a common desire to see the interests of southerners perpetuated no matter how much they may have come to dislike Lansana's administrative methods and his fondness for Sir Albert Margai. The most advantageous moment for this particular clique to declare its independence vis-à-vis the brigadier was not to come for several days.

Around 2:30 in the afternoon of March 21, word reached David Lansana and his friends of the governor-general's intention to swear in Stevens as prime minister. Lansana immediately ordered Captain Foyah to surround State House to keep the crowds at bay. He then requested Commissioner Leigh, under threat of arrest, to proceed directly to Flagstaff House rather than accompanying Mr. Stevens to the governor-general's office. Leigh complied with the brigadier's order because, as the commissioner expressed it, "if the army wants to do something, there is nothing the police can do as our function is to keep the peace. . . . The army is trained to fight."[32] Thus it can be said that Leigh was ordered against his will to participate in a military takeover. For this reason, the police role in the Sierra Leone coup differed considerably from that in Ghana where Commissioner John Harlley, according to some sources, plotted with the army officers at least two-and-a-half years before the February intervention.[33]

The actual seizure of power in Sierra Leone paralleled those operations common to most "golpes d'estado" in countries with minimal political and infrastructural resources. Upon learning of Stevens impending arrival at State House, Lansana ordered Sir Henry's aide-de-camp, Lieutenant Norman, to meet with him at Hill Station. There at Flagstaff House in the presence of a large contingent of SLPP stalwarts and senior army officers, the brigadier told Norman to return to State House, to seal off all the entrances, and to place Stevens and the other APC leaders under house arrest. Upon his return to the State House compound, Norman announced that no one would be allowed to leave the premises and that anyone attempting an escape would be shot on sight.[34] Captain Foyah then issued each member of his Tower Hill Company five rounds of ammunition and Norman arrested Siaka Stevens, C. B. Rogers-Wright, Mohamed Forna, Soloman Pratt, Ibrahim Taqi, and the assistant commissioner of police, Alpha Kamara, as well as Sir Henry himself. All told, the APC was in power for approximately one hour before being toppled by the Sierra Leone army in conjunction with members of the opposition SLPP.

Once having arrested Siaka Stevens and the other APC leaders, the commander of the Sierra Leone army worked swiftly to consolidate his grip on the country's political life. Late on the afternoon of March 21, the brigadier drove from Flagstaff House to the Goderich Transmitting Site and at 5:55 addressed the nation as "custodian of state security." Lansana told Sierra Leoneans that in order to "protect the constitution and to maintain law and order" he was compelled to declare martial law. The force commander also claimed that in his early morning audience with Sir Henry, the governor-general had promised not to appoint a prime minister until informed of the results of the paramount chief elections. Lansana spoke of "a widespread rumor put out by the APC . . . that the Governor-General has appointed Mr. Siaka Stevens as prime minister." "This rumor," he continued, "[was] an attempt to ignore the Constitution, and seize power by force"; all of which could only bring on "chaos and civil war." The brigadier concluded by noting that "from now on the army is in control and will use its power to see that the Constitution is not violated."[35]

Given our knowledge of the actual course of events on March 21, it is not especially difficult to discount most of Brigadier Lansana's ex-post facto arguments for having arrested Sierra Leone's prime minister. His charge that the APC had endeavored to "seize power by force" perpetuated a deceit of the highest order while talk of an impending civil war bore little resemblance to prevailing conditions. These facts were hardly lost on the people of Freetown who shortly after the force commander's broadcast massed in the streets to vent their anger. Crowds of APC supporters moved from Freetown's east end toward State House and "cut down trees which they used in blocking the streets [along] with scrap vehicles, drums and piled up stones."[36] Apparently some of the more zealous "red shirts" blew up the Hastings bridge outside the city limits and endeavored to do the same at the Congo Cross bridge in Freetown only to run short of explosives. Another group attempted to free Colonel Bangura from Pademba Road prison but were foiled by soldiers guarding the former deputy force commander.

Soon there ensued direct confrontations between army troops and defenseless civilians particularly in the area around State House and Independence Avenue. In the melee that followed, the army used liberal amounts of tear gas and, on several occasions, opened fire with automatic weapons. Estimates vary as to the number of deaths recorded that evening, but at least ten civilians were killed by army bullets with scores more sustaining injuries.[37] By the morning of March 22, soldiers patrolled most of the main streets, and an uneasy calm eventually prevailed.

With order apparently restored in the capital, Brigadier Lansana turned his attention away from the commonplace demands of peace-keeping to the somewhat more delicate problem of sustaining his yet unchallenged right to rule. To do so, it was necessary for the brigadier to maintain the fiction that he, unlike the governor-general, had only acted to protect the constitution. Thus on the morning of March 22, SLBS announced the results of the paramount chief elections, noting that of eleven districts reporting, ten had been declared SLPP.[38] At 8:15 AM, the brigadier requested all members of the "present government" as well as newly elected MPs to come to Freetown to meet together and to resolve the so-called constitutional crisis. In this way, the brigadier could convey the impression that he had merely protected the lawful—read SLPP—government of Sierra Leone against APC-inspired subversion.

This twisted logic eventually assumed the form of a long, detailed radio broadcast on the night of March 22 in which Lansana sought to describe in greater detail the reasons for his behavior. Once again he repeated his dubious constitutional arguments and once again he lied about the election returns. To these misrepresentations, was added the false scenario of a country "on the brink of intertribal warfare" as a result of the efforts of political propagandists. One particular section of the speech deserves quotation in full:

I want to make it clear that the Army—and I say this after consultation with my senior officers—does not, I repeat, does not, intend to impose a

Military Government on the people of Sierra Leone. This country has a record for Constitutional Government.

Nevertheless, as soldiers, when the Constitution is violated and violation is likely to lead—and in this case was actually leading to a breakdown of law and order, I and my officers felt that, in accordance with established practice, we should come to the aid of the civil power to restore Constitutional Government and law and order.[39]

Much of this resembles the kind of statements that we have come to associate with some Latin American coupmakers who, like their African counterparts, may intervene to "protect" the constitutions of their respective homelands. On the internal security question, Christopher Clapham points out that "newly installed military governments are prone to call in the spectre of civil war to justify their seizing power" but that such appeals do not "function as part of any general conception of human nature or of government responsibility but rather as a language appropriate to back up military appeals for support."[40] Blake and company would also resort to such arguments in their initial quest for respectability.

In a superficial sense, Lansana's declaration of martial law appeared to give the SLPP a measure of breathing room. According to the prevailing rationale, it was believed that by convening a meeting of all members of parliament including the paramount chiefs, it might be possible to keep Sir Albert's regime intact. Of course, this regime necessarily would have differed radically from its predecessor. Even were Sir Albert to retain nominal control of the premiership, David Lansana and the army as a whole could have been expected to exercise a pervasive influence over the functioning of the system. Had Lansana consolidated his position and exercised authority through an SLPP figurehead, we might have had the first instance in black Africa of what Finer terms "indirect-complete military rule."[41]

By entrusting their political future to Brigadier David Lansana, the SLPP leadership, together with their followers in the civil service and among the professions, gambled on a man who possessed a very limited constituency. Among APC supporters, of course, Lansana and his relationship to Sir Albert Margai personified all that was corrupt in the SLPP's modus operandi. Once Lansana had declared martial law, most APC members of parliament immediately went into hiding. For this reason, the brigadier's notion of convening a special session of the House of Representatives "to resolve the constitutional crisis" seems in retrospect a reflection of his total ignorance of the political milieu in which he operated. Within the SLPP itself, men such as Kutubu Kai-Samba and Luseni Brewah held as much contempt for the force commander as for Sir Albert himself.

Among senior members of the police force, David Lansana was almost universally disliked. When on the afternoon of March 22 Leigh broadcast a statement in support of the army takeover, the tone of the message clearly conveyed the commissioner's somewhat less than enthusiastic response to the events of the preceding day:

This is the Commissioner of Police speaking. No doubt you have heard the statements made by the Force Commander at 17:55 hours yesterday. As Police Officers we have no alternative but to fall in line. Therefore, from now on, until the situation is resolved, you are ordered to remain at your posts and continue your work as Police Officers. You will receive your orders through me from the Force Commander.[42]

Thus Leigh was really resigning himself to the inevitable—namely, that no matter how much the police officers may have objected to the Brigadier's line of action, Lansana and Lansana alone controlled all the guns.

## THE ARREST OF LANSANA—THE FORMATION OF THE NATIONAL REFORMATION COUNCIL

While opposition from the APC, from SLPP dissidents, and from the gazetted officers of the Sierra Leone police force might conceivably make things a bit unpleasant for Brigadier Lansana, none of these groups by themselves could actually overturn a Lansana-Margai alliance. The real threat to the brigadier came rather from within the ranks of his own officer corps. Lansana's poorly disguised attempt to rescue the Margai regime afforded an ideal opportunity for the only remaining group of anti-Lansanites in the army to rid themselves of a man they considered a total incompetent.

Almost from the initial moment of Lansana's takeover, Majors Blake, Jumu, and Kai-Samba adopted a unilateral strategy of their own. This is not to imply that these officers opposed the underlying spirit of Lansana's maneuvers. They had all been present at Flagstaff House when the brigadier directed Lieutenant Norman to arrest Siaka Stevens and had, in fact, encouraged him not to waver in his designs. As army officers of southern origin, they shared with Lansana a common ethnic and regional perspective and thus were not prepared to stand idly by while a northern-based government assumed power. Finally, all four officers no doubt lived in fear of losing their jobs should the APC have been allowed to assume power.

A shared ethnic and regional consciousness, however, does not necessarily guarantee a lasting mutuality of interests, especially at a time when sheer opportunism both within the army and within the larger political system had become the order of the day. We have already shown that by the time of the general elections, fissures began to appear in an ostensibly homogenous officer corps. Thus while Majors Blake, Jumu, and Kai-Samba identified with the preservation of southern hegemony they leaned toward the Kenema faction contesting Sir Albert's leadership of the ruling party. They also opposed Lansana's evident disregard for their opinions on strategic matters, his gross ineptitude in providing sound management of the military, as well as his excessive reliance on a civilian patron—this last trait perhaps mainly a function of the brigadier's sense of insecurity vis-à-vis the newer generation of direct-entry officers holding secondary school certificates. In any case, these tensions became demonstrably more acute during the forty-eight hours following Lansana's martial law declaration and eventually led to the establishment of direct military rule in Sierra Leone.

A latent mistrust between David Lansana and his junior officers surfaced almost immediately following the brigadier's takeover of State House. If we grant at least a reasonable degree of credibility to some of the testimony delivered at the treason trial, the following sequence of events emerges. Once it became known that Lieutenant Norman had arrested Siaka Stevens and other APC ministers, Blake, Jumu, and Kai-Samba suggested formation of a national government with mixed APC-SLPP membership, a government which, taking its cue from the army, undoubtedly would be required to perform according to the whims of that southern-dominated organization. According to Blake, this suggestion was made ''in order to avoid a national disaster.''

The three budding conspirators then took leave of the brigadier and went directly to Sir Albert's house at Lumley. There, the SLPP leader, now perhaps somewhat less of an extremist than the force commander and his civilian followers, agreed to accompany Blake and the others to meet with the governor-general and to discuss with Sir Henry the possibility of arranging some form of coalition government. Once at State House, however, Blake received a call from Lansana who ordered his staff officer to abandon any efforts at negotiating a compromise and to return with Jumu and Kai-Samba to Flagstaff House. Upon joining the brigadier, these officers learned firsthand of his formal declaration of martial law and received a dressing-down for their efforts to ''circumvent'' the brigadier.[43] Blake offers us a revealing portrait of Flagstaff House as a kind of battalion headquarters under the direct supervision of the force commander.

That night [March 21], I learnt that the Brigadier had stored a good quantity of ammunition in Flagstaff House. I also learnt that Lt. Gbassa had been made officer in charge of Flagstaff elements. I was surprised to know this since as a general staff officer, I should be informed of pending operations. I observed that night live ammunition was being issued to some soldiers in certain cases by private soldiers without any record of quantity to whom it was issued. I also observed that ammunition was being issued on a sectional basis.[44]

The brigadier had by now become undisputed master of his own domain and no longer could be said to speak for the Sierra Leone army or its officer corps. Jumu claimed, furthermore, that the decision to saturate Freetown with troops on the night of March 21 never involved prior consultation with all the senior officers, something which is "never done."[45]

On the following day, Blake, Jumu, and Kai-Samba—now fully cognizant of the brigadier's handling of the Freetown mobs and determined to undertake further mediating or referee duties, again attempted to bring the waring political factions together. Under the coalition envisaged by the majors, the army would recognize Siaka Stevens as prime minister but would require an SLPP deputy minister to serve with him. Furthermore, each party would be allotted an equal number of government portfolios. In deference to Sir Albert's opponents within his own party, the officers also believed that "since the leadership of the S.L.P.P. was in dispute . . . [the] plan would only work if a deputy leader is elected by S.L.P.P. Parliamentarians."[46] This move, of course, could have easily opened the way for either K. I. Kai-Samba or Jusu-Sheriff to gain control of the SLPP.

Late on the afternoon of March 22, the three army majors along with Berthan Macauley again visited Sir Albert. By this time, the military leader of the SLPP and his political counterpart no longer seemed to be acting in unison. For his part, Sir Albert had become more and more receptive to an army-backed coalition while Lansana and his civilian colleagues favored a far more intransigent position. The prime minister, in any event, showed every willingness to cooperate. Had they all been able to reach State House, Blake and company planned to present Sir Albert and Siaka Stevens with an ultimatum to join in a coalition.[47] At this juncture, however, the brigadier telephoned Sir Albert and ordered him not to leave his residence. The force commander then spoke with Blake and Jumu, criticizing them for undertaking an initiative without his prior approval. The rift between the army commander and his subordinates was now complete.

As Lansana continued to broadcast his fruitless appeals for a meeting of all newly elected members of parliament, Blake and the other officers began mapping a strategy of their own. All contacts between the brigadier and these officers ceased as of the night of March 22; and, on the following morning, Blake, Jumu, and Kai-Samba visited Police Commissioner Leigh and sketched out their plans for the day's operations:

. . . we discussed the difficulties confronting the security forces, should the situation develop into a nation-wide tribal conflict. We informed him also that it was obvious to us that Brigadier Lansana had a plan to impose Sir Albert as Prime Minister once the Paramount Chief election results were obtained. We were apprehensive of a situation where a Prime Minister had already been appointed, and other persons aspired to fill the same post. We believed that the consequences of such a situation at the time would have cause for far reaching disaster in this country, and so informed the Commissioner of Police that we had no choice, but to take over from the Brigadier.[48]

Leigh welcomed these developments and pledged to extend the full backing of the police. The army officers then offered to provide for full police representation on the soon-to-be-established National Reformation Council.

Blake arranged for all units of the battalion not deployed on internal security duties to assemble at the Wilberforce parade grounds. He also planned to invite the brigadier to address the troops "in order to clear certain speculations about the elections which were now becoming prevalent among the soldiers."[49] Lansana, however, concerned that his battalion commander and staff officers no longer bothered to meet with him at Flagstaff House, went straight-away to the parade grounds and spoke with the troops even before receiving Blake's formal invitation. Jumu then requested the presumably quite confused Sir Albert to meet with the junior and senior army officers. Jumu promised to provide Sir Albert with an armed escort for his trip from Lumley to Wilberforce and claimed that he was only acting on the orders of the force commander.

Once inside the Wilberforce officer's mess, Sir Albert Margai and his long-term army associate, Brigadier David Lansana, had passed the point of no return. Pleading total ignorance to reports that he had conspired with Lansana to impose himself as prime minister of Sierra Leone, Sir Albert soon became engaged in a heated argument with a number of senior officers and was immediately whisked off to Pademba Road prison. Moments later, at around 2 PM, a young northern lieutenant, M. Kanu, grabbed the force commander's arms and shouted "You are under arrest sir."[50] Blake then relieved the brigadier of his revolver and soon afterwards, Major Kai-Samba escorted the now deposed army commander to Pademba Road. Siaka Stevens was also formally arrested and imprisoned. Lansana's forty-four hour reign as "custodian of state security" thus came to a swift end, with no one remaining to lift a finger in his defense.

Five hours after the arrest of Brigadier David Lansana and Sir Albert Margai, Major Charles Augustine Blake delivered a curt statement to the nation announcing the overthrow of the army commander and the formation of a military government. Sections of that broadcast, presented in unusually businesslike tones, deserve our close attention. Blake, speaking on behalf of the "senior officers," remarked that he and the others had initially agreed with the brigadier's view that the election results "had demonstrated a clearly tribalistic attitude of the country motivated and aggravated by the propaganda campaigning of the two parties." They had also shared what they claimed to be Lansana's original view of how to best deal with the political crisis, that is, by bringing "both parties to the conference table to discuss the establishment of a national government representative of every section of the country." However, the senior officers "had since noticed that the attitude of the brigadier was not to bring about the creation of a national government but to impose Sir Albert Margai as the Prime Minister of this country." Confronted with Lansana's obstinacy, they were left with no choice but to "disassociate [themselves] from the Brigadier's line of action" and "to divest the Brigadier of control of this country." Perhaps in order to avoid rehashing Lansana's justifications for intervention, Blake also mentioned the "economic situation." Furthermore, as a means of demonstrating that the reason for the military takeover was not the self-aggrandizement of those who participated in the takeover, Blake indicated that the newly formed National Reformation Council would not "enhance the social standard of its members."

Included in the initial list of those who would serve on the National Reformation Countil (NRC) were Lieutenant-Colonel Ambrose Genda and Lieutenant-Colonel Andrew T. Juxon-Smith, two officers who, because of their anti-Lansana intrigues of the previous year, were living abroad. The chairmanship of the council was allotted to Genda while William Leigh, the commissioner of police, became deputy chairman. The other members of the council included Blake, Kai-Samba, Jumu, and Alpha Kamara, the assistant commissioner of police. The inclusion of Kamara reflected Blake's precoup conversation with Leigh.

In their endeavor to present themselves as a viable alternative to Lansana, Blake and his fellow coupmakers only obscured the central issue—that the net effect of their anti-Lansana coup was to continue to thwart a lawful transfer of power from the SLPP to the APC. By proposing formation of a coalition government—no matter how superficially equitable—and then seeking to impose this coalition upon the people of Sierra Leone, the NRC clique differed from the force commander only in a matter of semantics. Furthermore this group of coupmakers was more conscious of the need to act with some deference to public opinion in order to appear saviors. They were not as skillful at this task as they might have been, however; and, in one short sentence, Blake revealed the essential shallowness of the NRC's rhetoric. He assured "all [his] fellow citizens that the army does not propose to take cognizance of the past, to mount exhaustive inquiries into the liberty and possessions of the individual but to turn a new page in the history of our beloved country."[51] Given most of the council members' close ties with the SLPP, this was nothing more than a pledge to paper over the obvious wrongdoings of the former civilian government and, with only slight alterations in the interest of tactics, to renew indirectly efforts in defense of their civilian patrons. It therefore seemed on March 23, 1967 that Sierra Leone's government by soldiers would hardly differ in its values and policies—to wit, in its view of politics—from government by politicians.

The untimely intervention of the Sierra Leone army on March 21 and 23 brought to a sudden end the established patterns of civil-military relations in that country. Since independence in 1961, the relationship between the two subsystems had been based on a foundation of civilian supremacy. During Sir Milton's time, civilian control of the military remained largely an expatriate concern since British officers held most of the staff and line commands. Sir Milton is known to have viewed with some alarm the long-term repercussions of rapid Africanization upon colonial or quasi-colonial systems of civilian control and occasionally voiced these fears in conversations with his cabinet members. Other SLPP members of more recent vintage such as Sir Albert Margai and Madam Gulama took opposing views and wanted their indigenous army brothers to replace the white man as soon as possible. Sir Milton's opinion on the subject eventually prevailed with the result that not until after his passing would a postcolonial system of "interest convergency" assist in mediating relations between military and civilian.

Once Sir Albert had assumed office, he immediately turned his attention to the problem of civilian control of a military organization managed by African officers. His counterpart leader in Ghana, Kwame Nkrumah, when faced with this same delicate issue opted to "redefine civil-military relations in terms of party-military relations."[52] Therefore a brief and generally half-hearted attempt was made to transform Sandhurst-educated army officers into CPP ideologues, an attempt which floundered since "Ghana's military leaders believed in instrumental values and took their cues from the British political system."[53] Given also the ethnic, class, and educational dichotomies between CPP leaders and Ghanaian army officers, party control of the military was soon abandoned and replaced by a counterintelligence network and by the establishment of the POGR.

In Sierra Leone, the lack of a mobilizing or centralizing political framework required Sir Albert and the senior members of the SLPP to adopt an entirely different approach to the question of subjective civilian control. Instead of there emerging a polarity of interests between civilian and military, the two groups joined together in the defense of mutual interests. On the most elementary level, a common ethnic and regional identity helped fashion an alliance between army officers and civilian influentials once

Mendes came to predominate in the upper echelons of both sectors. Client-patron ties between army small boys and civilian big men—facilitated by the close physical proximity of army barracks and ministerial quarters in Free-town—also helped mediate civil-military interaction and eventually allowed for the development of a kind of symbiotic relationship between the two elites. The army officers needed identification with prominent civilians to raise the formers' status in the wider community and, indirectly, to further their military careers. The politicians required the assurance that in the event they could no longer hold the public trust, the army, guns drawn, would remain at their sides.

The quagmire of assorted plots, martial law declarations, and coups d'état that characterized Sierra Leone's civil-military relations in February and March 1967 demonstrated the failure of Sir Albert's attempts to control the army. This substitution of chaos for ordered patterns of civil-military relations cannot be traced to the usual kinds of factors so often cited in the literature as precipitating army takeovers. In asking why soldiers so often repudiate civilian control, scholars usually assign considerable weight to such things as the "faltering economy" or the visible excesses of the politicians in contrast to the moral righteousness of the officer corps. We have endeavored to show that, at least in Sierra Leone and presumably in a number of other black African states, the breakdown in civil-military relations cannot be explained in such terms. Thus, while it is true that in Sierra Leone the economy was "faltering," Brigadier Lansana did not declare martial law to deal with balance of payments weaknesses or runaway inflation. Even Blake's mention of the "economic situation" was at best a perfunctory sop to public opinion.

As to the image of politicians held by Sierra Leone army officers, we have shown that one of the most important elements of Sierra Leone's civil-military relations was the ongoing intimacy, both overt and covert, between officers and important civilians long before the coups of 1967. Lansana's relationship with Sir Albert was only the most public of a whole series of army connections with the SLPP. Even the Blake-inspired cohort, while against Sir Albert, the APC, and Brigadier Lansana, did not strike out at the politicians as a group. No more proof of this fact is needed than Blake's pledge "not to take cognisance of the past [or] to mount exhaustive inquiries into the liberty and possessions of the individual." These were hardly the observations of an army man who favored a pogrom against politicians and bureaucrats associated with the SLPP regime.

If there was any single factor of macro-proportions in Sierra Leone's civil-military relations that led to Brigadier Lansana's intervention, it probably was that set of army duties and obligations carried over from the colonial past into the first postindependence decade. Throughout most of Lansana's testimony at the treason trial, there appear innumerable references to the problems of internal security and of the necessity for an appropriate military response in order to prevent a complete breakdown of law and order. Even while the brigadier's description of ravaging street mobs concealed the true state of affairs in Freetown prior to the martial law announcement—most of the rioting came as a *result* of that declaration—he may well have recalled in some detail the army's involvement in the Freetown disturbances of 1955. Richard Kershaw has commented on the impact of colonial patterns of civil-military relations upon army intervention in Sierra Leone:

> During the colonial period, after all, there was not even a pretence of democracy on the part of the British government. "Good government" was maintained by force—if necessary by bringing in the military. There is a respectable case to be made that this is what the army has at least tried to do in Sierra Leone . . . and that the military takeovers have *been very firmly in the colonial tradition.*[54]

Lansana probably regarded each and every taxi-driver who supported the APC as a potential threat to the survival of "good government" in Sierra Leone.

Given his long period of tenure in a British-officered army there can be little doubt that the brigadier viewed his troops as the prime enforcer of internal security. The very decision to declare "martial law" and to act as "custodian of state security" hints at a special concern with order for order's sake. In this way, the clashes between civilians and army troops on the night of March 21, 1967 hardly differ from similar clashes on the afternoon of February 12, 1955, some twelve years earlier. In 1955, the army was called upon to aid the civil power while "unruly crowds roamed the city, manned road blocks, stoned and broke up property . . . and clashed head on with the police."[55] This is just about the way Freetown must have appeared to Sierra Leone's force commander before he gave the order to deploy companies of troops.

To the colonial system of civil-military relations was later added, under Sir Albert Margai, the intricate network of reciprocal obligations binding together army officers and members of the civilian elite. In comparison with his colleagues, David Lansana was the one officer most conspicuously enmeshed in this network of relationships which became the core feature of subjective civilian control in Sierra Leone. In the week or so preceding the military takeover, I would argue that the colonial and the postcolonial notions of army in society became one. Thus as more and more people in Freetown took to the streets to demonstrate their support for a populist leader, a military solution to "crowd control" became inevitable. A show of military force also became inevitable as Lansana found himself obligated, by dint of his relationship to Sir Albert and the SLPP, to defend the ruling circle at any cost—to prevent, as it were, the mobs from storming the gates of the castle. The specter of civil disorder thus fused with the idea of military assistance to a decaying regime to make Lansana's martial law declaration very logical.

Majors Blake, Jumu, and Kai-Samba were also affected by many of the same forces that influenced their force commander, including a distaste for civil unrest and at least partial assimilation by members of the SLPP government. However, the willingness of these young officers to "disassociate themselves from the Brigadier's line of action" and, by so doing, inaugurate formal military rule in Sierra Leone suggests the presence of forces that eliminated cohesion.

Perhaps the very conduct of the coups themselves—stumbling, random, ad hoc—affords us a meaningful clue as to those factors leading to the imposition of military government in Sierra Leone. The coup of March 23 seems to demonstrate that fundamentally the same dynamic motivates both intra-army cliquism as well as outright military praetorianism—in short, the feuding that arises over the issue of leadership in any tenuously institutionalized organization. Thus the dispute between Lansana and his subordinates hardly differed in style from the other instances of bickering in the officers mess throughout 1966 and early 1967. Whereas the first batch of disputes led to relatively mild forms of protest and to eventual exile for the rebellious officers, the feuding of March 22 and 23 brought the full wrath of the army into Sierra Leone's political life. What variable, we may ask, was added to this equation to broaden the impact of disintegration within the military hierarchy? The answer to this question is the particular form of politics—namely the politics of cliques and ruling families, whether at the local or at the national level. The transformation of purely organizational disputes into unrestrained military praetorianism was made possible by the "grafting on" to these highly particularistic situations differences over the leadership of the SLPP. Thus as Sir Albert's standing in the SLPP became increasingly untenable, so too did David Lansana in the Royal Sierra Leone Military Forces face the same dim prospects.

Army cliques and political cliques instantly overlapped because of the ease with which messages could be transmitted across civilian-military boundaries. In the highly charged atmosphere of Flagstaff House and Wilberforce Barracks on March 21, 22, and 23, the self-styled leaders of these military or politicomilitary cliques jettisoned rational discussion in favor of more dramatic deeds such as arresting and counterarresting. Therefore the almost instant demise of Brigadier Lansana followed by the almost equally swift appearance of a Blake-led conspiracy is not at all surprising.

Robert Price believes that "broadly speaking, there are two types of interests which motivate officers to intervene in the political system—societal interests and professional interests." Thus, according to Price:

The former are operative when officers intervene either to make or to prevent some change in the total society or one of its subsystems. Included in this category are coups which are staged to end corruption, mismanagement, or chaos; to overcome political immobilism; to introduce or to stop some social or economic policy such as land reform; and the like. . . . The second type of motivation to intervene involves professional interests rather than societal ones. In these cases, the officers involve themselves in politics to protect specifically professional interests in contrast to more diffuse societal interests.[56]

I would argue that based on the evidence presented in Sierra Leone one may add "primordially inspired clique interests" to societal and/or professional interests when attempting to explain army takeovers. In this manner, Blake, Jumu, and Kai-Samba might not be viewed as intervening simply to "overcome political immobilism" but in order to resolve intraorganizational deficiencies that had been inflamed by outside political manipulation. Military government came to Sierra Leone not because the army took revenge on the politicians in defense of a professional standard or in pursuit of a unique vision of society but because of irreparable fissures within a civilian-military coalition.

# 8
# THE NATIONAL REFORMATION COUNCIL ASSUMES OFFICE

The National Reformation Council, Sierra Leone's first experiment with military government formally came into being on March 25, 1967. On that date, the NRC's "Proclamation for the Interim Administration of Sierra Leone" appeared in the official gazette. Once again the prospect of "an almost total breakdown of law and order, bloodshed and imminent tribal war" became the official explanation for the intervention of the army. The council itself was formed, according to the proclamation "in order to ensure the maintenance of law and order, ensure domestic tranquility and the future enjoyment of the blessings of liberty . . . "[1] The council also dissolved the House of Representatives, banned all political parties, suspended most sections of the 1961 constitution, and, in a broadcast on March 24, ordered all newspapers except the government-owned *Daily Mail* and the pro-SLPP *Unity* to discontinue their operations so as "to enable the Council to work out proper guidelines, designed to avoid any publication that will revive political and tribal feelings in the country."[2] The NRC also threatened to detain any person "where it considers it necessary in the interest of public safety or public order to do so."

## MUSICAL CHAIRS

Before this vague potpourri of goals could be transformed into actual policies, there remained the unpleasant albeit crucial matter of selecting an NRC chairman.[3] The leadership issue was raised almost immediately following the initial designation of Lieutenant-Colonel Ambrose Genda as chairman of the council. Genda's receipt of the chairmanship was based on several paramount considerations. First, at the time of his forced retirement from the military, Genda was the third most senior officer behind Brigadier David Lansana and Colonel John Bangura—Bangura, of course, was still in jail. Assuming that Blake and the others still regarded Genda as a brother officer, this made him eligible for the chairmanship on the basis of seniority alone. In addition, Genda's southern origins coupled with his well-known dislike for Brigadier Lansana and Sir Albert rendered him an eminently suitable candidate for recruitment into the NRC. Finally, the recall of Genda seems to have followed a kind of "swing man" principle whereby an outside military leader is called upon to head a government which has toppled the previous regime by force of arms. By entrusting the leadership of the NRC to someone who had not directly participated in the coup, Blake and his fellow conspirators could refute more easily charges that they had intervened solely for purposes of self-enrichment.

On Saturday March 25, Major Blake stated that knowing "Colonel Genda as I do . . . he is a great patriot . . . and I am confident that he would do anything to reform the country."[4] However, two days later, Genda's name was suddenly dropped from the roster of NRC members and that of Lieutenant-Colonel Andrew T. Juxon-Smith substituted in its place.[5] By this time Genda had arrived in London where he joined up with Juxon-Smith on March 27. At a stopover in Lisbon on their way to Freetown, a reporter from a London newspaper informed them of the switch in leadership.[6] They then proceeded to Las Palmas where they "learned by listening to the radio that Genda had been dropped." Genda was ordered to "sit tight and wait for instructions," while Juxon-Smith was told to proceed immediately to Freetown.[7] The NRC also requested Major Abdul Turay to abandon his degree course at Cambridge and become a member of the junta.[8] This addition to the council was apparently made at the suggestion of Mr. Davidson Nicol, the Fourah Bay College principal, who initially remained in close contact with Major Blake.[9]

The reason for the NRC leadership switch—a switch perpetuating the musical chairs atmosphere of the previous week—may forever remain obscure. It is likely that in their weakly articulated endeavor to seem publicly accountable and not simply a mirror image of the SLPP, Blake and the rest of the young majors decided that a non-Mende chairman would be more appropriate. Blake is rumored to have been under considerable pressure from his Creole family connections not to entrust leadership of the country to a Mende such as Genda, no matter how well-established were the latter's anti-Margai credentials.[10]

Even if Juxon-Smith was only partially Creole, he did possess a good Creole-sounding name, was married to a Creole nurse, and had distinguished himself during his years in secondary school. Blake possibly viewed the appointment of Juxon-Smith as a relatively painless way to gain some political capital with the Creole community in Freetown upon whom the NRC would have to rely for bureaucratic and managerial expertise. Leigh subsequently heeded the concept of ethnic balance, remarking in a press conference that the original council members wanted two men from each of the three provinces plus the western area. Thus, "with Genda on, it would have meant three from the south, so we have put it straight."[11]

Other theories may be offered for the sudden dismissal of Genda as nominal chairman of the National Reformation Council. Genda is alleged to have cabled Freetown from Las Palmas and to have urged the young majors to hand over power to the APC, whereupon they decided to transfer their allegiance to an alternative "swing man," albeit one who was known to be far more politically ambitious.[12] According to Blake, the junta, not wanting to offend domestic and international sensibilities, deemed it necessary not to appoint as chairman a man who had previously been dismissed from the army "on the grounds of misconduct." Blake emphasized the NRC's "apprehension in the early stages . . . in the fact that the country was inundated with foreign press men who might capitalize on this abnormality thereby destroying the image of the government."[13] Actually Blake overlooked the real issue—that the image of the NRC was bound to suffer by the mere fact of the new government's readiness to change leaders at all so soon after seizing power.

The leadership mess was only partially overshadowed by the apparent resoluteness with which the NRC undertook to revamp government machinery. The military council itself replaced the former civilian cabinet and was designed to include a total of eight members, including two representatives of the Sierra Leone police, Leigh and Assistant Commissioner Kamara. Fourteen civilian ministries were reduced to nine NRC "departments" each to be headed by an NRC representative. In some cases, considerable consolidation of ministerial functions took place. Thus the Department of Social Services came to include all the functions of the former Ministry of Information and Broadcasting, the Ministry of Social Welfare without the Adult Education Section, and the Labor Division of the former Ministry of Lands, Mines, and Labor. The NRC Secretariat which was to become the administrative nerve center of the government handled all the duties of the former prime minister's office, the cabinet secretariat, the Ministry of Defense, and the nonbudgetary activities of the former Development Office.

The announcement of an administrative reorganization was followed by the assignment of portfolios on March 29. The NRC Chairman assumed charge of the Secretariat, the Department of Finance, and the Department of the Interior. Commissioner Leigh, the NRC deputy chairman, was assigned to head the Department of External Affairs. Major Blake handled the Department of Trade, Industry, and Agriculture; Major Kai-Samba, the Department of Works, Transport, and Communications; Major Sandi Jumu, the Department of Health; and Major Abdul Turay, the Department of Education.[14] Alpha Kamara became the NRC representative at the Department of Social Services while Captain Foyah, a minor figure in the Lansana coup, became an NRC member with special responsibility in the council Secretariat.

## LEGITIMIZATION

One scholar has observed that "in early years of the behavioral revolution when attention was shifted away from such macro-concepts as the 'state' and 'sovereignty' to the actual actions of individuals, political scientists came to have less and less to say about the nature of such collective and abstract concepts as authority and legitimacy."[15] Students of African military regimes, however, would be well advised to resist this trend and to pay special attention to the unique legitimization-related issues posed by the intrusion of ostensibly nonpolitical actors into African political life. By examining the manner in which military regimes cope with what Pye terms the "legitimization crisis," we shall be in a better position to assess their contribution to political development. Army officers are, after all, often propelled from total obscurity into the public eye in a matter of hours—the only exception to this rule being the occasional force commander such as Lansana or Amin who manages to acquire a certain amount of notoriety in the years preceding a military takeover. Given their lack of grounding in local, regional, or national politics—in short, their lack of a constituency or political base —leaders of military governments are likely to face special difficulties in endeavoring to comprehend and to respond to the political demands of civilian groups. These officers must also work to convey the impression that their authority derives from something other than their control over the instruments of violence. To make up for their political inexperience, juntas may be compelled to invent ideologies or images in order to appear "of the people," on the one hand, or representative of the "nation" on the other.

In the Sierra Leone case, most of the army participants in the coups of March 21 and 23 were individuals of relatively "middling" origin who, although having achieved a certain measure of notoriety within the elites as a whole by dint of their links with the civilian ruling group, were nevertheless unknown quantities as far as the general public was concerned. Since their intervention was motivated largely by particularistic and ethnocentric grievances, it was essential that they succeed in creating certain positive symbols of authority by which to legitimize their rule.

In Sierra Leone, the act of legitimization required a far greater measure of tact and sensitivity than in other West African states such as Ghana and Nigeria where army intervention generally has been greeted with a widespread sense of relief—in short, a feeling of liberation from past burdens. In Sierra Leone, however, discontent rather than relief accompanied the military takeover, discontent inspired by the knowledge universal in the Freetown area that Lansana, Blake, and their civilian supporters had behaved as opportunists rather than as dedicated nationalists. Jubilant crowds lined the streets of the capital to cheer Siaka Stevens and Ibrahim Taqi rather than David Lansana or Charles Blake. When Juxon-Smith arrived in Freetown following a flight from Las Palmas on the afternoon of March 28, "he received a full-dress military welcome but was greeted with a sullen silence from the few hundred people lining the hot and dusty streets."[16] Four days later, on April 1st, Major Turay slipped quietly into the capital city and took up his official duties with the NRC.

The public cynicism and anger confronting the NRC made it incumbent upon that regime to weigh carefully its method for acquiring a wider public audience. To be sure, the regime could count on at least the tacit support of any person or group opposed to the Lansana-Margai team. Thus on the night of Blake's takeover, he and his fellow officers approached two outspoken critics of Sir Albert, Dr. Sarif Easmon and Davidson Nicol, to assure them of their personal safety. Obviously others regarded the intervention as the only way to end the violence that followed Lansana's martial law declaration. Token gestures in deference to public opinion, however, could never substitute for meaningful attempts to gain acceptance.

Before seeking to appraise the regime's approach to the acquisition of a broader base of political support, we must first describe what, for want of a better term, may be called the political philosophy of the National Reformation Council. Kenneth Grundy's notion of the military coup as a "cleansing experience," where the evil visited upon the people by the scheming politicians is rooted out and destroyed forever will be considered followed by the examination of the methods adopted by the NRC to construct arenas of civilian support.[17]

The attempt by the Sierra Leone military government to introduce, and sometimes to impose its particular vision of national life upon the populace might be described more accurately as the attempt by Lieutenant-Colonel

Andrew T. Juxon-Smith to remake the country in his own image using ritualistic exhortations to work hard and to eschew corruption. Had Juxon-Smith remained at his staff course in England rather than returning to Sierra Leone to assume the chairmanship of the NRC, that regime might have engaged in a simple holding action, leading to a purge of some of the more obviously corrupt SLPP leaders, and finally culminating in the restoration of southern hegemony under the guise of a so-called national government. Certainly this seems to have been the original intention of Majors Blake, Jumu, and Kai-Samba when they finally removed Brigadier Lansana, Sir Albert Margai, and Siaka Stevens from the stage. Although it is a fact that before Juxon-Smith's arrival in Freetown, the original NRC members did abolish the two political parties, this was only done as a means of nullifying the election results without appearing partisan to the SLPP. The March 23 group definitely did not consist of men who, out of loyalty to a general moral code, sought to purge the political system of slackness and wrongdoing. The injection of this kind of rudimentary ideology—so prevalent in the military psyches of developing countries—was first occasioned by the return of the flamboyant lieutenant-colonel to serve as head of state. According to Grundy:

> Nowhere are the "puritan" characteristics of militarism more evident than in the military leader's own perceptions of his role in the development of his nation. He might, for example, conceive of himself as embodying all that is "good" in his people. In contrast, he might see himself as superior to the nation itself, and all that it stands for.[18]

Perhaps to a greater extent than any other senior officer in the Sierra Leone army, Lieutenant-Colonel Juxon-Smith embodied Grundy's description of a junta chairman.

Albeit delivered in a somewhat garbled fashion, Juxon-Smith's political viewpoint became evident immediately upon his arrival at Lungi airport on March 28. There, in a radio interview, he asked all Sierra Leoneans to behave as members of the "tribe of Sierra Leone" and not according to the dictates of ethnicity. He asked further that everyone behave as "friends and brothers and sisters" so they could "learn how to compromise and make the best out of any situation." He then invoked the memory of Sir Milton Margai: "Let us, let us, make sure . . . that we will continue his good works and take this our country, which, you watch and see what will happen in the future, take this our country to the greatest heights which is where its place is."[19] In a brief press conference held immediately after debarking at Government Wharf, he reiterated the tribal theme, stressing that, being of mixed tribal ancestry, he was a man "of all tribes."[20]

Within a few days after his return to Freetown, the puritan ethic in the leader of the National Reformation Council emerged in full strength. For the first time in the NRC's embryonic reign, the notion of the army as a purifying agent became a crucial aspect of the regime's gospel. After promising that the NRC would "cremate" tribalism and "bury it . . . into . . . a dark abyss," Juxon-Smith turned his attention to what he called "a demoniac and hydra-headed monster and that monster is bribery, corruption and nepotism, especially so in high places." He also spoke about all those "palatial buildings . . . that these people [that is, the corrupt politicians] built for themselves wherein they wasted our country's money." He also decried corruption in the civil service and asked why the "labourer . . . must find two pounds or four leones to bribe somebody before he can get a job."[21]

The chairman then went to great lengths to emphasize the need for obedience to authority—presumably the authority of the National Reformation Council and its civilian allies. Political activity of any sort was equated with malicious "rumour-mongering," and those "planning trouble" under conditions of martial law should, if apprehended, be prepared to face death by firing squad. He also warned against disloyalty or "subversion" among army officers or enlisted men, stating that as long as he was in charge of the National Reformation Council, "the Sierra Leone soldier would never revolt." As for the paramount chiefs—who in Sierra Leone still wield considerable authority—Juxon-Smith stated that "there would be no curtailment of their power or interference with their status by the NRC in view of their position as natural rulers."[22] The work ethic was then given its due. On the subject of performance within the civil service, he offered some revealing insights into the army man's perceptions of the bureaucratic sector:

Governments come and go, the civil service stays. So that a civil servant must be a devoted person, must be devoted to his job . . . He must be somebody of some integrity. He must be a reliable person . . . A civil servant must be prepared to work for 24 hours for the state, if the need should arise. He should not be late for work.[23]

Civil servants in Sierra Leone were soon to be known as the "24-hour men."

The NRC's attitude toward political behavior came into even sharper focus during the first few months after the new government came into being. On March 31, it was announced that the Freetown City Council had been replaced by a Committee of Management consisting of NRC appointees. On that same day the NRC dissolved such quasi-political organizations as the Settler's Descendants Union and the Aborigines Rights Society. On April 14, all town councils and district councils were abolished to be replaced by Committees of Management. District commissioners served as chairmen of the district Committees of Management. In May, the NRC

issued a decree banning all public meetings except for "sports and recrea-
tional meetings," "gatherings at market places and shops," and at other
explicitly nonpolitical functions.[24] Under a "preservation of peace" decree,
no person was allowed to "engage in any act likely to promote the formation
or operation of any political party."[25] Furthermore, the governor-general
was asked to leave the country and on April 30, he departed for Great Britain as a kind of "roving ambassador."

One uniquely Margai innovation—the mammy queens—was also decreed
into oblivion. Mammy queens were prominent women, usually Mende by
tribe, who helped rally local support for Sir Albert and often served on chiefdom councils. In late April, a conference of district commissioners based in
the southern province was held in Bo, the provincial capital. Taking its cue
from the NRC chairman, the conference decided that mammy queens constituted a "political institution which must die following the banning of
political activities." "These mammy queens," the conference noted, "were
very effective political agents and did very little or nothing to enhance the
prestige of their womenfolk."[26] On June 28, the NRC issued a directive
formally abolishing the institution of mammy queens. A suggestion by the
provincial commissioners that "women chiefs" be appointed in place of the
mammy queens was rejected outright; the NRC apparently taking the view
that women chiefs "would fall easy victims to unscrupulous politicians."[27]

In the name of eradicating tribalism, the NRC on April 5 ordered the
deletion of all references to tribe in government forms. The government
printer was instructed to "take special note that whenever supplying forms
to departments he must make sure that the section referring to tribe is either
omitted or replaced by the word 'nationality'."[28] Four and one-half months
later the NRC also abolished the institution of tribal headman, which, the
junta claimed, above all "fosters tribalism."[29] This emphasis of Sierra
Leone's military government on the abolition of politics and ethnic identification resembles a " 'non-political model' of nation-building which fails to
recognize the conflict of interests and values inherent in any society, but
particularly prevalent in one undergoing rapid social change, and which
consequently makes no provision for mediating conflict and reconciling
interests."[30]

The transformation of a military holding action in favor of a particular
group of civilian leaders into a kind of Calvinist vendetta against prevailing
value systems, tribalism, and political institutions was made possible, as we
have said, by the return of Lieutenant-Colonel Juxon-Smith and reflected
his special impact on the council's philosophy. At least one writer attributes
Juxon-Smith's zeal for "cleaning house" in Sierra Leone to a "psychopathic
personality."[31] Certainly he often displayed a number of eccentricities including his most famous one of all—he belonged to both the Islamic and

Christian churches simultaneously and believed he was a messenger of the deity. However they might have suffered grammatically, his statements differed very little in content from those of such military purifiers in black Africa as Major Nzeogwu who, in his plan for a new Nigeria, threatened to "gun down all the bigwigs."[32] He was unquestionably subject to the same influences as an Nzeogwu or an Ocran including participation in an organization that, at least theoretically, venerated the concepts of obedience and discipline. Like Brigadier Afrifa, Juxon-Smith was heir to the Sandhurst tradition with its subtle emphasis on love for the patria; but his excessive puritanism in the context of Sierra Leone's civil-military relations has yet another special meaning.

That factor in Juxon-Smith's personal history which set him somewhat apart from Blake, Jumu, Kai-Samba, among other senior army officers— his lack of close links with important civilian politicians—probably helped to dispose this particular officer toward a more excessively reformist view of society. Since he never enjoyed the benefit of a high-ranking SLPP patron nor participated in politicomilitary intrigues such as those at Flagstaff House, he never had any special reason to feel protective of civilians. This fact may have impelled him to overturn Blake's initial pledge "not to take cognisance of the past [or] to mount exhaustive inquiries into the liberty and possessions of the individual."

As we shall see in our chapter on the growth of opposition to the NRC, Juxon-Smith, becoming more and more pushy in his dealings with interest groups and individuals, ended up carrying his reformist fervor to almost absurd heights. He often told stories about how soldiers were mistreated in the past, at one point declaring that "we the soldiers are the most important element of any country" and that "no civilian can do what we as soldiers can do." For redressing past grievances, he pledged "to transfer the army barracks to Tower Hill . . . so that the people will know we are always in their midst."[33] These sentiments might have been especially acute for this thirty-five-year-old lieutenant-colonel if only because he had never been closely linked with the former ruling group in such a way as Lansana or Kai-Samba. He perhaps sensed a need to "get back" at prominent civilians which may have contributed to his interest in ridding Sierra Leone of civilian-induced "impurities."

Even though the NRC chairman had noted that "no civilian can do what we as soldiers can do," the size of the military organization imposed very real constraints upon the ability of the NRC to conduct the government business without substantial civilian support. The tiny army scarcely had the means to do little more than replace the former civilian ministers with army majors and captains. For this reason, both the judiciary and the bureaucracy remained almost fully intact and postcoup, military-role expansion was just not in the cards. Thus on Sunday, March 26, three days before the return of Juxon-Smith, judges of the Sierra Leone Supreme Court and those of the Appeal Court were sworn in during what one broadcaster described as a "short, businesslike, but nevertheless impressive ceremony" at the Wilber-force Officers Mess. Included in the initial lineup of judges were Gershon Collier, formerly Sir Albert's chief justice, and Sir Samuel Bankole Jones, the president of the Court of Appeal who was a supporter of Siaka Stevens. Deputy NRC Chairman, Police Commissioner Leigh, noted that the presence of the judges at the Officers Mess signified their "full support for the National Reformation Council."[34]

Apart from a few changes in nomenclature, the regime scarcely tampered with the preexisting alignment of permanent secretaries, and immediately following the Blake coup, an urgent appeal was made to all civil servants to remain at their duty stations. Thus Peter Tucker, Sir Albert's personal secretary, became the NRC secretary-general while Ade Hyde, the former secretary to the cabinet became secretary to the soon-to-be-appointed civilian advisory council. John Kallon, a member of the Flagstaff House group, stayed on as the establishment secretary. Other Margai supporters such as S. B. Daramy and Thomas Decker continued to hold key posts, Daramy as secretary to the Department of Finance (which superseded the former Ministry of Finance but included the budgetary operations of the development office) and Decker, the former permanent secretary in the Ministry of Social Welfare, as secretary to the Department of Social Services. All but one of the former provincial secretaries remained at their duty stations but were now termed "provincial commissioners" to correspond to the transformation of permanent secretaries into "secretaries" of their respective departments. The appointment of district commissioners to head the various Committees of Management actually enhanced the position of the former since as civil servants they now performed political functions which, in the precoup days, had been exercised by the elected members of the District Councils.

The NRC's reliance upon the civilian bureaucrats to keep the government machinery in operating condition seems to have developed in recognition of a convergence of interests between the two groups. On the emergence of a civil-military bureaucratic coalition, Dowse has noted:

> . . . the army does not have the expertise or the numbers to run a country and if they did run it, it might cease to be an army. On the other hand, the bureaucracy cannot bring down a government: that is the army's task. But when the government has been displaced, the bureaucracy is still necessary and by no means powerless. There must be a coalition of sorts, and hence an accommodation between the partners; whatever the conditions of the coalition, the fact of its existence is a certainty.[35]

The late Kwame Nkrumah underlined the same point:

In many cases, the officer class and the civil servants have shared similar educational experiences in elite schools and colleges . . . They tend to distrust change . . . Bureaucrats alone cannot overthrow a government; and the military and police have not the expertise to administer a country. Therefore they combine, and bring about a state of affairs strikingly similar to that which operated in colonial times, when the colonial government depended on the civil service, the army and police, and on the support of the traditional rulers.[36]

No one has yet to dispute the presumed inevitability of this "alliance of convenience" although some recent evidence concerning the Uganda military regime points to a monopolization of the decision-making function by an army council accompanied by widespread dismissals of experienced civil servants.[37]

Given the NRC's unquestioned need for civilian expertise as well as the regime's image of itself as the standard bearer of discipline opposed to corruption and mismanagement, it was only natural that Juxon-Smith, especially, would want to enlist the apolitical civil service in the task of reformation. Between the months of April and September 1967, the NRC chairman personally visited scores of government departments in order to "rally the troops." On April 8, for example, he told workers at the Department of Finance to "be honest, intelligent, abhor corruption, bribery, and nepotism." During similar visits to other departments, he appealed to civil servants to do a full day's work, to respect discipline and authority, and to support the regime in its efforts to create a world free of corruption and the other vices associated with the politicians of the Margai period. Department heads often responded favorably to these kinds of pronouncements. During his August visit to the Sierra Leone External Telecommunications Office, a senior official exclaimed that "from the time the National Reformation Council took over the reigns of Government, under the Chairman's leadership much has been done in correcting certain issues that had gone astray, and in rooting out malpractices and corruption from all sources . . . "[38]

Army efforts to cultivate the support of the civilian bureaucracy for regime goals was paralleled by a similar campaign directed at the traditional authorities. The reasons for the NRC's interest in this particular group are not difficult to list. In the first place, a number of the council members, notably Jumu and Kai-Samba, were intimately connected with traditional rulers through extended family relationships. Both officers, as we have shown, would have been inclined to resent Sir Albert's meddling in local chiefdom politics through his support of certain "young men" opposed to the chief in power or his backing of candidates for chieftaincy positions who were not "sons of the soil." In the second place, the NRC's stress on authority and discipline struck a responsive chord among chiefs, most of whom blamed disturbances in their respective chiefdoms upon a breakdown in respect for their authority. Finally, there was the simple fact that the NRC needed civilian allies and could not afford to be choosy. To acquire legitimacy in the provinces it was therefore deemed necessary to garner the support of those who, it was felt, could speak on behalf of the government in Freetown and who would serve as focal points of communication between the regime and the masses at large.

The NRC's original pledge to preserve the status and prestige of paramount chiefs was, of course, warmly received in the up-country chiefdoms. While Sir Albert had adhered in principle to the institution of chieftaincy, he was not at all adverse to deposing or banishing chiefs who seemed in any way disloyal to the SLPP government. Once having assumed office, therefore, the NRC was inundated with resolutions of support from paramount chiefs and chiefdom councillors who viewed army rule as a possible respite from past meddling by the central government in local affairs. Even those chiefs who had received the backing of the SLPP were quick to bless the "government of the day." In June, for example, one of Sir Albert's most ardent supporters, Paramount Chief Bai Sebora Kamal of Makeni in the Bombali District, came forth with what was to become a standard affirmation of loyalty:

All of us Paramount Chiefs today have pledged our loyalty and support to the NRC because we want to assist them to go a good job, the benefit of which could be said to be our own. We are happy for their taking over control of the Government as non-politicians. All the Chiefdoms are getting quiet and peaceful. We want this to go on and on. God bless the NRC. Long live the NRC.[39]

Other chiefs including those who had been harassed by Sir Albert soon voiced their support for the military regime. As a response to this kind of favorable signal from the provinces, the NRC acted almost immediately to reinstate a number of paramount chiefs who had either been deposed by the SLPP or prevented from taking office following rigged chiefdom elections. For example, Major Jumu's uncle, Foray Vangahun, whose efforts to gain the paramount chieftaincy of the Nongowa Chiefdom had been constantly frustrated by the former prime minister, was allowed to contest again; and on May 23, Vangahun, using his newly acquired influence in official circles, was returned unopposed.

As a further means of acquiring legitimacy in rural Sierra Leone, Juxon-

Smith despatched members of the NRC to the provinces to explain government policies and, most important of all, to help the paramount chiefs achieve "peace and quiet" in their respective chiefdoms. In the first several months of army rule, almost all the NRC members toured the provinces to recapitulate the junta's "message to the people" and to settle chiefdom palavers. The usual practice was to send officers to their respective home regions or districts, where, to the extent that these officers enjoyed the special respect of individual chiefdom officials or other local notables, they might more easily bring their positions to bear on the settlement of disputes. By mid-July onward, most of the responsibility for these rather unglamorous duties was borne by the young army captains who, beginning with Captain Sahr James Foyah, served directly under Juxon-Smith in the Department of the Interior on a three-month, rotational basis.

On their often whirlwind tours through the provinces, the junta officers worked assiduously to promote the army's vision of a new and "cleaner" Sierra Leone. For example, in an address to chiefdom officials in the Kono district, seat of Sierra Leone's illicit diamond mining and smuggling, the NRC chairman "emphasized that his Government was determined to make [Kono] clean."[40] At the time of Major Jumu's early summer visit to some twelve chiefdoms in the eastern province, a brief prepared for the major included a wide range of topics for discussion with chiefdom councillors. Jumu was asked in particular to point out that although the NRC planned to uphold the tenets of chieftaincy, it opposed all "oppression, victimisation and corruption" and "was determined to wipe out these evils which have been inimical to the progress of this country."[41]

In its search for civilian allies, the NRC took an active interest in settling long-standing chiefdom palavers. Given the NRC's simplistic view of local politics, chiefdom disputes were usually considered an unfortunate legacy of past intriguing by SLPP politicians who "had inflamed the situation."[42] Almost inevitably, the NRC regarded with suspicion the presence of "disruptive forces" within the chiefdoms and went to great lengths to back up the authority of the natural rulers. Chiefs were generally portrayed as repositories of virtue while their opponents were considered irresponsible rabble rousers. The young captains attached to the Department of the Interior proved especially zealous advocates of the NRC position on chiefs. Throughout July, August, and September, Captain Mboma (who on July 3 replaced Captain Foyah as the eighth member of the NRC) spent much of his time in the southern province delivering speeches supporting the institution of paramount chieftaincy. At Jaiama chiefdom, for example, he told chiefdom councillors that the NRC would effect the immediate return of the Bongor section to Jaiama since de-amalgamation of the chiefdom during the Margai regime was "on account of politics." Anyone who refused to accept the re-amalgamation of the chiefdom or who refused to pay their taxes to the chiefdom treasury would "be sent to a place where it will be difficult to breath 'fresh air'."[43] Mboma almost always threatened severe reprisals, including detention, for any persons who showed disrespect for a paramount chief or for the authority of his office. A report issued by the civilian National Advisory Council in September 1967 noted that "almost invariably, Chiefs and their followers against whom there are genuine complaints by the people, have danced for days upon hearing these speeches by Captain M 'boma'' and drew the logical conclusion that "some chiefs consider it a license to further victimise their people."[44]

Since civil servants and traditional rulers constituted only a small fraction of the NRC's wider audience, the junta was also required to shop around for other allies. As is common to all military regimes, the new government faced the problem of how to involve civilians, if only on a token basis, in the process of decision making. Army juntas in sub-Saharan Africa have experimented with several approaches to the question of participation by non-military influentials. For example, the then General Yakubu Gowon in Nigeria called on a number of former politicians to head government departments, styling them "Commissioners" because "of the Government's awareness of the public reaction of apprehension when the idea of bringing civilians into the administration of the Federal Military Government was first announced by the Head of State."[45] In Ghana, the National Liberation Council (NLC) was at first "unwilling to place former opposition politicians or community elites in official decision-making posts" and formed instead in June 1966 a twenty-three-man Political Committee "to advise it on past decisions and policy alternatives."[46] However, in June 1967, "the NLC decided to divest its members of many of their ministerial functions by appointing civilian commissioners to most ministries . . . , thus leaving more time for army and police duties."[47]

Juxon-Smith himself favored the original Ghanaian as opposed to the Nigerian approach, which meant the restriction of all portfolios to members of the army officer corps and the creation of some form of civilian advisory body in accordance with Major Blake's initial pledge to do so in his broadcast of March 23. Thus in early April, the NRC invited a number of former politicians as well as civilian professionals to become members of the soon-to-be-formed National Advisory Council. A membership list was made public on April 24, and on April 26, the twenty-five-member National Advisory Council held its first session.[48]

When the projected membership of the advisory council was initially discussed, some thought was given to the inclusion of former APC politicians; thus Juxon-Smith's boast that "members . . . would be drawn from . . . the public, including politicians, regardless of their political affiliation, creed or status in life.''[49] (Sir Albert Margai and Siaka Stevens were deliberately excluded.) This was clearly an unrealistic objective, as unrealistic as Lansana's earlier plea for a "meeting of all newly-elected parliamentarians." In mid-April he met with a number of APC leaders including Sembu Forna, Solomon Pratt, and M. O. Bash-Taqi to invite them to join the advisory council. All but Solomon Pratt refused his offer outright because they feared being overwhelmed by the NRC's hand-picked "stooges."[50] By refusing to collaborate with the chairman, the APC left the way open for the appointment of only those individuals having a vested interest in army rule.

Upon publication of the completed list of advisory council members, it was clear that with few exceptions all the members were sympathetic to the SLPP and thus, by implication, with elements on the NRC. From the northern province—the central core of the APC's strong showing in the general elections—came five men who at one time or another served in parliament under the banner of the SLPP.[51] One of these northern representatives, Mr. U. H. Koroma, who had been defeated by the APC candidate for Port Loko Southwest, became deputy-chairman of the advisory council. The southern and eastern delegations were also dominated throughout by SLPP loyalists although the presence of several independents, notably L.A.M. Brewah and K. I. Kai-Samba, gave this group some degree of stature. To these civilian representatives were added six paramount chiefs who hardly could be expected to offer critical assessments of NRC policies. Such conservative groups as the Catholic Mission and the Sierra Leone Chamber of Commerce were allotted positions. Perhaps only Dr. S. T. Matturi, principal of Njala University College, added any real distinction to the whole undertaking and was subsequently elected chairman of the council. However, even Dr. Matturi had been at least covertly identified with the Margai regime and was thus not prepared to question the right of the NRC to control the political destiny of Sierra Leone. The overwhelmingly pro-SLPP bias of the National Advisory Council undermined Juxon-Smith's pretensions of having created a politically objective team of civilian advisors.

The status quo outlook of the National Advisory Council and the fact that it included only a single member of Sierra Leone's most important political party, the All Peoples Congress, necessarily circumscribed the NRC's efforts to win acceptance among the civilian intelligentsia and among the Sierra Leone people as a whole. Perhaps in recognition of this fact, the army turned to more flamboyant gestures for securing at least a modicum of public approval. One tactic commonly employed to this end by military regimes involves the establishment of commissions of inquiry. To the extent that such commissions undertake a full-fledged investigation of the wrongdoings of the past, they become a visible extension of the army's verbal commitment to "eradicate evil."

During its thirteen months in office, the NRC instituted a number of commissions of inquiry whose specific task was to expose as precisely as possible all the corruption and nepotism of the second SLPP government. In an introduction to the Forster Commission which, beginning in May, examined the assets of all former ministers, deputy ministers, and civil servants earning no less than Le 3,200 per annum, the three-man commission (which included an army captain appointed by the NRC) revealed its philosophy on the subject of civilian political leadership in Sierra Leone:

The period commencing immediately with the death of the late Prime Minister, Sir Milton Margai, and culminating in the General Elections of March this year is one of which no self-respecting Sierra Leonean can be proud. Two characteristic assumptions marked this period, firstly that the government could do no wrong and secondly that the government would live forever . . . Stealing from the government was as common as petty larceny of private property . . . . There was such a widespread disregard of General Orders, Financial and Administrative Instructions that one is reminded of certain biblical times when there was no king in Israel and everyone did as he pleased, and might became right.[52]

By the time it submitted its final report in February 1968, the Forster Commission had exposed all the ingenious methods by which virtually everyone in positions of responsibility came to amass personal fortunes. Some forty-two persons in all, including most of the key figures in the Lansana takeover, were subjected to intense grilling by the commission chairman, Justice S. J. Forster, and his two assistants. Sir Albert, who several times collapsed under the strain of testifying, clearly emerged as a superstar when it came to using political office for personal gain. He was ordered on February 27, 1968 to pay back to the state a sum totalling almost Le 800,000. George Panda, at one time Sir Albert's personal secretary, was discovered to be worth around Le 151,000, while Peter Tucker held Le 44,000 in assets.[53] The NRC actually took possession of only a small proportion of these sums since most of the money was held in foreign bank accounts; all physical property, of course, was confiscated.

The zeal with which the Forster Commission pursued its exposure of the SLPP regime naturally struck a responsive chord in Freetown and its immediate environs where the SLPP had been almost completely repudiated in the recent elections. Taking note of this the NRC instituted other commissions, including the Beoku-Betts Commission of Inquiry into the activities of the Sierra Leone Produce Marketing Board—most of whose profits had ended up in the pockets of the party bosses rather than with the farmer. At all of these commissions, loudspeakers were set up to accommodate the crowds who gathered to jeer their fallen idols. The presence of the commissions reduced some of Freetown's initial hostility to the NRC, and at one point the chairman of the Dove-Edwin Commission of Inquiry was required to warn "APC backers" against molesting witnesses.[54] The NRC had to call attention to "a wide-spread rumour" that it was out to "victimise Mendes" and stated that while the "present enquiries . . . inevitably involve former members and supporters of the SLPP," the NRC was "not against any tribe."[55]

The junta took two other steps to curry favor with the man on the street. In May, Juxon-Smith established a Public Relations Committee whose function was "to help destroy wild rumours and destructive news which were likely to cause confusion in the Community." The committee, under the direction of Major Bockarie Kai-Samba, was given only the vaguest of guidelines including, among other things, the task of bringing "our community into a fuller understanding between the Government and the people so that our beloved country could be brought back to the good old days of fraternity and prosperity."[56] Then in late July, the NRC announced formation of an "anti-corruption squad" made up of "selected Army and Police Officers" instructed to apprehend persons suspected of corrupt undertakings. The squad was supposed to devote most of its time to stopping and boarding trains and buses in the hope of catching anyone in the act of overcharging the public on fares. In December the NRC issued a formal decree that empowered members of the squad to "enter upon any Government Department or Office or the premises of any Corporation" and to arrest without warrant persons suspected of being involved in, or "connected with corrupt practices."[57]

With the return of Lieutenant-Colonel Andrew T. Juxon-Smith to head Sierra Leone's junta, what had begun primarily as an exercise in military adventurism disguised as a war on political "disunity" and "tribalism" suddenly became a kind of religious crusade with the brash young officer playing the part of chief evangelist. Throughout the first several months of its rule, the National Reformation Council focused most of its attention on what had been roughly diagnosed as a general malaise in Sierra Leone society. Corruption came to be regarded as the handmaiden of politics and vice versa. Disrespect for authority and "slackness on the job" were made objects of an NRC vendetta.

In its campaign, then, to alter the underlying values of the polity and thereupon to cleanse that polity, the National Reformation Council soon grew wedded to no more than the symbols and imagery of reformation. B. J. Dudley has shown that with respect to the Ironsi regime in Nigeria "vague statements about 'cleaning' the system are no substitutes for well-worked-out policies, and this, in any case, the Army was in no position to do for the simple reason that what has to be 'cleaned,' the extent of the 'cleaning' to be done, etc. are not issues which are intuitively obvious."[58] However, by the NRC's logic, if one banned political institutions, then political behavior and political thought would simply disappear. By issuing continuous warnings against "rumour-mongering" one could prevent people from "causing mischief and confusion"; or by threatening to eliminate all opposition to paramount chiefs, one would somehow be upholding the idea of unquestioned obedience to all power holders. The formation of an anticorruption squad to "root out evil" epitomized the NRC's simplistic response to the problem of corruption for, as Anton Bebler notes, the squad "could not, without intelligence training and special skills, uncover the most economically damaging forms of corruption—those related to diamond smuggling, customs evasion, wholesale trade, etc. . . . ."[59] The NRC apparently regarded the establishment of a public relations committee as an effective means of reaching the citizens of Sierra Leone when, in fact, it was little more than a misconceived attempt to acquire legitimacy. As for the National Advisory Council, it was instituted with possibly noble intentions but contained very few people capable of exercising an independent judgment in matters of state. Even the various commissions of enquiry, which to be sure were useful in disclosing the wrongdoings of the second Margai government, were nevertheless instituted by the NRC primarily to drum up some much needed support from APC sympathizers in Freetown.

As long as the NRC insisted on allowing its highly mechanical view of human weakness to color its approach to dealing with sociopolitical forces in Sierra Leone, the possibility of political disintegration as opposed to substantive development seemed ever more apparent. The ability of the NRC to contribute to a reduction of tensions in Sierra Leone was further contingent upon the willingness of the regime to establish a meaningful dialogue with persons as yet unswayed by Juxon-Smith's rhetoric. Protestations of loyalty from certain paramount chiefs may have seemed comforting to the military rulers, but there remained the unpleasant chore of reconciling those who "far from being relieved by the efficient intervention of the military, felt intensely thwarted by it."[60] In addition there was always the chance that the regime might alienate through its own incompetence those groups—traditional authorities and senior bureaucrats—that had been considered the natural allies of the new administration. Life would become particularly difficult for the NRC when it tried to cope with the politics of demilitarization. It was, in fact, on this broader issue of the return to civilian rule that the NRC's legitimization efforts would meet their severest test.

# 9
# OPPOSITION TO THE NATIONAL REFORMATION COUNCIL

Perhaps to a degree unprecedented in the combined experiences of African military regimes, the National Reformation Council was required to confront a great deal of opposition to its continuation in office. Most never coalesced in any formal manner since organized politics had been banned, but nevertheless it was a reflection of an almost universal resentment at the spectacle of Sierra Leone soldiers acting as government administrators and goal setters. If these various components of opposition, ranging from university professors to army privates, had a common objective, it was to do away with military rule and to reestablish some form of civilian government. Of course, card-carrying followers of the outlawed APC became the most vociferous element in this loosely aggregated opposition movement, but they also had their sympathizers even in the supposedly apolitical civil service.

According to one scholar, the military, "once having achieved power . . . must develop political organizations of civilian types or work out viable relations with civilian political groups."[1] The majority of junta leaders in black Africa usually engineer some kind of direct accommodation with the civilian elite in lieu of the more Nasserite creation of a dynamic political myth or the development of alternative political institutions.[2] The NRC, as we have seen, adopted the former approach largely because of Juxon-Smith's distrust of organized politics.

This chapter reviews the nature of civilian discontent and the kind of response it evoked from the NRC leaders. Except where politicians have been discredited completely and army officers subsequently venerated, military regimes sooner or later must face the possibility of covert unrest and attempt to foster communication channels with dissident civilian sectors. Often this unrest is merely a reaction to an army officer's personal deportment while in office in addition to the broader issues like the rate and philosophy of "demilitarization." The thirteen-month experience of NRC rule in Sierra Leone, culminating in the private's mutiny of April 18, 1968 and the restoration of civilian government shortly thereafter, offers us a sufficient gestation period with which to measure the army's ability to sustain a dialogue with the civilian elites under conditions of military dominance. We can also gauge the army's response to growing civilian disaffection, particularly the alienation of Sierra Leone's intelligentsia.

## THE ALIENATION OF THE INTELLIGENTSIA

One can determine that opposition to military rule in Sierra Leone began at the precise moment of the army takeover on March 21—witness the crowds of APC supporters who, upon demanding the release of "our prime minister," were answered with Lansana's bullets. The decision of the NRC to ban all formal manifestations of political power meant, however, that pressure groups or individuals sympathetic to the APC but not explicitly political had to take up the party's cause. Most of the APC politicians were not in a position to provide leadership once they had rejected Juxon-Smith's offer to serve on the National Advisory Council. Furthermore, the more radical members of the banned party, fearing detention, escaped from the capital and went into hiding, some with the assistance of secret societies in the provinces.

With most APC leaders no longer an activist force in the political system, other groups surfaced to assume the mantle of protest. Especially influential during the first month of army rule were those twin pillars of the intelligentsia—the teaching staffs of Sierra Leone's two principal colleges and the members of the bar association. Both the academics and the barristers challenged the fundamental tenets of Sierra Leone's military government. In a memorandum to the NRC chairman dated April 3, the bar association reaffirmed the constitutionality of Siaka Stevens's appointment as prime minister, deplored the killings of "peaceful citizens" on the night of March 21, and expressed deep concern at the banning of political parties and "certain other associations." It also viewed "with considerable alarm" the NRC provision for detention without trial and concluded with an offer by the bar association to assist the NRC "in its effort to facilitate the speedy return to Constitutional and democratic government."[3]

The two constituent colleges of the University of Sierra Leone—Fourah Bay College and Njala University College—also became centers of opposition to the NRC. During the 1967 General Elections, Fourah Bay students had actively campaigned for APC candidates, and on the morning of March 19, they marched to the residence of the governor-general, bearing a resolution calling upon him to appoint Stevens as prime minister. Since independence, most of the African faculty members at Fourah Bay have been Creole and thus, like the students, supported the APC. On March 31, four days before the delivery of the bar association protest note, eighty-three members of the Fourah Bay teaching staff (including expatriates) wrote the NRC chairman and, in relatively mild tones, urged him not to curtail freedom of expression and publication. The petitioners also supported the "ideal of government in accordance with the will of the people as shown by free elections."[4]

A little over two weeks later, yet another memorandum from Fourah Bay—this one receiving wide public circulation—was delivered to Juxon-Smith. This particular resolution noted "with dismay that many of the citizens of Sierra Leone have become apprehensive of discussing, even in private, the large problems which face the country at the present time, fearing reprisal if they offer an opinion . . ." The signers also backed the efforts of the bar association and denounced the NRC's suppression of the freedom of the press. They implored the military government not to squelch debate and suggested that "if opinions expressed are unsympathetic to the National Reformation Council or adversely critical of its policies and actions they must be answered by rational justification and reasoned argument."[5]

The Fourah Bay College memorandum was soon followed by similar activity at Njala, the main provincial institution of higher learning. Thirty Njala staff members in a memorandum dated May 1 gave their support to the Fourah Bay and bar association resolutions but proposed further that the NRC "immediately hand over the government to the constitutionally appointed Prime Minister."[6] In making this latter demand, the Njala staff rejected the NRC's claim that Steven's appointment had violated the constitution. This was to challenge the legitimacy of the regime at its most vulnerable point and in a political system where blind obedience to authority had apparently become a virtue, these various memoranda brought a predictable response from the NRC.

On April 7 the Secretariat issued yet another of its almost daily warnings—this one in response to the bar association memo and probably to the faculty unrest at Fourah Bay College:

The Chairman wishes the public to note that all constitutional matters relating to the establishment of the National Reformation Council are a matter for the council. Certain persons have however made it their business to give advice calculated to create mischief. These persons and all other members of the public are warned that activities of this nature are subversive to the peace and good government of Sierra Leone and any person found indulging in them will be severely dealt with.[7]

Soon after this announcement, members of the bar were summoned before the chairman and threatened with detention. In a press conference on April 11, Juxon-Smith openly denounced the bar association memorandum and called for the immediate deportation of a prominent Ceylonese-born lawyer, J.E.R. Candappa.[8] Then on April 26 and 28, hundreds of women loyal to the APC demonstrated in front of the now vacant parliament building. They criticized the first public session of the National Advisory Council as a gathering of "collaborators" and some later lay down on the road to prevent the passage of army vehicles.[9] Challenged now by street mobs as well as by a large percentage of the professional bourgeoisie, the NRC once again found it necessary to warn, to threaten, and in some instances to detain. On May 1, the Secretariat announced that the regime would no longer "tolerate this blatant disregard of its authority." The statement referred to "disruptive elements" who had "set to work again to bring about disunity leading to disturbances and even bloodshed." The NRC also reiterated unequivocally that it had never recognized the appointment of Stevens as prime minister and that the governor-general's action "in purporting to make the 'appointment' was both unconstitutional and indiscreet."[10]

Relationships between the NRC and the university community soon deteriorated rapidly. Contrary to the army officers' hopes of winning the approval of the nation's intellectual elite, the two college faculties—especially the Creole members—could scarcely hide their distate for a government run by soldiers with limited education and administrative capabilities. The Fourah Bay principal, Davidson Nicol, was invited to serve as a representative on the National Advisory Council as he had been in contact with Major Blake before the return of Juxon-Smith. However, within several weeks of the appointment (which triggered adverse faculty comment) Nicol resigned, primarily because of fundamental differences between himself and the NRC chairman and because "it did not appear . . . that the majority of the Advisory Council were anxious for a speedy return to civilian government."[11] The Fourah Bay principal soon came out publicly in defense of academic freedom, announcing that he would not be intimidated by the military junta. The NRC responded to this "act of defiance" by threatening to halve the government's recurrent grant to the college. Although this threat was never actually carried out, Sierra Leone's military regime, through its total disregard for the arts of compromise and bargaining, had succeeded in eliminating any semblance of a political constituency among Freetowners.

The single quality most characterizing the NRC's response to open challenges to its legitimacy in these early months was an acute defensiveness punctuated by a constant stream of warnings to all who would not respect authority. Each statement of criticism or public demonstration was interpreted as an example of insolence or insubordination that the regime could not tolerate. The simplest explanation for the NRC tendency to equate political dissent, however mildly couched, with outright defiance is to say that the army officers were simply transferring the norms of their military experience to the political sphere. Military organizations do place a premium on disciplined modes of behavior; and, no matter how far it might have been removed from the British model, the Sierra Leone army had no doubt stressed these values as well. Once again, however, this writer believes that the NRC's insensitivity to debate and discussion—in short, to ideas—may be given an alternative explanation.

The bulk of those statements emanating from the NRC Secretariat that warned everyone "to obey or else" were largely the responsibility of the chairman himself and of the young captains on three-month assignments to the Department of the Interior. A content analysis of addresses delivered by the original members of the NRC reveals that, as a rule, Majors Blake, Jumu, and Kai-Samba avoided threats in dealing with their respective audiences. Their approach was largely factual in substance and conciliatory in tone as opposed to the blustering, threatening pronouncements of the NRC captains and Juxon-Smith, who was well known for his habit of scolding anyone who "got out of line"—including petty officials as well as important dignitaries like Davidson Nicol and Sir Samuel Bankole-Jones, president of the Sierra Leone Court of Appeal.[12] Whenever someone in a room Juxon-Smith entered did not instantly stand to attention, that person would be ostracized and often, if in government employ, dismissed from service.

The National Advisory Council would later record in detail the behavior traits of Captain Sam Mboma as he conducted his weekly tours of southern and eastern provincial chiefdoms. The council paid particular attention to Mboma's way of intimidating all those "in opposition."

We have a report from the Njaluahun Chiefdom of the detention of Mr. J. C. Barnett and three others by Captain Sam Mboma in H. M. Prisons, Kenema, because they arrived late for a meeting with the Captain, even though their late arrival was due to the fact that they had been to the burial of Mr. J. C. Barnett's grand child that morning. When representations were made to him on behalf of the persons detained, he stated that *they had been disrespectful to him by arriving late,* thus leaving out of consideration altogether the justifiable cause of their late arrival.[13]

Lists of trouble-makers who failed to show proper respect for the paramount chiefs (implying an equivalent lack of respect for the NRC) were handed over to the young army officers who often detained the individuals in question.

Both Juxon-Smith and the NRC captains seem to have enjoyed the exercise of apparently limitless power—in short, the power to demand respect (as opposed to earning it) and generally to order people around. This kind of behavior was indicative of another response to a sense of status deprivation. By treating most civilians with whom they came in direct contact as little more than small boys the NRC member could, in effect, compensate for the civilian's negative image of soldiers during both the colonial administration and under the two Margai governments. Some of the young captains who served in the Department of the Interior were especially disposed to behave with arrogance if only because of their low rank in the officer corps, their up-country origins, their inferior educational qualifications, and their lack of prominent connections with SLPP big men. In any event, this kind of arrogance rendered it extremely difficult for certain junta members to reconcile or mediate political differences including the most minor chiefdom palavers.

## INTRA-JUNTA FRAGMENTATION

Thus the political opposition in the early stages of the National Reformation Council can be described as an external condition that impinged upon the civilian-military partnership. Before discussing the politics of demilitarization we must consider the nature of dissension within the civilian-military administrative structure. Beneath the seemingly calm facade that the NRC and its civilian coworkers presented to the Sierra Leone people lay serious rifts that, when combined with opposition mounted against the regime as a whole, eventually led to its downfall.

The strains that developed within the ruling army-civilian coalition assumed two forms. First, there was the continuing problem of building consensus within the officer corps itself that only became aggravated once these officers found themselves in charge of an entire state apparatus and not simply a 1,500-man battalion. As in the past, quarreling among senior army officers hinted at a special linkage between organizational tensions and political cliquism.

Closer scrutiny also reveals, moreover, that shortly after the NRC had seized power, its supposed allies—the civil servants and the advisory council representatives—were not always sympathetic or uncritical partners. To be sure the alliance did not crumble completely. Most of the permanent secretaries continued to man their posts, and the National Advisory Council continued to dispense political advice. But there were enough important points of cleavage in the relationship between the army and the civilian components of the NRC to necessitate our critical scrutiny of such a relationship before we comment upon its "naturalness" or "inevitability."

If opposition to the NRC rule as a government began with Lansana's martial law declaration on March 21, then opposition within the NRC to the leadership of that regime commenced almost immediately upon the return of Lieutenant Colonel Juxon-Smith on March 28. Unlike the original members of the Blake clique which included Commissioner Leigh and which had participated in a united strike against Brigadier Lansana, Juxon-Smith had been called back to Sierra Leone largely as an afterthought. However, Blake and his fellow conspirators grossly miscalculated the outcome of this decision. By inviting back an officer who did not share their sense of fealty to the anti-Albert faction of the SLPP but who instead harbored only contempt for all forms of civilian politics, they risked sabotaging the holding-action spirit of the March 23 coup. They had also entrusted the overall command of the council to an individual whose self-righteous posturing clashed with the more pragmatic, low-key style of a Blake or a Jumu.

The issues that led to frequent bickering within the NRC displayed themselves in the first several months of army rule. On the most elementary level, Blake, Leigh, and the other senior army and police officers arrayed themselves against the chairman because of his excessive moralizing fervor, his autocratic methods of decision making, his penchant for secrecy, and his apparent refusal to be held accountable by no one. Leigh notes that when Juxon-Smith assumed chairmanship of the council, "he [Juxon-Smith] was talking a lot and I later advised him to be respectful to people and talk less."[14] After the NRC had held its first formal session, he always "threw his weight around and tended to be very arbitrary."[15] Even though the council was theoretically required to reach decisions by a majority vote, "Juxon-Smith was a dictator" and "did not allow anybody's name who is a member of the council to be put down on the minutes as not in agreement with him."[16] In a move somewhat imitative of his public crusade against rumor-mongering and idle gossip, Juxon-Smith also warned his fellow officers not to discuss "sensitive matters" with prominent civilians on the grounds that such discussions inevitably endangered national security. Early in April, for example, he reprimanded Charles Blake and several others for chatting about council decisions outside the meeting room.[17] Often when challenged by his colleagues, he would reply, "You will all die as sinners."[18]

The disintegration of the National Reformation Council into one- and two-man cliques was soon heightened by the usual quibbling over the military pecking order. Perhaps the first army officer to openly quarrel with the NRC chairman on this matter was Major Blake.[19] Following Juxon-Smith's return to Freetown, Blake was entrusted with operational responsibility for the Royal Sierra Leone Military Forces, thus allowing the NRC chairman to concentrate solely on his duties as de facto head of state. Once Blake had gained physical custody of the Sierra Leone army with Juxon-Smith assuming the title of commander-in-chief (superseding the now deposed governor-general) the two men feuded over that perennial issue in Sierra Leone military affairs—''who's *really* in charge here.'' At several meetings of the NRC, the chairman harangued Blake ''for taking certain decisions on his own without consulting the chairman.''[20] Blake apparently retorted to the effect that ''you can't be Force Commander and Chairman at the same time.''[21]

Beneath the administrative nitpicking dividing the two senior army members of the NRC were larger political questions that produced a broad-based alliance against Juxon-Smith, the ''outsider.'' Conflict arose first over the subject of those primarily northern officers who had been arrested and imprisoned by Sir Albert in early February. Juxon-Smith wanted them all released, some to be reinstated at their former rank and others, especially Bangura, to be sent overseas on diplomatic assignments.[22] This plan aroused the ire of Major Jumu who under the belief that he would have been killed had the February coup plot succeeded, wanted all of the conspirators either court-martialed or required to confess their guilt in public. Juxon-Smith later stated during the treason trial that ''it took him some three weeks coaxing Major Jumu that they should all try and forgive their brother officers.''[23]

Also particularly unsettling to Majors Jumu and Kai-Samba was Juxon-Smith's operation ''spring clean'' which symbolized a repudiation of the NRC's original promise not ''to take cognisance of the past'' or ''to mount exhaustive enquiries into the liberty and possessions of the individual.'' The commissions of inquiry which were established only served to humiliate a number of civilian patrons and the SLPP in general. These commissions were resented therefore by the two Mende officers having extensive connections in the former ruling elite. Juxon's distaste for civilian politics and civilian politicians was also an irritant since most members of the NRC had originally wanted to entrust a fairly prominent advisory role to key members of the anti-Albert wing of the SLPP, including Kutubu Kai-Samba. Major Blake had also intended to allow such well-known Creole professionals as Davidson Nicol and Sir Samuel Bankole-Jones an important say in running of the military regime. Juxon-Smith's bellicose public image and his moralizing antics dashed these hopes and limited civilian access to the new government. Major Jumu, for his part, objected to the NRC chairman's decision to close down most of the SLPMB plantations—one of the more significant trademarks (and from Jumu's point of view, achievements) of the SLPP period.[24]

By late August and early September the internal politicking that had sabotaged any residual cohesion in the NRC reached a climax. Major Turay had already left the council and was replaced by Major Mark Koroma, a northerner.[25] Blake and Juxon-Smith were no longer on speaking terms, and at one point each threatened to arrest the other. Juxon-Smith then proceeded with a long list of charges against his acting force commander including the usual references to nepotism and administrative malpractice.[26] The chairman and Police Commissioner Leigh also clashed, partly from differences in age and experience (Leigh regarded Juxon-Smith as a pompous young upstart) and partly from Juxon-Smith's distrust of any police involvement in policy making. Leigh tendered his resignation but was persuaded by Assistant Commissioner Alpha Kamara to remain on the council. Kamara argued that Leigh's departure would "finish" the NRC.

Meanwhile in early September, Leigh and Jumu were despatched to an OAU Ministerial meeting in Kinshasa before proceeding to New York for the opening session of the U. N. General Assembly. Once back in Freetown Jumu apparently contemplated arresting both Blake and Juxon-Smith but was dissuaded by Commissioner Leigh who himself had come to appreciate the folly of such a course of action and its potentially disastrous impact on army rule in Sierra Leone. Cooler heads eventually prevailed with some sort of compromise arranged between the council chairman and the army commander.

The petty feuding and clique formation that became endemic to the NRC leads us to several conclusions. First, intraofficer cleavages under military government conditions hardly differed in form or substance from those under conditions of civilian dominance. Thus Blake versus Juxon-Smith, Leigh versus Juxon-Smith, or Jumu versus Juxon-Smith and Blake belonged to a tradition of disputes dating back to January 1966 when the contestants for the seat of power were Lieutenant-Colonel Ambrose Genda and Brigadier David Lansana. Second, the almost ritualistic threats of coupmaking that took place within the council severely inhibited its ability to grapple with the problems of "reformation." Most of the junta's time and energy was of necessity channeled toward the reconciliation of its own members' grievances rather than toward the legitimate grievances of all Sierra Leoneans. Obviously a house divided against itself cannot stand for very long, as will become apparent in the next chapter.

## DISSENSION IN THE CIVIL SERVICE AND THE NATIONAL ADVISORY COUNCIL

In our discussion of the NRC's quest for regime supports we noted that some members visited government departments in an effort to rally the civil service to their cause, primarily as a response to a perceived identity of values between the two groups—the junta requiring the technical and administrative skills offered by the bureaucrats; the civil service in turn relying upon the army to control the political system and to "liberate" them, as it were, from the meddlesome interference of SLPP ministers and other party leaders. One student of Ghana's first experiment with military government in the form of the National Liberation Council (NLC) has suggested that:

Apart from the broad area of agreement between military men and civil servants on policy, relations between the two were also helped by greater agreement, compared with the CPP period, on the line of demarcation between administrative and political territory. Officials who served under the CPP were able to list instances of political interference in what they regarded as administrative matters, and of the contempt shown for the administration through by-passing the proper channels.[27]

When we attempt, however, to apply to Sierra Leone this scenario of army officer and civil servant conducting the affairs of the nation in perfect harmony, we immediately encounter some difficulties. In certain instances, a new kind of interference from above replaced that experienced by civil servants under Sir Albert Margai and the SLPP.

At least in the early months of NRC rule, the military-bureaucratic alliance seemed to work reasonably well. For example in May 1967, the NRC established an Economic Advisory Committee to assist in the implementation of the IMF's stabilization program for Sierra Leone, a program originally undertaken by Sir Albert the previous November but considerably watered down prior to the intervention of the army. The committee included among its members Dr. G. Conrad, a West German economic adviser; S. B. Daramy, the financial secretary; Mr. S. B. Nicol-Cole, governor of the Bank of Sierra Leone; and V. A. Nylander, secretary of the Development Planning Division in the NRC Secretariat.[28] Most of those on the committee eventually developed a viable working relationship with the NRC chairman and were instrumental in persuading him to jettison strictly political considerations by closing down the SLPMB plantations (which employed some 2,000 workers) and to phase out the unprofitable Sierra Leone railway. Juxon-Smith who apparently fancied himself a "financial wizard" because of his earlier experience in the army pay and records office, was usually receptive to the kind of advice dispensed by his team of international and domestic technicians.[29]

There was one other locus of civilian-military interaction at the government level where NRC department heads and senior administrative officers developed a healthy respect for one another and policy was left largely in the hands of the civilian secretaries. Aside from the NRC Secretariat, the Department of the Interior, and the Department of Finance all under the personal supervision of Juxon-Smith, the remaining departments were headed by army and police officers engrossed almost solely with their military and police responsibilities. Thus though Commissioner Leigh and Assistant Commissioner Alpha Kamara were NRC members responsible for the Departments of External Affairs and Social Services, respectively, they devoted most of their time to police duties (which were considerable given the increased preoccupation with internal security under the NRC). Leigh might be trotted out on occasion to make a foreign policy speech or to attend an overseas conference but, apart from these occasional forays into the foreign policy realm, his very able permanent secretary, H. E. Maurice-Jones, actually ran the Department.

The other senior officers—Blake, Jumu, Kai-Samba, and Major Mark Koroma—also had their military duties. Blake, of course, as nominal head of the Sierra Leone Military Forces had very little opportunity to report for work at the Department of Trade, Industry, and Agriculture and spent, at most, an hour or two per day in his "ministerial quarters." Jumu, the battalion commander, and Major Koroma, the deputy battalion commander, found little time to act out their nonmilitary administrative functions. Major Kai-Samba almost never appeared at the Department of Works, Transport, and Communications. Major Jumu explained to this writer how "he had no interest in the day-to-day running of the administration in the Department of Health and left everything with his permanent secretary."[30] Almost by default, therefore, the secretaries in most of the NRC-controlled departments were given almost a completely free hand in the management of their respective departments. No doubt the lack of interference from above rendered life in the senior echelons of the civil service rather palatable.

Even though we have managed to identify areas of harmony between some members of the NRC and senior civilian administrators, the Sierra Leone civil service was often as demoralized and harassed under the NRC as under the preceding SLPP regime. In its initial endeavor to mirror the political alignments of the past, the NRC first risked alienating those civil servants who had been appalled by Sir Albert's tendency to appoint certain persons to senior posts on the basis of their personal loyalties to the SLPP and to the prime minister himself. Thus when it soon became known that such noteworthy backers of the Lansana coup as Peter Tucker, John Kallon, S. B. Daramy, and others—several of whom were Mende—would not be dismissed, the Creole elements in the civil service grew apprehensive about the junta's willingness or capacity to revive the theoretically apolitical nature of the bureaucracy. As in other cases of disaffection within the political system, the regime issued its usual "severe warning:"

The National Reformation Council has heard with grave concern rumours that are being spread by malicious people . . . to the effect that certain people have been allowed to remain in their posts . . . and suggesting that this is done for tribal reasons. The public is hereby warned . . . that any further rumour of this nature . . . will be pursued to its source, and the persons responsible severely dealt with. The Council wishes to take the opportunity to assure all civil servants that it will not tolerate victimisation of any officer for any past conduct in political affairs.[31]

This last statement was clearly a pledge to protect civil servants such as Peter Tucker and John Kallon who had southern backgrounds from victimization for their past association with the SLPP inner circle.

Once Juxon-Smith had become chairman of the NRC, those civil servants not tainted by prior allegiance to Sir Albert gained some satisfaction from the forced resignation of Attorney-General Berthan Macauley, and Chief Justice Gershon O. Collier in early April as part of a general program of spring cleaning. In mid-August, the Forster Commission began its inquiry into the assets of Peter Tucker, George Panda, and other known SLPP sympathizers with past or present experience as public servants. However, though the activities of the Forster Commission served to revoke the NRC's pre-Juxon-Smith commitment to shield prominent civil servants from criticism for "past conduct in political matters," only Peter Tucker, the NRC secretary-general, was actually replaced. Thus by the time of the military regime's demise in April 1968, many of those regarded by the Creoles as collaborators were still at their posts, and their continued presence weakened the morale of the non-Mende civil servants.

In those departments under the overall supervision of Juxon-Smith and the young army captains the relationship between the NRC and the civil service suffered irreparable damage. In one of his early press conferences, Juxon-Smith outlined his philosophy of public service:

Fixed time for work is 8 o'clock; some people never get there till 8:15, or 8:30 or 9:00 o'clock. Some . . . leave their work and go out . . . to attend to their private businesses. Now I am the person responsible for the civil service [the establishment office was located in the NRC Secretariat]. Whoever does that will be dealt with.[32]

A few weeks after this broadcast, Juxon-Smith attempted to practice what he had so vigorously preached. It is not unreasonable to assert that he expected his departmental secretaries to perform like robots since the NRC chairman was of the impression that all matters even remotely connected with policy needed instant attention. Those senior civil servants working directly under the chairman often found themselves lining up for hours outside his office to advise "on the most minor of points which he failed to grasp."[33] The secretary-generals who diligently copied the minutes of all council meetings were also subject to undue stress. Sometimes the NRC would meet virtually every day of the week, from early morning until late evening. NRC members enjoyed talking for hours on end, thereby wasting their own time as well as the time of the secretary-generals. Ultimately, most of the latter "were driven crazy" by the excessive length of the meetings and by the tendency of NRC members to argue incessantly throughout the course of their deliberations.[34]

Civil servants not living up to the chairman's expectations might expect to receive nasty little notes ordering them to embrace their tasks with renewed energy and always to show the proper respect for their military superiors. Following Juxon-Smith's first tour of the provinces, the NRC Secretariat sent a memorandum to all provincial administrative officers chiding them for their "disrespectful treatment" of the NRC chairman and pointing out to them "that it is their duty as civil servants to give the utmost respect and accord the greatest courtesy to all members of the NRC particularly to the Chairman who is the Head of State." One of the NRC's major complaints was that the district commissioner in Kailahun had failed to "dress properly"; the poor chap forgot to wear a tie during his meeting with the chairman![35] Several months later the council reprimanded all district commissioners for allowing some Lebanese nationals to visit the Kono diamond area in violation of specific orders forbidding these persons to enter Kono. District officers were warned "that instructions are not issued for fun," and that "disciplinary action will be taken against any officer who is found guilty of disregarding instructions issued to him."[36] According to one informant, the NRC chairman went so far as to dismiss civil servants not agreeing with his views or failing to demonstrate respect.[37]

Apart from receiving threatening messages from the top, provincial and district administrators were subject to other forms of what they viewed as NRC arrogance and interference. On the surface, the NRC did not tamper with the structure of regional administration apart from altering some nomenclature. Furthermore, unlike in Ghana where army officers served on regional committees of administration, all NRC members carried out their duties from Freetown, and no military governors were ever appointed. Yet though there was no permanent military presence outside of the capital, relations between the NRC and the provincial administrators were hardly cordial. First, provincial and district commissioners were often asked to serve as apologists for the NRC. Obviously the removal of all political brokers whether of the APC or SLPP variety meant that the NRC needed to recruit as many nonpoliticos as possible to spread the message. Thus on May 5, 1967, the regime instructed "all provincial and District Commissioners to make more frequent tours of their provinces and to explain to the people the policies of the National Reformation Council."[38] Because of the overtly political nature of this exercise, provincial administrative officers began to resent the imposition of a military government.

Even more resented was the behavior of the young captains assigned to the Department of the Interior. On their frequent trips up-country, they attempted to solve most chiefdom palavers without showing any deference to the views of provincial administrators. The latter particularly disliked the way Captain Mboma and the others sought to impose solutions "without gathering all the pertinent facts."[39] The situation became so serious that even Juxon-Smith himself apparently criticized the captains "for sticking their noses in too many things."[40] When Captain D.D.K. Vandi replaced Mboma in October as the NRC's eighth member, he is said to have antagonized provincial administrators with his simplistic approach to settling chiefdom disputes. One source claims that Vandi, like the politicians preceding him, "bullied" all those civil servants who took issue with his method of operation and in November demanded, unsuccessfully, that all district commissioners be dismissed from their posts.[41]

From the examples presented above it is safe to assume that the much vaunted alliance between army officers and civilian public servants under conditions of military rule does not necessarily function as described in the literature. Particularly galling to those Sierra Leoneans who had the misfortune to come into direct contact with a Juxon-Smith or a Vandi was the element of regimentation. Most disliked the way some members of the NRC ordered them around like just another company or battalion of troops. No one in the public service (especially a college graduate) appreciated some army captain—perhaps ten or fifteen years his junior and possessing only a secondary school degree, if that—telling people "to behave" or risk dismissal. Even those departmental secretaries who found themselves playing a greater advisory role than in the past could rarely disagree with the NRC chairman or the NRC captains without incurring their wrath. A number of informants told this writer that though decisions under the military were often made with "commendable speed," the civil servant had to display at least tacit obedience at all times "since they were working at gunpoint."[42] Here was clearly an element of class differentiation at work once small boys, thrust overnight into positions of authority, began to lord it over holders of bachelor degrees from Creole families.[43]

Once dissatisfaction with the style and performance of military government in Sierra Leone had succeeded in undermining the morale of both the civil service and the NRC itself, it was not long before the National Advisory Council began to experience its own summer of discontent. Part of the problem was that, with Juxon-Smith at the helm, the regime no longer felt committed to maintaining a dialogue with any group of politicians, including those of the SLPP variety who toiled for the Advisory Council. At least in the first month or so following the army takeover, a man like Kutubu Kai-Samba, the former leader of the SLPP "revisionists" and a leading member of the advisory council, enjoyed considerable influence with the junta. His brother, after all, was Major Bockarie Kai-Samba who, along with Blake and Jumu, had staged the March 23 coup at least indirectly on behalf of those within the former ruling party wanting Sir Albert removed as their leader. Thus according to an underground newspaper that appeared in late April, the NRC received much of its "legal advice from Kai-Samba, the Ex-Minister who [is] not interested in saving Sierra Leone from the dangers of military rule, but only to see those who were against him in the cabinet and during the elections punished."[44] Some well-known Creoles including Sir Samuel Bankole-Jones were also, as we have already shown, quite friendly with the regime through their association with Major Blake even though they did not actually serve on the advisory council. However, once Juxon-Smith had unmistakably stamped his peculiar brand of puritanism on the NRC, no one, either on or off the advisory council, could expect to receive a truly sympathetic hearing from the chairman.

There soon appeared still other impediments to a productive effort by the National Advisory Council. Indeed the very terms of reference elaborated at the council's first session on April 26 posed some special difficulties. At this session, the advisory council was formally requested by the NRC:

1. To work out ways and means of calming down political feelings and bringing about national unity, free of tribalism and separatist agitation.
2. To work out steps leading to a peaceful return to civilian rule after a general election.
3. To work out a Constitution designed to incorporate the results in (1) above and to obviate all the underlying causes of the previous conflicts and corruption.
4. To advise on all matters referred to it by the National Reformation Council.
5. To advise on any other matter which is in the general interest of the nation.[45]

Perhaps the major drawbacks to these terms of reference were their essential vagueness and their implicitly biased interpretation of the events surrounding the general elections in March. By entreating members of the advisory council to somehow magically discover "ways and means" of restoring national unity under the aegis of a regime that denied the existence of the APC, the NRC inadvertently imposed its own simplistic model of "development without politics" upon the council's deliberations. It was furthermore presumptuous for the NRC to transform the advisory council into a de facto constitutional commission. Sierra Leone already possessed a number of constitutions including one which came into being on independence day as well as the SLPP republican constitution bill passed in the House of Representatives the previous February. Certainly the political excesses of the past, particularly corruption, could hardly be blamed on prevailing constitutional arrangements but rather on the behavior of individual ministers, civil servants, and party hacks.

The NRC also diminished the prospects of the Advisory Council's playing a meaningful role in reformation and reconciliation by asking council members "to work out steps leading to a peaceful return to civilian rule *after a general election.*" This request demonstrated once again the army's unwillingness to accept the APC victory of March 21, thereby restricting the advisory council to an academic and sterile discussion of the civilian rule issue. Theoretically, an advisory body that, because of slanted terms of reference, could not examine objectively the reality of political sentiments in Sierra Leone would tell the junta only what it wanted to hear. Those members of council who saw little or no need for the holding of "fresh elections" might soon be placed on the defensive.

In the months following its first meeting in late April, the National Advisory Council debated issues of minimal relevance to the specific context of government by soldiers. Reams of position papers were churned out on every conceivable subject from the delimitation of constituencies based on revised population statistics to altering the composition and functions of the Electoral Commission.[46] In its August meeting, lasting from the 21st to the 29th, the council examined the case for a monarchical constitution, for a republican constitution with an executive president, and for one with only a ceremonial president as head of state. Also considered during this session was a plan for the "re-regionalization of the whole country to ensure integration among tribes." Along these lines, the council suggested abolition of the long prevalent distinction between the largely Creole Western Area and the rural provinces which are almost exclusively inhabited by indigenous Africans. Furthermore, the council, in its rather superficial quest for a "solution" to tribalism, recommended that "in principle there should be as much admixture of tribes as possible in boarding schools" and "the present restriction imposed upon the movement of Paramount Chiefs should be lifted" so that a Temne chief might visit "a fellow Chief in the heart of Mende Land."[47] Not until late September did the council initiate a discussion of the vital question of a return to civilian rule.

As consideration of issues of questionable relevance continued to monopolize the council's agenda, relations between it and the NRC began to deteriorate. Particularly objectionable to members of the council was Juxon-Smith's insistence on "reforming" the state through this or that decree. In

June, for example, he asked the council to consider a change of name for Sierra Leone, arguing that "in a united entity a new name should be adopted."[48] The NRC chairman also asked the advisory council to explore the possibility of "a change of time from GMT to local time" and providing "a halfday on Friday, or making suitable arrangement for Muslims to pray, between 12 noon and 3 p.m."[49] Many council members believed such issues to be of only marginal importance, and some were thought to be an affront to the members' intelligence. A number of council representatives went to great lengths to inform Juxon-Smith that, if only because of the costs involved in altering the letterheads on official government stationery, the idea of suddenly changing the name of the country during a period of financial retrenchment was "unrealistic."[50] Many of the items presented for the consideration of the advisory council seem to have reflected little more than the whims of the NRC chairman.

There were still other areas of disagreement between the military regime and its civilian advisors. In discussions held with the advisory council chairman, Dr. S. T. Matturi, Juxon-Smith emphasized that once Sierra Leone had returned to civilian rule, the country should immediately adopt a republican constitution with an executive president. The council then challenged Juxon-Smith's views. The chairman was informed that:

To introduce the B.2 constitution [republic with executive president] would be most unfortunate because it would definitely open up the sores created in the minds of people by the S.L.P.P.'s attempt to introduce the "One Party System" which became inextricably woven with the idea of the Republican Constitution . . . An attempt to introduce the B.2 Constitution would be tantamount to undoing the good work now being done by the N.R.C. and thereby jeopardising [its] prestige. It would be a sure way of getting the people to lose confidence in the N.R.C. and in the Advisory Council.[51]

The council proceeded to recommend eventual adoption of a republican constitution with a ceremonial president and by so doing incurred Juxon-Smith's displeasure.

Throughout August and September, relations between the NRC and the advisory council continued on their downward slide. In September, council members were piqued by Juxon-Smith's failure to consult with them prior to appointing a new board of directors for the Sierra Leone Produce Marketing Board. The NRC chairman was then told that "the quality of the membership which constituted the newly appointed Board of Directors would not easily win public confidence." Also singled out for special attention were the antics of the army captains in the settlement of chiefdom disputes. The council was especially critical of Captain Mboma's proclivity to jail anyone giving the slightest indication of "infidelity" to his chief. In late September the excessive use of detention as a means of forcefully resolving chiefdom palavers provoked the council to draw a fairly somber assessment of the state of the nation:

As a result of all these happenings, there is general disquiet and unrest in the country. We feel that it is our duty as Members of the Advisory Council to implore the National Reformation Council to devise immediate remedial measures to rectify these things, otherwise the authority and standing of the National Reformation Council among the people is likely to be considerably undermined with very unfortunate results.[52]

By the mid-point in the NRC's thirteen-month reign, the advisory council emerged as one of the more perceptive behind-the-scenes observers of the nation's mood. That this council should almost overnight be transformed from a timid collection of NRC "yes men" into an astute critic of that very same regime demonstrates unequivocally how widespread was the spirit of dissent in the land. By failing to heed the views expressed by members of the advisory council, the junta eventually fell victim to those "very unfortunate results" mentioned in the council's warning to the NRC chairman.

# 10

# *THE NRC*
# *AND THE*
# *POLITICS OF*
# *DEMILITARIZATION*

During the first wave of successful coups d'état in sub-Saharan Africa, most of the regimes that followed these usurpations of civilian authority promised an eventual return to government of the politicians. They key word of course was "eventual." In some cases, pledges assured that civilian rule would be restored after a specified time—in Nigeria, the Federal Military Government originally promised a handover to civilian leadership in 1976. In other cases, a return to the barracks was made contingent upon the exorcism of corruption or the liquidation of foreign debts. By attaching such conditions to the voluntary demilitarization of the system, one could delay the process indefinitely. Furthermore, although it is possible for a military regime to preside over a relatively swift and orderly transition from direct army control of the system to a democratically elected government, as did Ghana's National Liberation Council, handovers are still subject to compromise by such statements as those made by Ghana's Major-General Ocran—"in the final analysis it is the future government's performance that will either keep the soldiers in the barracks or bring them out again, rifle in hand, to seize power."[1] It goes without saying that Colonel Ignatius Acheampong's coup of January 1972 has demonstrated the fragility of a return to civilian rule not accompanied by an effective restoration of civil control over the armed forces.

More recently some coup leaders in black Africa have not even bothered to pay lip service to the former sacred shibboleth of recivilianizaton. Acheampong, for example, has made no mention of an eventual return to civilian rule; and in July 1973, Major Mathieu Kerekou who engineered Dahomey's most recent successful coup was forced to discount "fantastic and intentious rumours" of an impending handover to civilians, noting that "the Dahomean Revolution" would continue merrily on its course.[2] This was in marked contrast to the efforts of certain predecessor military regimes in that country to schedule democratic elections within months after seizing power. Certainly the prospects for voluntary military disengagement have never been bleaker. In Upper Volta, General Sangoulé Lamizana promised in 1973 that he and his fellow officers would "rentrer à la caserne" in 1974 and that his own special role as an "arbitre" between competing political factions would be formally concluded. Steps in this direction were actually taken as early as December 1970 when the army permitted national elections followed by the creation of a general assembly and a joint civilian-military cabinet headed by Premier G. K. Ouedraogo. However on February 8, 1974, the army reestablished full control over the system, abolished the assembly, and deposed the premier while Lamizana remained on as president. Even in Nigeria where the essential fairness of the crop of military leaders headed by General Gowon would have seemed to have boded well for a handover in 1976, the announcement in September 1974 that a return to civilian rule would be postponed indefinitely was not unexpected given the high degree of institutionalization of the regime and its civilian technocratic allies.

In Sierra Leone, a small group of warrant officers and NCOs acting on behalf of the army privates, overthrew the military regime of Brigadier Andrew T. Juxon-Smith on April 18, 1968 and within less than ten days managed to effect a complete restoration of civilian government. Prior to the so-called "privates' mutiny" of April 18, the whole detailed subject of a return to civilian rule became a matter of overriding concern for both military and nonmilitary elites in Sierra Leone. How the NRC tackled the problem of a return to the barracks and how the junta's willingness to manipulate the politics of withdrawal ultimately failed to satisfy the demands of articulate civilians for an immediate end to rule by decree are important to analyze. There are those factors that militated against an NRC withdrawal from active participation in the governing of the state as well as those, both of a political and of an organizational nature, that made it incumbent upon the regime to hand power back to the politicians. There were groups sanctioned by the NRC as well as those operating independently who joined together in a debate over the mechanics of demilitarization that must be described before investigating the background to the mutiny of April 18, the formation of the National Interim Council (NIC) headed by Colonel John Bangura, and the swearing-in of Siaka Probyn Stevens as prime minister on April 27, 1968.

## REASONS FOR AND AGAINST A WITHDRAWAL

No doubt taking his cue from the statements of brother army officers throughout West Africa, Major Charles Blake in his March 23 radio broadcast announced the formation of a "National Reformation Council" strictly as "an interim measure." Speaking for all the members of the NRC, Blake stressed most emphatically that "we are soldiers, and want to remain soldiers, and politics is not our mission." The new regime, Blake continued, would "do all in its power to bring about a civilian government in the shortest possible time," but added one small caveat—such a handover would have to wait "until the situation is favorable." This was a classic enunciation of the position Perlmutter has attributed to the "arbitrator-type" of praetorian army which "imposes a time limit on army rule" and "has no independent political organization and little interest in manufacturing a political ideology."[3]

The arbitrator spirit of the March takeover persisted well into the early months of army rule. In an address to members of the advisory council on April 26, Juxon-Smith stressed that the regime probably would stay in power only for fifteen months "before handing over to a civilian government."[4] In early June, Major Kai-Samba, addressing a group of paramount chiefs and commoners in Tonkolili District, indicated that a handover would occur within fifteen months' time (presumably taking the March coup as a starting point.)[5] This reference to a fifteen-month interim administration was diluted somewhat, however, by the subtle hedging of bets which began to appear in NRC pronouncements. Thus Kai-Samba's June speech stated that there could be no handover until the various commissions of inquiry had completed their purge of the system. Kai-Samba added that "there is also the task of holding a fresh general election before we hand over, because we are convinced that the last general election was not conducted fairly and properly."[6] In late August, Juxon-Smith emphasized that the NRC would hand over following a fresh election because the results of the March balloting had been declared "null and void."[7]

The NRC's increasingly muddled commitment to a withdrawal from the political arena can be blamed on the internal contradictions posed by the continued presence of uniformed military men as the country's leaders. First, there was the problem of the NRC chairman, who, according to a *London Times* reporter, had "privately told friends here in the past that he will be Sierra Leone's first president.''[8] Unlike most of the other members of the NRC who, with few illusions of budding political careers, had initially forsaken the comforts of barracks life to protect civilian friends from displacement by the APC, Juxon-Smith appears to have regarded himself as destined to rule Sierra Leone even in a post-NRC era. Through his unabating references to the examples set by past Sierra Leonean political leaders (Sir Milton Margai and I.T.A. Wallace-Johnson were two of his favorites), his obvious enjoyment of the pomp and circumstance accompanying his duties as head of state and his fondness for a republican constitution with an executive presidency, he created a self-image of more than a humble army officer on a ''rescue mission.''

Juxon-Smith's obvious political ambitions together with his scarcely concealed disdain for civilian leadership of recent vintage sharply reduced the credibility of the NRC's protestations of an imminent return to the barracks. Credibility was so strained that the NRC failed to groom a proper set of civilians to whom there could be an eventual handover. Claude E. Welch, Jr. has noted that ''the ease and speed of military withdrawal vary directly with the availability of potential successors deemed appropriate by the armed forces.''[9] In Ghana, the extensive involvement in NLC activities of bourgeois elites sympathetic to the tenets of the ''February revolution'' helped nurture a smooth transfer of power from Brigadier Afrifa to Dr. K.A. Busia and his Progress Party supporters. However, in Sierra Leone a suitable fit between the military regime and its civilian heirs never really materialized because of the NRC's annoying proclivity to alienate potential civilian backers.

To whom, one might ask, was the NRC planning to hand over the reins of government? One group, the leaders of the All Peoples Congress, seemed a most unlikely choice. For their part, Siaka Stevens and the other APC principals, regarding the military regime as treasonable, viewed as collaborators those civilians, including the National Advisory Council, who allied themselves with the NRC. The possibility of a reconciliation between the junta and the APC was almost entirely ruled out on May 1, when the NRC stated that it would never recognize the appointment of Stevens since this '' 'appointment' was both unconstitutional and indiscreet.'' Thus it was not the intention of the council ''at any time to hand over power to Mr. Siaka Stevens as Prime Minister as a result of the last election.''[10]

Most of the old line SLPP stalwarts, thoroughly discredited by the various commissions of inquiry, were also not available for potential recruitment. About the only politicians with any degree of influence in the increasingly circumscribed army circles were former members of the anti-Albert faction within the SLPP such as Kutubu Kai-Samba and L.A.M. Brewah; however, this clique, standing alone, could hardly constitute a viable future government. Faced with an almost nonexistent civilian constituency, the NRC lacked a precise vision of the mechanics and political ramifications of demilitarization, an unpleasant fact that rendered as sheer tokenism many of its statements and, as we shall see, some of its actions in this area.

Economic recovery and the participation of the NRC in that recovery provided the regime with an additional incentive for the continued exercise of power. Clearly the intervention of the army inaugurated a more mature relationship between Sierra Leone and its international creditors, specifically the International Monetary Fund. The military takeover led to the timely introduction of a fiscal stabilization program in contrast to the economic fiasco of the Margai period. Under the terms of the IMF grant (November 1966) to Sierra Leone of a $7.5 (Le 5.4) million standby credit for a one-year period, the civilian government was asked to freeze most vacancies in the civil service, to reduce budgetary appropriations for travel and supplies, to impose a number of special surcharges, to restrict borrowing from such institutions as the Central Bank for financing its budgetary deficit, and to avoid accepting more supplier's credits if inconsistent with the country's ability to service its short-term debts.

Faced with an impending general election, Sir Albert chose to evade most of these measures. As a case in point, the SLPMB continued to divert monies from its "stabilization fund" into unprofitable palm kernel, cocoa, coffee, and ginger plantations and processing plants. This meant that there remained almost no working capital with which to purchase cash crops for export. "Confidence in the board was shaken," an IMF study notes, "and there were indications that the produce was being smuggled to neighboring countries."[11] Payments to farmers were usually made in the form of chits, and, for political expediency, at artificially inflated prices. Primarily as a result of the SLPP's disregard for the proper fiscal and monetary management of the produce marketing board, Sierra Leone's net external reserves fell from Le 23 million at the end of 1964 to Le 11.4 million at the end of 1966.

Faced with these harsh economic realities and with the need to strengthen its initially flimsy arguments for intervening, the NRC publicized the nation's economic crisis and launched a "massive deflationary effort whose influences went much beyond the target areas of public finance and external reserves."[12] It was expected that the implementation of certain deflationary measures would reduce the overall budgetary deficit expected in fiscal year 1966-67 from Le 19.2 million to Le 7.2 million. For fiscal year 1967-68 economies in government spending were to be highlighted by a 43 percent drop (Le 22.9 to 12.8 million) in development outlays—the NRC agreed not to enter into any further contractor finance schemes. Supplementary measures were expected to provide additional revenues of Le 3.4 million as another means of reducing the government deficit. Surtaxes of 15 and 10 percent respectively were added to the company tax and the personal income tax; the Turnover Tax on companies was increased from 2 to 5 percent, and early in June diamond dealers were assessed a "once and for all levy" expected to yield an additional Le 5 million in revenue.[13] The NRC also raised duties on most imported and capital goods and levied higher excise taxes.

The most impressive achievement of the NRC in the economic realm was the revival of the SLPMB. First, the regime replaced all of the SLPP political appointees who had previously managed the board. Then, those plantations that had proved economically unviable were closed down. Finally, in November 1967, the devaluation of the leone followed that of sterling, and the regime was able to raise some producer prices by the percentage of the devaluation. A sharp reduction in administrative expenditures permitted the SLPMB to make all its payments to farmers in hard cash, and, with the price differentials narrowing between Sierra Leone and Liberia, the board could liquidate most of its short-term debt owed to British commercial banks.

When it was ejected from office on April 17, 1968, the NRC had begun to make a significant impact on the Sierra Leone economy. As a result of decreasing expenditures and sharply increased revenues, the actual budgetary deficit for 1966 and 1967 was only Le 5.9 million on both current and capital accounts. For 1967-68, the overall deficit was only Le 1.1 million. The balance of payments situation also improved markedly, reflecting a reduced demand for imports together with an increase in the prices and volume of cash crops grown for export. By the end of 1967, total external reserves had risen to approximately Le 13 million and by April 1968 to almost Le 16 million. Recognizing these improvements the IMF negotiated a second standby agreement with the Sierra Leone government in January 1968; this one provided a credit of up to $3.6 (Le 3) million for a one-year period. True, there were some unfavorable side effects resulting from this NRC/IMF enforced austerity. Drastic cutbacks in government spending brought increased unemployment (the closing of SLPMB plantations alone affected some 2,000 persons) and "consumer prices showed upward trends on all fronts while money wages virtually remained constant."[14]

Accountable to almost no civilians, the NRC did not particularly see fit to gauge the political consequences of its austerity measures with the same degree of sensitivity as might a civilian government. Juxon-Smith stressed this view in a "State of the Nation" address in February 1968. "Never again," emphasized the NRC chairman, "must the timely implementation of national economic policies be delayed or even prevented because the government in power is more interested in party politics than in the wellbeing and prosperity of the nation as a whole."[15] Nonetheless, the NRC deluded itself if it thought economics could be divorced so easily from politics. Since it had succeeded in attracting only marginal civilian support, the NRC could not operate as if politics, particularly the politics of demilitarization, was just something to be swept under the rug at the convenience of the regime. As much as Juxon-Smith and his messmates enjoyed tinkering with the economy, others in Sierra Leone believed that a return to civilian rule counted for more than straight economic recovery under the direction of a tiny group of military conspirators. Thus when Juxon-Smith noted in his address that "although the National Reformation Council considered as its main task the resuscitation of the economy, we had nevertheless, *if reluctantly,* to deal with what *appeared* to be political issues," he had somewhat missed the point.[16]

Although Juxon-Smith's political aspirations together with the NRC's obvious enjoyment of economic management and its inability to develop a satisfactory coalition with potential civilian heirs inevitably complicated plans for an honorable retirement to the barracks, there remained a number of compelling reasons why the council should have withdrawn as soon as possible. Perhaps the NRC's most telling failure—its incapacity to win public trust as opposed to grudging obedience—alone made it imperative that the regime abdicate before some persons turned to possibly violent measures to rid the country of army rule. As the regime evolved into a rigidly enclosed system, its vision of the popular will become so impaired that it could no longer retain the support even of those whose loyalties were automatically directed to the "government of the day." Thus in January 1968—ten months after the March intervention—the council, through a woefully inept try at altering the composition of the chieftaincy staffs of office, managed to alienate many traditional rulers who had initially welcomed the military government with open arms.

The NRC chairman believed that the colonial staffs held by paramount chiefs should be abolished and replaced by staffs bearing insignia that reflected the independence of Sierra Leone.[17] Though to the western observer the chairman's plans seemed relatively innocuous in scope, Sierra Leone's paramount chiefs, who often regard the institution and staff of chieftaincy as one and the same, sharply opposed the brigadier on this key issue. Rumors of an impending military decree to abolish the chiefdom administrations filtered down to some of the most remote provincial chiefdoms. Just as in the past situations of this sort, the NRC reacted harshly to what it had diagnosed as simple "rumor-mongering." On March 10, a press release from the NRC Secretariat outlined the army's position:

The National Reformation Council states that the attention of the Council has been drawn to the current ugly rumour now circulating in the country to the effect that the Council was deliberating on a policy to abolish the institution of Chieftaincy in the country. The National Reformation Council wishes it to be known that there is no modicum of truth in these rumours.

The Council . . . wishes to repeat its warning to all those who indulge in the habit of propagating false rumours that all such rumours will be traced to the source and those responsible for their propagation severely dealt with.[18]

The damage had already been done so no NRC denial could erase the impression among most traditional rulers that the continued presence of a military government in Sierra Leone was inimical to their interests. By arousing the apparently implacable hostility of once natural allies, the NRC ended up severing its remaining ties with the outside world and retreated further inward. In light of these realities, a prudent course for the regime would have been to withdraw gracefully and with honor.

An even more pressing reason for the NRC's swift handover of power was the ominous specter of intensified bickering within the council itself. We have already documented the extent to which intraofficer quarreling had become the modus operandi of NRC deliberations. With the basic tendency for members to feud over very particularistic concerns, there was the chance that, as long as the NRC clung tenaciously to power, the junta literally could fragment over issues of greater magnitude. A possible catalyst for friction lay in the substantive differences in political perspective between the NRC chairman and his subordinates. As Juxon-Smith evidenced an increasing proclivity to sabotage the caretaker spirit of the March 23 coup, he risked isolating Majors Blake, Jumu, and Kai-Samba who perceived their role in Sierra Leone political life as a limited exercise. Thus while Juxon-Smith favored the possible transformation of the NRC from an arbitrator-type regime into a more permanent ruler-type arrangement, the others sought to preserve the spirit of the initial model. Unless military rule ended immediately, the clashes over the divergent philosophies regarding the proper sphere and duration of the NRC's influence might eventually trigger a countercoup similar to that which ousted Brigadier David Lansana. Furthermore, despite his best efforts at secrecy, word of the increasingly bitter differences between the chairman and his fellow officers was absorbed easily by the Freetown rumor mill, thereby undercutting further the government's pretensions of restoring "national unity" in Sierra Leone.

All in all, the reasons for an immediate return to civilian rule far overshadowed those favoring a continuing political role for the army. Most Sierra Leoneans regarded the NRC as obstructionist, not reformist. Once the commissions of inquiry had completed their appointed duties, there was little remaining for the NRC to discredit. Economically, the regime had made an important start in dealing with the mistakes of Sir Albert's SLPP, but this accomplishment was vastly overshadowed by the fact that medium- and long-term prospects for economic growth would be jeopardized by the inherently destabilizing nature of rule by alternating military cliques.

## THE DOVE-EDWIN COMMISSION AND THE CIVILIAN RULE COMMITTEE

Though the NRC failed to orchestrate the politics of demilitarization with the precision and commitment demonstrated by the NLC in Ghana, the regime never skirted completely the issue of a return to the barracks. In fact, on many occasions the junta proceeded as if it were deeply aware of public sentiment favoring an immediate return to civilian rule. A number of committees and commissions of inquiry were established for the sensitive task of extricating the military government from direct charge of the political system. The rub came when some of these bodies failed to dispense advice that meshed with the NRC's attitudes toward the scope and timing of withdrawal. The input from the civilian sector on this important issue served only to exacerbate preexisting tensions within the council.

The first civilian attempt to grapple with the politics of demilitarization came, albeit somewhat indirectly, in the proceedings of the Dove-Edwin Commission. Established in June to examine "the conduct of the 1967 General Elections in Sierra Leone," the Dove-Edwin Commission undertook an extensive inquiry into the "compilation and operation of the Register of Voters . . . the custody of ballot papers . . . " and the behavior of the two political parties during the course of the election.[19] The commission was also called upon to determine the true standing of the two political parties as of March 23, 1967.

When the Dove-Edwin Commission completed its work on August 19, it had recorded the testimony of scores of witnesses involved in the March elections. These included returning officers, electoral commissioners, as well as paramount chiefs and ex-ministers. Throughout the inquiry, the story of the SLPP's attempts to manipulate the outcome of the election largely through ballot-stuffing, intimidation of voters sympathetic to the APC, and falsification of some returns became a matter of public record. On September 23, the commissioners submitted their findings to the NRC thereby condemning the SLPP's attempt to rig the general elections:

The whole of the Government's arrangements for the 1967 elections was rigged and corrupt. At all levels, before, during and after the Elections this corruption was evident. They were determined to use all means fair or foul to win and remain in office and if all failed to get Brigadier Lansana to take over.[20]

The report delivered to the NRC noted further that, as of March 23, the APC had won thirty-two contested seats, the SLPP, twenty-two contested seats (not including the six declared unopposed), with the remaining six seats going to independent candidates. On the basis of all the evidence presented in testimony, the report concluded that the "A.P.C. won the Elections on their own merit," that the governor-general was "constitutionally right" in appointing Siaka Stevens as prime minister, and that this latter action *"cannot be properly challenged."*[21]

By declaring the APC a clearcut victor in the general elections, the Dove-Edwin Commission automatically repudiated most of the NRC's ex post facto arguments for seizing power and, in particular, its claim that Sir Henry had erred in appointing a new prime minister. The junta was now placed clearly on the defensive. If it accepted the findings of the commission, it was left with no choice but to declare that peace had been restored to Sierra Leone followed by a handover to the APC. But if the regime refused to be held accountable by the Dove-Edwin Commission and decided to reject the findings outright (the most probable course), there would remain few legitimacy "reserves" capable of future exploitation. It was impossible for the junta to deny the APC its rightful place in the sun and yet, at the same time, to expect Sierra Leoneans to regard its plans for a return to civilian rule as sincere. Try as he might, Juxon-Smith could not have his cake and eat it too.

For over a month following the submission of the Dove-Edwin report to the NRC, the junta refused to issue any form of public statement, a fact that suggested uncertainty within the council as to an appropriate response. When a white paper was finally released on November 29, the NRC reiterated many of the shopworn arguments, first put forth by Brigadier Lansana, that the governor-general should have waited for the results of the paramount chief elections before appointing a prime minister, and that his action to appoint Stevens "gave rise to an increasing tension throughout the country." The white paper also contained a scathing attack on Justice Dove-Edwin who had apparently visited the governor-general's residence prior to Stevens's appointment and thus, in the opinion of the NRC, "should have tendered his resignation" as chairman of the commission. Perhaps as a crude method of salvaging public opinion on the matter, the council stated that "it appreciates the earnestness of local aspirations for a return to civilian rule at the earliest possible time" and announced plans to establish a broadly-representative civilian rule committee.[22] As usual, this allowed the NRC to postpone confronting the real political issues.

More to the NRC's liking were a series of recommendations on the return to civilian rule emanating from the National Advisory Council. It will be remembered that one of the original terms of reference drawn up for the advisory council in April called upon members "to work out steps leading to a peaceful return to civilian rule after a general election." Since the council consisted almost entirely of individuals committed to forestalling an APC takeover while harboring visions of a return to former political glories, a go-slow approach to the question of an NRC withdrawal from political life is not surprising, especially if it presaged a transfer of power from the army to Mr. Stevens. In late September, for example, the advisory council informed the NRC that it would be desirable "that the NRC should allow circumstances to dictate the time factor and they need not keep to the original deadline [presumably the fifteen months] if the financial and economic situation and also other factors do not justify the handing over to a civilian government." As an interim measure, it was further suggested that the NRC appoint "emminent civilians with integrity . . . [to] share responsibility and work conjointly with the National Reformation Council members in the running of government departments." By April 1968 these civilian "commissioners" would be "left in charge of the departments but the broadly based National Reformation Council should remain the Government." In November 1968 a referendum on a proposed republican constitution with a ceremonial presidency would be held. Sometime in 1969, the NRC would call for new general elections to elect a Constituent Assembly which would in turn choose a prime minister and a "national government" by means of secret ballot. A return to party politics would be delayed for five years. The advisory council hoped that "only a national government will help to get rid of tribal feelings."[23]

The advisory council recommendations to the NRC on the subject of demilitarization seem in retrospect to have been little more than an ill-conceived endeavor to apply a Ghanaian-type solution to a non-Ghanaian set of political circumstances. A phased, orderly movement from army to civilian rule like that of the NLC in Ghana was not possible in Sierra Leone where only an increasingly isolated minority within the civilian elite subscribed to the NRC's view of the mode and pace of withdrawal. Since the APC's leadership or supporters would not accept the delay of another general election before the restoration of civilian rule, the advisory council proposals faced little chance of gaining public acceptance, however amenable they were to the NRC membership. On the contrary, the NRC now faced the possibility, unless it heeded the findings of the Dove-Edwin Commission and handed over to Mr. Stevens, of the politics of demilitarization soon falling beyond the pale of direct army manipulation.

As the thinking of Juxon-Smith and others on the NRC became increasingly divorced from political realities in Sierra Leone, the regime found it difficult to include civilian groups in its deliberations concerning the army's retirement from politics. Certainly many of the members of the most popular and most eligible successor group, the APC, were no longer available for recruitment. In fact, within a few months after the NRC takeover, the more radical elements in the party were already clamoring for blood because it was held that "military regimes never return to the barracks peacefully."[24] However with John Bangura now attached to the Sierra Leone embassy in

Washington and with the army firmly in control of southern officers, it was hard to see just how a countercoup might be staged on behalf of the APC.

Siaka Stevens himself favored adoption of a "diplomatic offensive" and, in late September, was granted permission to leave the country for London for "medical reasons." Both he and the former governor-general, Sir Henry Lightfoot-Boston, operating from their London base, wrote letters to the NRC urging the council to publicly acknowledge the findings of the Dove-Edwin Commission and to proceed forthwith to implement them. On October 19, Stevens informed the NRC chairman that in his view, "it would be in the national interest that immediate arrangements . . . be made for the handing over of power to the elected representatives of the people."[25] On November 17, Stevens issued a public statement in London, espousing a more militant line:

> Today the slogan in Sierra Leone should be: Immediate Return to Civilian Rule or No Co-Operation with the So-Called National Reformation Council which is violating our sacred constitution and trying to replace the ballot box with guns and bayonets.[26]

Shortly thereafter, the NRC released its white paper on the report of the Dove-Edwin Commission, and Stevens moved to embrace the more radical grouping within the APC leadership.

By the end of 1967, military and civilian in Sierra Leone had become totally juxtaposed rather than fusing together in a coalition along patterns noted in Ghana and Nigeria. In the absence of a viable civilian support mechanism under conditions of military control, it was unreasonable for the NRC to have assumed that token moves in the direction of recivilianization might substitute for open dialogue with the nonmilitary sector. Dialogue itself was generally subject to several constraints. First, the NRC government was never perceived as one to carry a mandate from any civilian group apart from a tiny minority of opportunists, some of whom served on the National Advisory Council and held civil service posts. Rather, the NRC's actions were interpreted as belonging to a special category of political intrigue favored by a discredited civilian-military clique. Initially only educated members of the bourgeoisie—senior civil servants, professionals such as lawyers and teachers, in addition to some politicians—objected to the intervention and subsequent performance of the men in uniform. Eventually however, disaffection with military praetorianism came to encompass such presumed allies of the NRC as the traditional rulers. Consequently, the civilian-military dialogue, largely rhetorical in tone, was devoid of the kind of consensus so evident in Ghana between 1966 and 1969.

Perhaps the most subtle and, concurrently, the most decisive obstacle to the emergence of a Ghanaian-type of military-withdrawal politics in Sierra Leone can be traced to a past legacy of civilian values around Freetown. One major theme of civil-military relations in both the colonial and also the immediate postcolonial eras was the recurrence of an underlying "class" hostility between soldier and civilian (see Chapter 3). Under conditions of civilian supremacy, it was possible for a number of senior army officers to surmount the suspicion-laden, "small-boy" barrier through the acquisition of civilian allies or patrons. Once the military had acquired control of the political machinery, however, the old image of the brash illiterate soldier—often thought personified by Juxon-Smith and his hand-picked team of young captains—regained its former prominence and hindered the NRC's efforts to manipulate the withdrawal process. Most of Freetown's educated elites would not countenance soldiers dictating the time and specifications of a return to civilian government. If for this reason alone, NRC-directed demilitarization was probably doomed to failure even before it had been set into motion. Thus the NRC announcement (January 17, 1968) of yet another committee formed to consider the question of a return to civilian rule, in accordance with a promise made in the government white paper on the Dove-Edwin Commission report, somehow contained an element of déjà vu.

With a few months remaining in its "term of office," the NRC again sought to regulate the politics of demilitarization. This time emphasis was placed on assembling a widely diverse collection of influential civilians who, it was believed, could help formulate plans for an NRC departure from overt involvement in Sierra Leone politics. The vehicle they designed for it was dubbed unimaginatively the Civilian Rule Committee. A full list of committee members, made public on January 30, immediately revealed a number of features that distinguished this committee from past groups such as the National Advisory Council. First, in marked contrast to the Advisory Council with its twenty-five members, some seventy-five persons were either appointed by the NRC or indirectly elected by various groups to the Civilian Rule Committee. Second, the new committee consisted of delegations from the banned SLPP and APC, as well as six independent candidates who successfully contested seats in the 1967 general elections. To these delegations were added nine paramount chiefs apportioned among the three provinces, three NRC appointees from each province, three members of the now defunct advisory council, one representative from each of the twelve committees of management (formerly the district councils), and other delegates from such diverse bodies as the Sierra Leone Ex-Servicemen's Association and the Sierra Leone Teachers Union. This was the group that the NRC, having "decided to hand over the Government of Sierra Leone to a civilian government," would invite to "deliberate and advise" on the following issues:

(i)    The necessity for fresh General Elections;
(ii)   If (i) above is in the negative, the method of forming a National Government; if (i) above is in the affirmative, the stages by which the hand-over should be effected;
(iii)  Any other action which the Civilian Rule Committee considers necessary to effect a peaceful hand-over.[27]

In contrast to the terms drawn up for the advisory council, the NRC granted the Civilian Rule Committee the option of accepting or rejecting the army's view that new elections had to precede an actual transfer of power to civilians.

Exactly what impelled the National Reformation Council to establish the Civilian Rule Committee is not really clear. A variety of conclusions may be drawn from this decision to renew the junta's political energies toward a return to the barracks. In a positive sense, the existence of the Civilian Rule Committee reflected at least the momentary triumph of individual NRC members who sought to thwart a conversion from a regime with limited arbitrator objectives to one intended as a permanent or semipermanent fixture on the political horizon. According to this interpretation, Juxon-Smith might have agreed to the establishment of such a committee if only to appease Blake, Jumu, Kai-Samba, and any others who wanted to maintain channels of communication with the civilian sector.[28] Although Blake and the others were not especially in favor of a handover to Stevens, they were prepared to withdraw from political activity as long as their actions could be indemnified by a future civilian government.

A cynic might argue that NRC strategies envisaged the formation of a Civilian Rule Committee as a diversionary tactic, designed to provide the elites with busywork. In this way, prominent civilians were lulled into believing that they might still control their political affairs when, in fact, the NRC expected to delay complete demilitarization for several more years. There is little doubt that this was Juxon-Smith's intention even if, on the occasion of the committee's opening session, he told the gathered members that the "National Reformation Council would like to look at the Civilian Rule Committee as a pro tem constituent assembly" and "that the task and responsibility placed squarely upon you are very sacred indeed."[29]

Whatever motivated the NRC to establish the Civilian Rule Committee, it was clear from the outset that the junta inadvertently had provided an ideal forum for a direct confrontation between military and civilian. Certainly the majority of the politicians were in no mood for more false starts on the question of demilitarization. As a concession to civilian opinion, the NRC in mid-January lifted the ban on political meetings to allow caucusing by the APC and the SLPP for selection of representatives to the Civilian Rule Committee. The APC delegation, announced on January 24, included C. A. Kamara-Taylor, the party's secretary-general prior to the military takeover; S. I. Koroma, self-styled leader of the APC's radical wing; as well as more moderate individuals including Soloman Pratt, the sole party member to serve on the National Advisory Council. From the perspective of these individuals, twelve months of NRC evasion and outright deceit on the civilian rule issue would now have to be exposed and the fact of the APC victory transformed into real political power. Curiously, the APC found a willing ally in the disgruntled SLPP leadership no longer shielded by a Juxon-Smith-dominated NRC.

The SLPP also chose a six-man lobby for the meetings of the Civilian Rule Committee. Included in the SLPP contingent were R.G.O. King, Sir Albert's finance minister; Maigore Kallon, the former minister of external affairs; and Julius Cole, the party's secretary-general. With the removal of Lansana, the homecoming of Juxon-Smith, and the institution of probes into the acquisition of assets by former SLPP ministers, some of these men had suffered considerably and by now had nothing to gain from continued military control. Many SLPP members were as antagonized by the antics of the NRC chairman and his band of supporters as the most militant member of the APC, if, admittedly, for different reasons. The resentment felt by both political groups toward a common enemy would eventually prove sufficient for the evolution of a joint APC-SLPP strategy on the necessity of fresh general elections.

The potential for an increasingly acrimonious debate between the NRC and its civilian opponents was dramatized at the committee's opening session on February 21.[30] At that time, Dr. Sarif Easmon, whose editorials in the APC journal, *We Yone*, had helped topple the Margai government, was elected chairman. In the person of Dr. Easmon, the committee acquired a spokesman for those who would brook no further compromise on the civilian rule issue. He immediately launched into a tirade against the NRC, thereby further reducing chances for a civilian-military reconciliation:

We are meeting under the guns of an army: not the guns of an invading and conquering army, but an army that is paid with our own taxes. I take it therefore that the most important duty of this committee is to decide that our soldiers go forthwith to their barracks and never again interfere in the government of this country.[31]

Following Easmon's address, the SLPP and APC delegates held a series of joint meetings on February 22 and produced a memorandum concerning the necessity for holding another general election. Both political parties agreed that fresh general elections would require a national population census, a redelimitation of constituencies, and a financial outlay of at least Le 2,000,000. Completion of these preparations was estimated to be in no less than three years and would thwart "the declared intentions of the National Reformation Council who have publicly stated that they have decided to hand over within the *shortest possible time* in an atmosphere of peace."[32] According to the APC and the SLPP delegates, the only remaining conclusion to be drawn was "that there is no necessity for a fresh General Election before the National Reformation Council hands over to Civilian Rule."[33]

Immediately following the submission of the APC-SLPP memorandum, the Civilian Rule Committee heard arguments for and against holding new elections. Then on February 23 it was moved "that this Committee does not consider it necessary to hold fresh General Elections before a return to Civilian Rule."[34] In the balloting which ensued, fifty-five members voted for the motion, with only eleven against and one abstention. The lopsided vote offered further convincing evidence of just how deep the currents of civilian disaffection with NRC policies ran. Not only did all the APC and SLPP members of the Civilian Rule Committee vote in support of the motion, but additional backing also came from a number of paramount chiefs as well as from four of those nine civilians originally selected by the NRC on the basis of their presumed adherence to the official NRC line. Representatives of the universities, the churches, the bar association, and other predominantly Creole professional organizations supported the motion. It was now clear that, judging from the opinions expressed at the committee meetings, civilian and military were diametrically opposed on the method deemed appropriate for extricating Sierra Leone from rule by soldiers.

Once the Civilian Rule Committee had delivered its opinion on the new elections issue, members undertook the problem of establishing a "national government" and endeavored to set a deadline for the termination of all military control. First it was agreed that a national government should consist "of elected members of Parliament with certain safeguards."[35] Such a government would include members of the two political parties, those returned as independents in the 1967 general election, as well as paramount chiefs. It also would be constructed to "inspire confidence and command respect at home and abroad." Regarding leadership for such a government, the "A.P.C. side stated beyond doubt that if it came to a point of considering leadership (which matter could or should not be avoided) that side would present Siaka Stevens and nobody else."[36] The APC's adamancy on the leadership problem rendered future discussion between the two parties somewhat less than promising since some SLPP representatives continued to express residual loyalties toward Sir Albert Margai. As a compromise, it was decided to let a future civilian parliament cope with the problem of choosing a leader who, given the APC's presumed majority, undoubtedly would be Siaka Probyn Stevens.

On March 18, the Civilian Rule Committee held its twelfth and final session at which time a fifteen-page report was prepared for delivery to the NRC chairman. The unity which had been so evident at some of the earlier meetings was diminished by the defection of those SLPP members who could not accept a provision calling upon the NRC to compel "those elected parliamentarians found guilty of corruption by the various Commissions of Inquiry . . . to resign their seats, and be disqualified from serving in Parliament for a period of 5 to 10 years depending upon the degree of culpability." The SLPP argued that the commissions of inquiry "were not Courts of Law, that the SLPP members had already been through enough and that most of the monies had been returned."[37] Yet even with an SLPP boycott of the final meeting, the Civilian Rule Committee report was adopted by a vote of fifty-three in favor, none against, and only five abstentions.

In its summary of recommendations, the Civilian Rule Committee report submitted to Juxon-Smith on March 21, 1968 maintained once again "that there be no Fresh General Election before handing over from Military to Civilian Government" and that "the National Government [should] consist of four groups of Parliamentarians elected at the March 1967 General Elections." The no-nonsense mood of Sierra Leone's civilian elite was also indicated in perhaps the committee's most startling recommendation, "that the restoration of Civilian Rule be not later than three calender months from the date the Civilian Rule Committee submits this Report to the National Reformation Council." During this period of civilian-military dyarchy (equivalent in some ways to the colonial dyarchy of the late 1940s and 1950s in West Africa), the NRC would summon a "mock parliament" to first choose a prime minister and then negotiate the terms of an act indemnifying past NRC actions. This would be followed by the appointment of a new governor-general, the restoration of the 1961 constitution, the convening of parliament, and, then, a formal handing over of the reins of government from Brigadier Juxon-Smith to the new prime minister. In concluding, the report of the civilian rule committee offered some frank comments on past and future patterns of civil-military relations in Sierra Leone and, in particular, on the formation of secretive cliques between politicians, civil servants, and army officers during periods of political instability. It mentioned "the collusion between the Brigadier [Lansana] and the ex-Prime Minister, Sir Albert Margai" and "deplored the way Sir Albert made both Senior Army Officers and Senior Civil Servants come, as it were, to swear personal allegiance to him, thus engendering an alliance so corrupting that these very officers, at a time of crisis, set their obligations to Sir Albert above their duty and loyalty to the country.'' As for the future, the committee could do little more than to resolve that "everything possible should be done by all concerned . . . to ensure mutual goodwill and confidence between Government and the people of Sierra Leone on the one hand, and the Army on the other.''[38]

## THE GUINEANS AGAIN

While the Civilian Rule Committee's proceedings offered an unparalleled opportunity for Sierra Leone's citizens to aggregate and articulate their views regarding demilitarization, the more overtly political factions within the APC were pursuing an alternative strategy on the grounds that the NRC had virtually no intention of withdrawing in the forseeable future. Although the APC has never publicly admitted that there was, in fact, such a strategy, there is enough circumstantial evidence to suggest that beginning around mid-1967 some party leaders began devising a plan to overthrow the NRC by force. A central feature of this plan involved reestablishing contacts with Sékou Touré in Guinea in the hope that the president would permit the training of Sierra Leonean guerillas on Guinean soil.[39] Mr. Touré, of course, was no stranger to Sierra Leone politics and, in particular, to its civil-military relations. His involvement with Sir Albert Margai, certainly no ideological bedfellow, had been predicated on the belief that Guinea must do all in her power to thwart army coups d'état in neighboring states before such practices spread to Conakry. With the NRC firmly entrenched, it was a relatively simple matter for Sékou Touré to place his bets on another horse. For the APC, the need for external assistance to carry out their plans no doubt helped erase unpleasant memories of the Margai-Touré ''mutual defence pact.''

Although details of the refurbished ties between Guinea and the APC remain shrouded in secrecy; it appears that when it became known that the NRC intended to reject the Dove-Edwin Commission findings on the subject of the 1967 General Elections, a number of the more radical party members entered into continuing discussions with President Touré. This decision to turn to Conarky for assistance was apparently reached without the approval of Siaka Stevens who was in London in pursuit of diplomatic recognition of the APC electoral victory.[40] In Stevens's absence, Sékou Touré agreed to supply both training facilities and weapons as his country's contribution to the ''just struggle'' against the NRC. Beginning around October 1967, several hundred unemployed youths and dockworkers were recruited in the Freetown area and smuggled across the border into Guinea near the Sierra Leone town of Kambia. Just how extensive was the training received by these guerillas is not known, but one told me that Soviet instructors and Soviet ammunition were involved. None of these latter claims can be documented, however, and they sound rather dubious.

By the end of 1967 and into early 1968, the whole Guinean venture represented a potentially credible threat to the survival of the National Reformation Council. In the first place, Siaka Stevens himself, perhaps embittered by the British government's refusal to aid his party, left London in mid-December, reestablished contacts with President Touré, and went into exile in Guinea.[41] Word of his voluntary exile in the Guinean capital soon spread to Freetown and served as a rallying point for those in the APC who sought the immediate ouster of the NRC. Stevens then met with APC leaders and other interested parties who slipped back and forth across the border.[42] According to Davidson Nicol, then the principal of Fourah Bay College, a number of students and faculty "risked their personal safety" in working "both overtly and covertly towards the achievement of civilian democratic rule." For example, "Dr. Ralph Taylor-Smith, Dean of Science and a Sierra Leonean [as well as a member of the Civilian Rule Committee] crossed the Guinea border at night evading army frontier posts, to visit and hold discussions with the Prime Minister in Conakry."[43]

Not long after Steven's arrival in Guinea, Colonel Bangura, leader of the February coup plot against Sir Albert, departed from his post at the Sierra Leone embassy in Washington to join with the APC leader. This was apparently accomplished with the assistance of Sierra Leone's ambassadors in Washington and New York, both of whom were Creoles with known APC connections. The return of Bangura presented the NRC with a particularly delicate situation for he was reported to be highly esteemed among the rank and file of the Sierra Leone army. In the event of a Guinean-sponsored invasion of Sierra Leone, Juxon-Smith might be hard pressed to rally the sympathies of the army's rank and file in defense of the regime.

The politics of peaceful demilitarization in Sierra Leone hinged on the NRC's reactions to the not wholly unrelated developments of the recommendations to the NRC by the Civilian Rule Committee that were being prepared and of the rag-tag band of APC zealots being trained in neighboring Guinea. The impact of the civilian rule discussion upon the NRC's political strategy involves a bit of guess-work because of the often self-serving testimony on the subject that appeared throughout the treason trials held in 1969 and 1970. However, the official NRC response both to the report of the Civilian Rule Committee and also to developments in Guinea is not difficult to ascertain. For example, during the meetings of the Civilian Rule Committee, the NRC deliberately obstructed efforts to obtain an official constituency-by-constituency breakdown of the general election results. On February 28, the committee received a letter from the NRC secretary-general to the effect that "the N.R.C. did not consider that it would serve any useful purpose if the information was made available.''[44] To some committee members this meant that ''the NRC did not accept the election results'' as they would further embarrass the regime.[45] Only a few months earlier, the NRC had rejected the findings of the Dove-Edwin Commission that the APC had emerged victorious despite the SLPP's best (or perhaps worst) efforts to prevent this from occurring. Juxon-Smith himself is alleged to have described those serving on the Civilian Rule Committee as ''fools and stooges'' and to have become incensed when the committee concluded that the NRC should phase itself out over a period of three months.[46] This illustrates once again the inherent conflict of interest between a ruler-type mentality (personified by the NRC chairman) and the desire of civilian elites to regain maximum control of the political system as soon as possible. Under such conditions a military regime's promise to withdraw may represent merely an amorphous goal that will only materialize when the ''situation is favorable.'' In some instances, an expressed willingness to withdraw may become so much empty rhetoric, if the commitment is not in fact discarded altogether.[47]

Even though the NRC avoided responding publicly to the report of the Civilian Rule Committee, it reacted harshly to intelligence accounts that Guinea was providing a sanctuary for political dissidents and made its feelings known in the press. Just three days after receiving the unfavorable news from the committee, the NRC resorted to its time-tested strategy of scolding and condemning its critics. In a published memorandum on ''subversion,'' it was noted that the NRC viewed ''with considerable concern and alarm reports now circulating throughout the country of subversive activities contemplated now and in the near future.'' The memorandum added that this concern acquired ''additional significance when certain events which have happened and are now happening in certain neighbouring countries are reflected upon, involving as they do considerable suffering on the part of many innocent people.''[48] If one reads between the lines, it seems that the NRC was offering a scenario of future civil war in the event the APC guerillas attempted to invade the country. Following the release of the memorandum, the NRC chairman accompanied by Jumu, Alpha Kamara, and several other lesser figures paid an official visit to Conakry. The Guineans hoped to impress upon the NRC that unless the army retired to the barracks immediately, Sierra Leone would have to face a major time of troubles. At Conakry airport Sékou Touré reportedly advised Juxon-Smith to devote more time to the politics of reconciliation and less time to the so-called politics of ''reformation.''[49] Juxon-Smith retorted that he had been kept fully informed of the APC's activities in Guinea and that ''Sierra Leone was ready for the guerillas and would fight them on land and sea.''[50] The Guinean president just laughed at these remarks and had the NRC chairman placed on the next plane back to Freetown. Needless to say, Juxon-Smith's abbreviated visit to Conakry represented something less than a diplomatic triumph. Worse still were the prospects at home for a civilian-military accommodation for, given the chairman's continued intransigence toward all those clothed in civilian garb, the NRC stood virtually alone without any visible means of internal or external support.

## THE OFFICERS RENEW THEIR FEUDS

Even in the twilight of military rule in Sierra Leone it appears that old fissures within the NRC were revived by the national debate over demilitarization. As might have been predicted, those officers who interpreted the March 23 coup primarily as a referee action seem to have regarded demilitarization somewhat differently from their boss, Juxon-Smith, now a brigadier. Even discounting the more obviously self-serving statements delivered by certain army and police officers at the treason trial, it still seems that most senior members of the NRC were not in agreement with the brigadier's position on returning to civilian rule. Perhaps the first defection from the official line was Police Commissioner William Leigh who had been bickering with the chairman almost from the moment of the latter's return to Sierra Leone on March 28, 1967. Leigh argued that the fratricidal tendencies of military administration and, in particular, "the quarrel between Major Blake and the Chairman" persuaded him "that the sooner we returned to Civilian Rule the better."[51] At the first council meeting held in late March 1968 to consider the report of the Civilian Rule Committee, Leigh recommended acceptance of all its provisions including that which set June 21 as the latest possible date for a complete handover.

The Civilian Rule Committee's finding also produced a measurable heightening of the already long-existent tensions between the military members of the National Reformation Council. Those original founders of the NRC—the self-promoted Colonel Blake and Lieutenant Colonels Jumu and Kai-Samba—by early April had become convinced that continued military rule could benefit no one (except perhaps the ambitious brigadier). They were necessarily more proficient than the NRC chairman at comprehending the civilian temperament because of their past involvement in civilian-military cliques. Although there is no direct evidence for this, it seems that they were far more receptive to private overtures from prominent civilians than the brigadier. They were also aware of the situation in Guinea and the possibility of a pro-Bangura mutiny, if not by the officers at least by the rank and file who had become exceedingly restless.

In order to deal with the problem of Guinea-Sierra Leone relations, the NRC postponed serious discussion of the Civilian Rule Committee report until April 16. At that council meeting those present included Juxon-Smith,

Blake, Jumu, Commissioner Leigh, Captain Jawara, and Major Mark Koroma.[52] Juxon immediately adópted a belligerent tone and asked the council to reject the recommendations of the Civilian Rule Committee and instead to support an enlargement of the NRC including a provision for portfolio-granting to civilian appointees.[53] Captain Jawara and Major Koroma are said to have voted in favor of an enlarged NRC with greater civilian participation. This should not have been a surprise given the obvious enjoyment of political power displayed by other junior officers in the past. For example, some two and a half months earlier, several younger officers, who did not serve directly on the NRC but who entertained notions of doing so, are alleged to have informed the chairman that "manpower was available in the army to have officers as Resident Ministers."[54] These were hardly the opinions of men anxious to preside over a speedy return to civilian rule.

As debate over the question of military withdrawel continued throughout the afternoon of April 16, Commissioner Leigh offered his resignation unless there was an immediate handover; to this, the brigadier "laughed and jeered."[55] At the council meeting the following morning, Colonel Blake and Lieutenant Colonel Jumu recommended adoption of the entire Civilian Rule Committee report.[56] Juxon-Smith refused even to record the views of his dissenting officers, a fact which signaled the end of all efforts to restore cohesion within the NRC. When the meeting had concluded around one o'clock, the three-man clique of Blake, Jumu, and Kai-Samba which had arrested Brigadier Lansana almost thirteen months earlier assumed an independent status once again. On the afternoon of April 17, the three officers met privately with Commissioner Leigh and agreed that during an NRC meeting scheduled for April 18, they would press Juxon-Smith to publicly acknowledge the NRC's readiness to accept in full the Civilian Rule Committee report. If the chairman persisted in his refusal to proceed with a handover during the time designated by the committee, he would be removed in a manner reminiscent of the arrest of Brigadier Lansana. The founding members of the NRC, now plotting the overthrow of Brigadier Juxon-Smith to restore Sierra Leone to civilian rule, did so with an acute sense of urgency; for while the NRC haggled over the details of recivilianization, there were those among the enlisted ranks of the army who had similar thoughts.

## INTERVENTION TO END INTERVENTION—SIERRA LEONE RETURNS TO CIVILIAN RULE

At approximately 10:00 PM on April 17, Police Commissioner Leigh received a telephone call from Blake informing him that "the boys have started." Leigh proceeded immediately to the Central Police Station where he was met by Kai-Samba who told of soldiers "making trouble" at Wilberforce Barracks. Kai-Samba requested armed police to quell the apparent mutiny, but Leigh "told him that he knows my policy as a police force will never fight the army."[57] Several hours later, a number of warrant officers arrived at the police station and placed William Leigh under arrest. Throughout the late evening hours of April 17 and on into the early morning, teams of warrant officers, NCOs, and privates searched houses and bars in Freetown for commissioned army officers and their counterparts in the gazetted ranks of the 2,400-man police force. Juxon-Smith was the first to be arrested at his Hill Station lodge because he held the keys to the armory. Once having acquired substantial numbers of weapons, the mutineers surrounded the officers' mess and began a systematic search for any officers thought to be hiding in Freetown. In some instances, cars belonging to officers were smashed; in others, individual officers including Bockarie Kai-Samba were physically assaulted. There was also a considerable amount of anomic behavior such as looting. According to a description provided by Ruth First:

The billiards room in the officers' mess was the scene of a brief tussle for control. The following morning, the debris was slight, some broken Coca-Cola bottles and cues lying awry on the green baize, and, in a ditch not far from the barracks, a car belonging to an officer who had tried to escape.[58]

All in all, some seventy-six army and forty-eight police officers were arrested and imprisoned during the course of the mutiny.[59] There was also some violence associated with the widespread arrests. During a gun battle between officers and mutineers, one NCO was killed and six army and police personnel wounded. Needless to say, the NRC meeting planned for the morning of April 18 was never held.

The privates' mutiny of April 17 and 18 was generally a flawless production bringing to an end months of discontent within the lower echelons of the army, most induced by the NRC's neglect of the rank and file. After the military takeover the previous March, enlisted men and noncommissioned and commissioned officers gained the impression that the army as a whole would benefit immediately as a result of pay raises, new uniforms, reconditioned barracks, the acquisition of new automobiles, and the like. Juxon-Smith's public statements to the effect that soldiers "were the most important element in the country" certainly contributed to inflated hopes. Some individuals, of course, did stand to gain from army rule. Most of the members of the NRC promoted themselves and thus drew higher salaries. They participated in numerous extended junkets abroad. They apparently spent most of their waking hours in Freetown nightclubs. Furthermore, the brigadier in complete violation of his call for fiscal austerity, "established a quota of car allowances extending down to the rank of first lieutenant.''[60] This meant that a number of officers who previously had ridden public transport or army landrovers suddenly appeared in brand-new Mercedes. Those who were not commissioned officers reaped few of these benefits.

As the NRC chairman became more impervious to the demands of civilians, he, along with the other NRC members, failed to monitor accurately the sentiments of his own army. Discontent began to mount in early 1968 when new uniforms, promised in March 1967, failed to materialize and when requests for pay increases were coldly rebuffed. All of this occurred when many rank and file believed that assets confiscated by the Forster Commission had been used to help officers finance purchases of new cars. Soon virtually all commissioned army officers (as well as all police officers) came to be identified with the National Reformation Council. *West Africa* remarked just after the mutiny that "even junior officers who might have been expected to sympathize with the men sided with the NRC, it was alleged, because they hoped to occupy the Council's junior position which was filled by a junior army officer every three months.''[61] Crudely lettered posters began appearing at Wilberforce, Murraytown, and Daru Barracks proclaiming the impending demise of the NRC clique. According to Commissioner Leigh, ''they [the privates and the NCOs] were asking for their own share of the money and . . . were not happy at all.'' This discontent was recorded in the police ''Special Branch Daily Report'' and the NRC chairman was duly informed.[62] Nothing however was done.

The actual logistics of the mutiny were the brainchild of a Temne private, Morlai Kamara. During a temporary posting at the Daru barracks, Kamara met with other soldiers who informed him that conditions at Daru paralleled those at Wilberforce. It was agreed that the arrests of army officers would begin at Daru in the early evening of April 17. A coded message would then be relayed to Wilberforce signalling all arrests in the Freetown area could commence. Perhaps as a means of acquiring an additional increment of respectability and to demonstrate how widespread were the anti-officer and anti-NRC feelings in the army, the privates recruited two warrant officers, Amadu Rogers and Patrick Conteh (some say, the latter were compelled to participate), to supervise the actual conduct of the mutiny. All facets of the operation successfully concluded at 8:00 on the morning of April 18, Conteh announced the formation of an Anti-Corruption Revolutionary Movement (ACRM) as the successor to the NRC.

The ACRM consisted of Conteh as chairman together with ten other warrant officers and two subinspectors from the police. In his address to the nation, Conteh noted that when the NRC assumed power "little did we realise that the people we had chosen to direct our Nation's affairs were more corrupt and selfish than the ousted Civilian Regime.'' The ACRM chairman added that ''the rank and file of the Army and Police have been ignored'' and suggested that the NRC had failed to ''fulfill their boastful promise to both Civilians and Members of the Armed Forces.'' Rather than retiring to the barracks, the NRC gave the impression of wanting ''to remain in office indefinitely.'' Conteh stated in closing that ''soldiers and police have no business in the running of this country'' and that ''a concrete announcement to this effect will be made in due course.''[63]

Conteh's veiled references to an impending return to civilian rule suggested that, at least in Sierra Leone, military intervention had been specifically tailored to end a previous armed intervention. Along these lines Ali Mazrui has written (in reference to the East African mutinies of 1964) that ''it is not enough that a mutiny should have political consequences before we call it political'' but that it ''should have *conscious political aims.*''[64] To the extent that Conteh and the other mutineers were aware of public feeling on the demilitarization question, their actions appear to have been consciously political. In this regard as well, the APC must have played more than a peripheral role. Several sources indicate that Colonel Bangura visited Freetown at least a week prior to the overthrow of the NRC and must have communicated with the privates either directly or through a third party. Any message from the APC in Guinea no doubt contained a pledge to upgrade conditions substantially in the army in return for a handover to a civilian regime. It was decidedly in Stevens's interest to back a surgical operation of the kind envisaged by the army privates rather than attempting an overthrow of the regime using ill-trained APC thugs recruited from the docks of Freetown.

Once the ACRM had completed its roundup of all army and police officers, a number of key military and political figures resurfaced in Sierra Leone to assume charge of the country's political destiny. On the afternoon of April 19, Colonel Bangura arrived by road from Guinea and Lieutenant-Colonel Ambrose Genda flew in from Liberia.[65] Both had been invited back by the ACRM and were committed to an immediate restoration of civilian rule. Genda, in an interview upon landing at Hasting Airport, stated that it was ''his determination and ambition to get back to the barracks as soon as possible.''[66] In order to further this pledge, the two senior officers aligned themselves wholeheartedly with the mutinous warrant officers and rank and file. Genda was picked to serve as acting force commander of an army now containing only two commissioned officers while Bangura became head of a newly formed National Interim Council (NIC) replacing the shortlived ACRM. A former police officer, Malcolm Parker, was brought out of retirement to serve as commissioner of police and deputy chairman of the NIC. The other NIC members included Patrick Conteh (who had promoted himself to captain), Amadu Rogers, a second warrant officer, a police inspector, and subinspector.

With Colonel Bangura in charge of that loose conglomeration of individ-

uals constituting the ACRM and the NIC, the interests of the All Peoples
Congress and of their leader, Siaka Stevens, were now easily transformable
into substantive political gains. In a broadcast to the nation on the afternoon
of April 20, Bangura stated that he agreed with those in the ACRM who had
argued that "political matters and the Government of a country are not part
of the duties of a soldier or a policeman." He stressed that the National
Interim Council would "restore Constitutional Government to this our beloved Sierra Leone in the shortest possible time."[67] Unlike similar pledges
that had been emanating from the NRC, this one seemed certain to become
a reality, for Colonel Bangura, rather than being identified with any military
or civilian-military clique, possessed an unofficial mandate from the APC
and, most important of all, from a broad section of the Sierra Leone people.

Before procedures for a return to the barracks could be set in motion, it
was imperative that the politicians meet to complete arrangements for a future civilian government. This involved an especially delicate round of negotiations for the SLPP which, prior to the 1967 general elections, had been
involved in a leadership dispute of its own. Sir Albert Margai, who arrived
from London several days after the mutiny, naturally hoped to retain his
post as party leader; but this was opposed by the younger members (notably
those from the Kenema area) backing Salia Jusu-Sheriff, a former minister in
Sir Albert's cabinet. At a meeting of the SLPP parliamentary group on April
25, Sir Albert was nominated but had so little support that no one even
bothered to second his nomination. He was then asked to "withdraw all his
interest in the party leadership," and Sheriff assumed the top post.[68]

While the SLPP was choosing a new leader to replace the Margai dynasty,
the National Interim Council made certain technical arrangements to pave
the way for a return to civilian rule. On April 22, the NIC announced the
appointment of Chief Justice Banja Tejan-Sie as governor-general and summoned all successful candidates in the last general election to meet at State
House on April 26. This was accompanied by a statement of the NIC's intention to hand over power to a civilian regime within a few days. The NIC
also made it known that it favored creation of a "national government"
although with Bangura at the helm, there was little question that no one but
Siaka Stevens would be acceptable as leader of this future government. On
the morning of April 26, Sheriff and Stevens (who returned from Guinea on
April 24) met and agreed to form the kind of government envisaged by the
NIC. In a projected fifteen-member cabinet, six portfolios would go to the
APC and four to the SLPP. The five remaining portfolios would be divided
among independents and paramount chiefs. Stevens would be appointed
prime minister of Sierra Leone's second experiment in democracy.

On the afternoon of April 26, 1968, seven years after Sierra Leone's entry
into a world of independent states and a little over thirteen months follow-

ing a military coup d'état, that country regained civilian rule. In a brief ceremony at State House, Siaka Stevens was again sworn in as prime minister, this time with the full backing of the Sierra Leone military.[69] Prior to the ceremony, Colonel Bangura stressed two preconditions for a complete military withdrawal from all political activity. First, no civil servant or member of the Sierra Leone army and police was to be retroactively subject "to any form of victimisation whatsoever" and second, "that it shall be necessary for an Indemnity Act to be passed almost immediately by Parliament to uphold decisions and actions taken within the last thirteen months by both the National Reformation Council and by the National Interim Council."[70] This later provision was meant to ensure Sierra Leone's international creditors and the diplomatic missions in Freetown that their interests would not be threatened by the change in governments. In a meeting between Bangura and Stevens these terms were agreed to and Stevens assumed the mantle of political leadership. On May 1, a seventeen-man cabinet was formed, although the final mix of the two parties in the cabinet favored the APC to a greater degree than originally contemplated.[71] The acting governor-general expressed the mood of all Sierra Leoneans when he praised the National Interim Council for having accomplished "in 9 days what others [had] failed to achieve in thirteen months."[72]

S.E. Finer has argued that military disengagement from overt control of the political system will occur as a result of three conditions: "the disintegration of the original conspiratorial group, the growing divergence of interests between the junta of rulers and those military who remain as active heads of the fighting services and the political difficulties of the regime."[73] To these factors, Claude E. Welch, Jr. would add "the disappearance or diminution of the conditions that initially brought about intervention; conscious civilianization of the military government, making it indistinguishable, in the long run, from a government with more 'ordinary origins' " and "overthrow of the military-dominated regime leading directly to a civilian-controlled government."[74] Had Brigadier Juxon-Smith been willing to accept the recommendations of the Civilian Rule Committee then our data for Sierra Leone would have confirmed a number of these observations. First of all, the NRC was characterized by institutional weakness almost from the moment of takeover. Intrajunta feuding developed along a number of axes. Blake, the acting commander of the armed forces, and Juxon-Smith, the chairman of the National Reformation Council, quarreled over their respective spheres of power, a fact which illustrates the second of Finer's hypotheses. Police Commissioner Leigh disputed the brigadier's right to let army interests prevail on the council. Jumu and Kai-Samba sought to further the position of the SLPP civilian-military cabal (or factions thereof) and were rebuffed by the chairman. All the anti-Juxon-Smith forces appear to have supported the proposal for an immediate return to the barracks both as a means of pacifying public opinion and more importantly, as a means of restoring cohesion in the military-police establishment. They were thwarted in their plans by the brigadier's obstinance and by the actions of the army rank and file.

Second of all, those conditions which the NRC claimed had prompted the original takeover were no longer in evidence. The corrupt within the SLPP had been exposed and the economy restored to a reasonably sound footing. The scattered violence or "breakdown in law and order" which had marked the general elections was now muted, although as long as the NRC stayed in power, it could have easily revived itself on a mass scale. Some NRC members were no doubt aware that the regime, having completed most of its cleansing and reformation operations, wanted to restore politics to the politicians. Only Juxon-Smith had any intention of traveling the Mobutu road to attempt a conscious "civilianization of the military government" with him as a future President of the Republic of Sierra Leone. It was really the chairman's dream of constructing a quasi-civilianized ruler type of regime which meant, ironically, that a return to the barracks could only be accomplished by an outright "overthrow of the military-dominated regime, leading directly to a civilian-controlled government." Peaceful demilitarization in Sierra Leone floundered on the inflated ego of the NRC chairman; support for this ego was forthcoming from a number of junior army officers with ambitions of their own.

Since it is reasonable to assume that the NRC's desire for a peaceful withdrawal only manifested itself in the last month or so of army rule (when it was too late), and then only among a select number of NRC members, it was more than just the brigadier's obstructionism that augured against a Ghanaian-type politics of demilitarization in Sierra Leone. Missing right from the outset was the kind of civilian-military consensus that must inevitably accompany an army withdrawal from politics. In Ghana, the National Liberation Council evidenced a basic commitment to the democratic way and, in particular, to the ethos of civilian supremacy. In affirmation of this value, the NLC actively encouraged a civilian-military partnership whose task it was to work out the technical details of an army return to the barracks.

In Sierra Leone, however, the NRC was little more than a coalition of one- and two-man army cliques that had stumbled into the act of intervention without much commitment to anything, let alone to a political program. The regime was especially incapable of building bridges to a popularly based civilian sector, epitomized by the APC and Siaka Stevens. Efforts toward a return to civilian rule were generally regarded as token because of the NRC's unwillingness to espouse the basic right of the country to be inspired by civilian political values. As long as the brigadier argued that soldiers deserved a special niche in society to the exclusion of all other groups, then there could be no Juxon-Smith-Stevens relationship to mirror that of Afrifa and Busia in Ghana. Looking back on events in the two countries and in other parts of black Africa, one must conclude that the whole Ghanaian formula has been the exception rather than the rule and was therefore responsive to a unique set of political conditions. Now, after Acheampong, this formula may be inapplicable to Ghana as well.

# 11

# CIVIL-MILITARY RELATIONS UNDER SIAKA STEVENS AND THE ALL PEOPLES CONGRESS

In light of the frequent comings and goings of the military in other African states, the restoration of civilian government in Sierra Leone scarcely constituted a guarantee against future army involvement in political intrigue. Rare indeed is the African army, once praetorianized, that can reemerge as a passive observer of civilian political instability. A typical postdemilitarization scenario usually contains further coups of varying degrees of success or lack of success. In the Sudan, for example, the army intervened in 1958, withdrew in 1964, intervened again in 1969, only to narrowly avert being overthrown by a countercoup in 1971. In Dahomey, the army has intervened successfully no less than four times since the original Soglo coup of October 1963. When Ghana's National Liberation Council restored power to Dr. Busia in 1969, many observers concluded that Ghana might serve again as an example of Westminster parliamentarianism in black Africa. The Acheampong coup, however, canceled out Ghana's brief revival of multiparty democracy as easily as Afrifa had swept away Nkrumah's "mobilization" party six years earlier. Meanwhile, the National Redemption Council has had to fend off an alleged pro-Busia coup plot in July 1972 and another civilian-military plot in September 1973.

Since transferring power to Siaka Stevens and the All

Peoples Congress in April 1968, the Sierra Leone army, like its counterparts in the Sudan, Ghana, and Dahomey, has been unable to eschew sporadic forays into politics. In the years following the 1968 handover, there have been numerous rumors of coup plots, frequent purges of the army officer corps, one coup plot which was ''nipped in the bud,'' a number of coup attempts and a countercoup in defense of the civilian regime. Though the army has not succeeded in establishing full control over the political system in Sierra Leone, it constantly threatens ordered patterns of civil-military relations and, with a little cohesion in its officer corps, probably could topple the present government with little difficulty, were it inclined. Civilian control of the military has become such a dubious proposition that the prime minister has been forced to rely increasingly upon the threat of intervention by the Guinean armed forces and the build-up of his own security guards.

Before we attempt to isolate some of the major themes in Sierra Leone's civil-military relations throughout the postindependence decade, let us consider the army's relationship with the APC and those in opposition to the regime. The *New York Times* noted that ''for Siaka Stevens . . . political leader of diamond-rich Sierra Leone, the problem has been to work out a stable relationship with his country's 1,500-man Army.''[1] Recognizing this fact, Stevens was in office less than two months before he purged the officer corps of several officers and warrant officers alleged to have participated with some SLPP politicians in ''attempts to stir up trouble again . . . after a return to constitutional Government.''[2] Among those dismissed and later arrested were the self-promoted Captain Patrick Conteh and warrant officers John Kengenyeh and Emadu Rogers. All three belonged to the Mende tribe and had joined with army privates to form the Anti-Corruption Revolutionary Movement. The detention of these men was followed by the forced retirement of Lieutenant-Colonel Ambrose Genda, a Mende, who together with Colonel John Bangura had constituted the entire officer corps of the Sierra Leone army since the privates' mutiny of April 18.[3]

Weeding out officers who, because of tribal affiliations, were thought to be untrustworthy became one of several tactics employed by Prime Minister Stevens to restore civilian control of the military. The first order of business was, of course, to reestablish a full-fledged army—that is, one under the command of commissioned officers—and then to fashion a cadre of officers loyal to the regime in power. To this end, Stevens began negotiating for the release of the seventy-six army officers still being held in Pademba Road Prison. In bargaining for the release of these officers, Stevens agreed to an immediate 15 percent increase in ''personal emoluments'' for all privates, NCOs, and warrant officers. At its first budget session following the return to civilian rule, parliament ratified the salary increase and also agreed to appropriate Le 54,000 for the purchase of new uniforms. Promises were also forthcoming that military expenditures both for weapon replacements and for improvements in barrack conditions would rise substantially in the coming years. Finally, and perhaps the crowning touch, twenty-one warrant officers were commissioned as second lieutenants on August 12, 1968.

By late September, almost all the gazetted officers in the Sierra Leone police had been released from detention and reinstated at their former ranks. In late November, thirty-four army officers were also released, and in March 1969, another thirty-two received their freedom. Nevertheless a number of prominent junior and senior officers still languished in prison. This group included most of the key principals in the 1967 round of coups d'état—David Lansana, William Leigh, Bockarie Kai-Samba, Charles Blake, Captain Sahr James Foyah, Captain Mboma, and Lieutenant Samuel Norman. Together with the major civilian figures in the March 21 coup, Lansana, Blake, Leigh, Kai-Samba, and Norman were charged with "conspiring together and with other persons unknown to overthrow the government of Sierra Leone." Juxon-Smith, Leigh, Blake, Kai-Samba, Major Mark Koroma, Captain Foyah, and Captain Mboma were also charged with usurping the constitution and in general with "preparing and announcing a complete takeover of the country by the Army and the Police."[4] On one level, their detention and trial eliminated them once and for all as future coup-makers in Sierra Leone. On yet another level, the treason trials were meant to affirm the supremacy of civilian values and of civilian control of the Sierra Leone military. The trials were designed also to "send the officers a message" and to dissuade future army malcontents from believing that their staging of a coup would be regarded by the general public as anything less than high treason. In August 1968, Soloman Pratt, the minister of development under the national government, was quoted as saying that "Sierra Leone wants to be the first country in Africa to let the military know [that] it is treasonable to take over power because you have a gun."[5]

To reward the army rather than only punish it, Stevens supervised a substantial increase in military expenditures. Whereas the 1968 estimates provided for defense expenditures of Le 2,091,824, in fiscal 1969-70 the figures for this same category had increased to Le 2,353,309. For 1970-71, the estimates called for military expenditures of Le 2,725,740, a 45 percent increase over an actual outlay of Le 1,500,000 in 1966-67, the last year of Sir Albert's administration. In June 1970, the APC government stated that it had recognized the "need for improved and modern accommodation for the Royal Sierra Leone Military Forces" and promised to construct new barracks. It also announced plans to create a second army battalion to be stationed at Teko near Makeni, capital of the northern province.[6] This would require an overall increase in army wages to cover the expected intake of new recruits, an increase provided for in the 1970-71 estimates (some Le 300,000). The government also pledged to replace outdated weapons and to acquire a number of Swiss-built armored cars—for an army that had never been called upon to fight a war and probably never would.

In a debate over the proposed military budget for 1969-70 one SLPP member offered his assessment of the APC's approach to civil-military relations: "The fact is that this Government is playing with Army rule under the cloak of civilian rule. Their strength lies in the Army and they will stay by force and rule by force. This is why they are spending so much money for the Army and carrying the Army like a baby."[7] The idea of the government buying off the Royal Sierra Leone Military Forces and then using those forces to suppress political dissent was not totally unfounded. In October and November 1968 troops were used extensively for internal security in the Bo and Kenema districts. The government had scheduled by-elections in those districts after a number of SLPP MPs were unseated by successful election petitions from APC candidates. Clashes between Mendes and "northerners" in a traditional SLPP stronghold led to the declaration of a state of emergency, the postponement of the by-elections, and the deployment of soldiers to maintain order. Several civilians were killed when members of the Daru rifle company opened fire on SLPP supporters near the town of Kenema. Contrary to past practices, the army rather than the police was ordered to carry out most arrests of the antigovernment demonstrators in Freetown and in the provinces.[8] In the Bo and Kenema districts—largely Mende in population and still loyal to the SLPP—the army was increasingly viewed as the paramilitary wing of the ruling party. Kutubu Kai-Samba, the SLPP representative for Kenema Central, stated in parliament "that as far as the people of the South East of this country are concerned they are under what looks like permanent military occupation." He added that, "in a town like Kenema . . . you have a few nightclubs and . . . it is not uncommon for private soldiers to enter there with guns on their backs and order people to leave."[9]

Stevens also sought army involvement in as much busywork as possible, perhaps recognizing the dictum that "it is more of a ceremonial army and because of the lack of full employment, finds a preoccupation in dabbling in politics."[10] Throughout 1969 and 1970, the prime minister deployed substantial numbers of troops along the Sierra Leone-Liberia border on the pretext that pro-SLPP mercenaries operating out of Monrovia might try to invade the country and restore Sir Albert to power. In September 1969, the APC created AMPOL, teams of army and police personnel recruited in the government's campaign against violent crime in the urban areas. These units were introduced eventually into the provinces to participate in the struggle against illicit diamond miners in Kono. Involvement in civic action programs—common in Latin America but relatively unknown in Africa—also was suggested as an additional nonmilitary chore for the army, apart from manning frontier posts and fighting crime. When the APC in June 1970 formally declared its intention to create a second battalion, the hope was also expressed "that a percentage of the new recruits will be artisans or men with special skills who will help to make the Army an economic and productive unit equipped to help itself with repair and construction work and to partici- pate in national development programmes particularly in the rural areas."[11] Keeping the soldiers preoccupied with constructive tasks, thereby hopefully relieving the boredom of barracks life, was clearly the goal of the post-NRC civilian government as part of its overall strategy for preserving control of the military establishment.

Even though Stevens altered Sir Albert Margai's policy of benign neglect of the army as an organization, he did revive the central pillar of the SLPP system of civilian control—the formation of an officer corps sympathetic to the regime in power and prepared to defend that regime against internal threats. The need for the renewal of cross-boundary linkages was occasioned by the removal of Lansana, Blake, Kai-Samba, Jumu, and their fellow con- spirators from the army list. Their departure brought about the destruction of the old SLPP civilian-military coalition; it was therefore necessary to con- struct a replacement. Since the APC received the bulk of its support from northerners of various tribes and from Freetown Creoles, it was clear that these groups would have to predominate among the army's senior ranks.

Throughout 1968 and 1969, the APC eliminated as many Mendes as pos- sible from the officer corps. Apart from those called upon to answer charges of treason, other Mendes were simply pensioned off without explanation. The result was that by the fall of 1969 there remained a single Mende among the ten most senior army officers.[12] Taking the officer corps as a whole, the Mende proportion was now 32 percent and the Temne propor- tion, 35 percent, which meant that an earlier imbalance in favor of the Mendes had been wiped out completely. Furthermore, and most startling, minority northern tribes now constituted 29 percent of the total. These were principally the Korankos and the Yalunkas which together represent only 4.4 percent of the Sierra Leone population.

Colonel John Bangura (promoted to brigadier on May 1, 1969) was ac- ceptable from a tribal standpoint and, because of his association with Siaka Stevens in Guinea during the waning hours of the NRC, an obvious choice for the position of force commander. The commander of the first battalion, Lieutenant-Colonel Joseph Saidu Momoh, belonged to the prime minister's minority Limba tribe and was untainted by prior involvement with military or civilian-military cliques. Both general staff officers were Temne, one of whom had been transferred from the police and possessed no prior military experience. This retribalization of the officer corps was no doubt expected to yield a group of men loyal to the APC, although it probably would be misleading to describe their relationship with the ruling group as one of a client to patron. Rather, these were officers who belonged to a postintervention era and who, like Ocran in Ghana, were now clearly the politicians' "equals." Such officers were fully aware of their special power to wring concessions from the civilian leadership in exchange for a pledge to back that leadership. As we are now aware, ex-Prime Minister Busia in Ghana failed to grasp this cardinal rule by neglecting the army establishment altogether.

Siaka Stevens's attempts to reestablish civilian control of the armed forces faced an important test during the latter half of 1970 and the first half of 1971, when there emerged in Sierra Leone an opposition movement clearly divorced from the rather moribund SLPP.[13] Stevens's time of troubles actually dated as far back as December 1969. A group of university graduates returned from abroad to form the Sierra Leone Provincial Organization (SLPO), an ostensibly nonpolitical group whose principal goal was "to promote and maintain a strong National consciousness and a sense of oneness thereby encouraging unity and understanding among the Provincials."[14] If one looked behind this rhetoric, it became clear that the SLPO was primarily the mouthpiece of Temne northerners who believed that Stevens had allowed the Creoles to perpetuate, if not to strengthen, their monopoly on senior positions in the civil service and elsewhere. On May 10, 1970 the SLPO was superceded by the National Democratic Party (NDP) which, although it held no seats in the House of Representatives, became Sierra Leone's third registered political party. The NDP was headed by Hamid Taqi whose older brother Ibrahim had served previously as the APC minister of information. The NDP charged that Stevens was planning to transform Sierra Leone into a republic, followed by the creation of an autocratic executive presidency of the Nkrumist type.

Temne cliquism soon began to surface within the APC itself in the form of a struggle between party "newcomers" and party "stalwarts."[15] The stalwarts included Stevens himself, C. A. Kamara-Taylor (the APC secretary-general), and others who had been among the party's original founders. Representing the newcomers were Dr. Mohammed Forna, Stevens' finance minister and Ibrahim Taqi, a backbencher. Both men belonged to the Temne tribe and represented the same Tonkolili District in parliament. Neither had served as an MP prior to the 1967 general election and, from the stalwarts' point of view, had missed out on six years of bitter struggle against the Margais. Both Forna and Taqi were known to covet the deputy premiership and apparently grew angry when the APC failed to appoint a successor to Stevens at its general convention held in May 1970.

Political dissent in Sierra Leone was considerably heightened by the return to Freetown in July 1970 of Dr. John Karefa-Smart, who served as Sir Milton Margai's external affairs minister before crossing over to the APC in 1965.

Since that time Karefa-Smart had been regarded generally as a potential claimant to the APC leadership; and when, upon his return, Stevens could only offer him (once assistant director-general with WHO in Geneva) a post as party "adviser," Karefa-Smart decided to assume charge of the APC dissidents. Like Forna and Ibrahim Taqi, Karefa-Smart was a Temne from the Tonkolili District. He eventually succeeded in persuading both men to resign from the APC on September 12.[16] In his letter of resignation, Forna accused Stevens of manifesting a "meglomaniac syndrome," of turning once again to prefinanced schemes in order to further the country's economic development, of seeking to impose an executive presidency upon the people of Sierra Leone, and of equating himself with Sékou Touré, Kenneth Kaunda, and Julius Nyerere.[17]

Stevens's reaction to his rebellious ministers was not long in forthcoming. On September 12 the government formally suspended the holding of public meetings. Two days later, following a series of violent clashes between supporters of the Tonkolili group and APC partisans, Stevens declared another state of emergency. In his broadcast speech, the prime minister referred to "clear indications that a small group of people who want to get into power by every possible means or who have lost positions of authority are doing their utmost to disrupt the peace and good government of this country."[18] Undeterred by Stevens's announcement, Forna, the two Taqis, and Dr. Karefa-Smart formed on September 20, the United Democratic Party (UDP), promising to "bring awareness to the people of Sierra Leone of the threat to their individual rights and to their freedom posed by the lust of the present leaders of the All Peoples Congress (A.P.C.) for unbridled power."[19] The UDP immediately incorporated Hamid Taqi's NDP and nominated Karefa-Smart as its provisional chairman. Stevens soon counterattacked, however, and on October 8 banned the new political party and detained thirty of its members under the emergency regulations.

If past experience was any guide, the renewal of feuding among Sierra Leone's political cliques posed an immediate threat to Siaka Stevens's efforts to preserve civilian control of the military. Perhaps the prime minister's first blunder was his deployment of the army to enforce the ban on the UDP, an action that required many officers to choose sides in the controversy. Thus on the night of October 8 and throughout the following week, the army was used to carry out the arrests of the UDP leadership including Dr. Karefa-Smart. According to a press release issued by the "Directorate of the Democratic Civil Resistance Movement," claiming to speak for the banned UDP, Mr. Stevens "handpicked some Limba, Yalunka, and Kuranko soldiers to arrest and attack opposition leaders."[20]

The decision to involve the army in the arrests of opposition politicians and some of the UDP's major supporters supposedly angered Brigadier Bangura who, although only part Temne, was known to be sympathetic with the Karefa-Smart group. Rumor held that Bangura had been contacted by Karefa-Smart and other UDP members on several occasions, and on September 10 the government had to dismiss a report "that for tribal considerations the Force Commander has been served with notice of retirement and is to be replaced by the Officer Commanding the 1st Battalion."[21] Clearly this referred to Lieutenant-Colonel Momoh, who commanded the battalion and was known to be circumventing the line of command to court the prime minister's personal favor. Just as an earlier Bangura-Lansana rivalry had been inflamed by struggles between the APC and the SLPP, feuding between the UDP and the APC was now clearly exacerbating relations between Bangura and Momoh.

On October 13, five days after the banning of the UDP, Bangura's standing was eroded even further as Stevens sought desperately to neutralize the army from the effects of the APC—UDP struggle. On that day, two senior officers—Majors Benedict Kargbo and Yankay Sesay, who were both Temne and known to be among Bangura's most trusted confidants—were suddenly pensioned off. Major Sesay was ostensibly retired because an American embassy official, Mark Colby, had been reported leaving Sesay's quarters at Wilberforce Barracks early on the morning of October 9. However, accounts appearing in the Government information services hinted that the two officers had been connected with a UDP-inspired coup plot that would have involved, among other things, the arrest of Mr. Stevens and his cabinet, followed by the release of the detained UDP leaders. The linking up of Sesay and Colby (who was thought to be in CIA employ) reflected the government's wish to portray the UDP as an agent of US "imperialism."[22] The opposition party was also said to have recruited another junior officer to carry on "propaganda work." Given that neither Kargo nor Sesay was courtmartialed, however, it was clear that the APC had little or no evidence to implicate them directly in a coup plot.

Immediately following the dismissal of Kargbo and Sesay, Stevens ordered the arrest of twelve army warrant officers and NCOs—most of them Temne—and charged them with violent mutiny on the night of October 13. When the first of these, Alex Conteh, was brought before a military tribunal in December, he admitted removing some 650 rounds of ammunition from the Wilberforce Military Store. Conteh stated that when Dr. Forna resigned from the APC and joined Dr. Karefa-Smart to form the UDP, he (Conteh) noticed the development of "a great split in the barracks" and, in particular, that the Temne rank and file feared being attacked by soldiers belonging to other tribes, especially the Koranko and the Yalunka.[23] The ammunition was taken to permit the Temne soldiers to "defend themselves" rather than to "fight the Government." Nevertheless, Conteh did mention the name of

Brigadier Bangura who, according to the defendant, was planning to stage a coup on the night of October 13 because he anticipated being arrested by pro-APC officers and "because two of his best officers [presumably Kargbo and Sesay] had been retired."[24]

While the degree of Bangura's involvement with the Temne warrant officers cannot be determined, his position in the army hierarchy was as tenuous as during the six months or so prior to his arrest in February 1967. There was no special reason, therefore, to believe he would not act to salvage his wounded pride. The UDP, in fact, offered additional encouragement for an antigovernment coup when, following its official banning, some UDP supporters, who had gone underground, called upon "the Military, its officers and other ranks, to arrest Mr. Stevens."[25] Furthermore, it was later claimed that the then Minister of Education, Mr. Barthes Wilson "publicly reviled the Commissioner of Police, whom he said was not supporting them [the APC] as well as Brigadier John Bangura, and promised that his Government intended to get rid of these, who will be replaced by party supporters."[26] As in 1967, intracivilian fragmentation now coincided with intra-army fragmentation, and the stage was set once again for a revival of military praetorianism.

The crisis in Sierra Leone's civil-military relations was only temporarily eased by the release in February 1971 of a number of UDP leaders including Dr. Karefa-Smart and Mohammed Bash-Taqi. However, Stevens refused to lift the ban on the UDP, and command patterns in the army could not be stabilized as long as the brigadier remained only a figurehead force commander. Curiously, the APC did not follow through with its pledge to oust Bangura; perhaps Stevens feared triggering a pro-Bangura coup if he dismissed the brigadier outright. Like Sir Albert before him, Stevens looked to Guinea to supplement his own domestic efforts at maintaining civilian control of the army. On March 19 he visited Conakry for discussions on a proposed Sierra Leone-Liberia-Guinea defense pact which, although ostensibly providing mutual assistance in case of external aggression against one of the consenting parties, was for Sierra Leone, at least, aimed clearly at internal subversion. Since mid-1970 it, in fact, had been believed that Stevens possessed his own bodyguard of Guinean troops although these were certainly not in evidence on March 23, the date of the APC leader's second major confrontation with the Sierra Leone army.

At approximately 1:45 on the morning of March 23, 1971, four days following Stevens's visit to Conakry and five years to the day since the Blake coup, a truckload of soldiers led by Major Falawa Jawara (who had served briefly on the NRC) attacked the prime minister's official residence and began riddling the surrounding area with bullets. Mr. Stevens, asleep when the soldiers commenced firing, managed to alert his guards who promptly returned the fire. In the ensuing gun battle two army privates belonging to the attack force were killed and several others critically wounded. When the coupmakers apparently ran short of ammunition, they were ordered to withdraw. Stevens miraculously escaped unharmed but would have to survive yet another assassination attempt before he could count his blessings.

On the afternoon of the same day as Stevens met with members of his cabinet to discuss the events of that morning, another lorry-load of soldiers attempted to finish the task which Major Jawara had bungled earlier. Around 12:30 PM troops attacked the prime minister's office in central Freetown, severely damaging its exterior. For several hours loyalist troops engaged the mutineers in a fierce gun battle. Once again, Stevens managed to escape and went into hiding, some say, at the residence of a professor at Fourah Bay College. While all this was taking place, antigovernment troops moved to seize the main radio station and began to arrest cabinet ministers, who were subsequently held to enforce the release of those UDP leaders still in detention. At approximately 3:00 the same afternoon, Brigadier Bangura appeared on Sierra Leone radio to announce that "owing to the current state of affairs, the army had been compelled to take control of the situation until further notice." He added further that his statement had the "full backing and support of all members of the armed forces" and warned that "any undue outside interference will be viewed with disfavour."[27] According to a *West Africa* correspondent, this latter statement "was taken as being a possible reference to the two unidentified jet aircraft, believed to have been MIGs of the Guinean air force which flew low over Freetown."[28] Earlier in the day, Guinean forces had been placed on general alert owing "to serious troubles affecting the fraternal peoples of Sierra Leone."[29]

Bangura's control of the Sierra Leone government lasted only a few hours, and at 9:00 PM a pro-Stevens army clique led by a Creole officer, Lieutenant-Colonel Sam King, announced that "a large percentage of Sierra Leone's armed forces" wished to disassociate themselves from Brigadier Bangura's coup.[30] King added that he and his fellow officers regarded "the present Government as the only legally constituted authority in this country." His countercoup was strikingly reminiscent of a similar action carried out against Brigadier Lansana by Majors Blake, Jumu, and Kai-Samba with one important difference. Whereas King, as leader of a progovernment countercoup came to the rescue of the civilian authorities, the countercoup staged on March 23, 1967 was designed to install a full-fledged military government in Sierra Leone.

The dramatic upheaval in Sierra Leone's civil-military relations wrought by the events of March 23, 1971 was not completely resolved by the King countercoup. Following the young lieutenant-colonel's radio broadcast, Brigadier Bangura was placed under arrest and a search conducted for other pro-Bangura army officers believed to have gone into hiding. On the morning of March 24, Major Tom Caulker, another loyalist officer, announced on Sierra Leone radio that "the statement made by Lieutenant-Colonel S. H. King and others [is] true and genuine" and that the army would continue to back Siaka Stevens and the APC. Caulker's broadcast was followed by a personal address from the prime minister in which he reported that "by the grace of God" he was still "alive and well" and recounted the details of the assassination attempts. On March 26, loyalist troops arrested six other officers alleged to have participated in the Bangura coup attempt. In the next several days an additional five officers including Major Jawara were apprehended and detained.

Not content merely to rely upon progovernment cliques within his army to ensure continued civilian control, Stevens decided to reintroduce the "Guinean variable" into Sierra Leone's civil-military relations. Sékou Touré, as usual, was more than ready to oblige, and on March 28 the two leaders announced the formal signing of a mutual defense pact.[31] The pact had been necessitated, Stevens stated in another radio broadcast on March 29, by "a terrible rift in our armed forces, a situation which has left the people unarmed and helpless." That same day, Guinean troops were airdropped into Freetown to take up positions at the prime minister's residence and other key points in the capital. By March 31 there were some 200 Guinean soldiers in Freetown with promises from Conakry to send the entire Guinean army if it were needed. According to Stevens, the two armies had "become one." Lieutenant Ahmed Kuyateh headed the Guinean troop contingent, and on March 30, the newly promoted Colonel Joseph Saidu Momoh succeeded Brigadier Bangura as force commander of the Sierra Leone army.

The Bangura coup of March 23 may be subjected to a variety of interpretations, none of which can be documented at this juncture. According to the *London Times* of April 2, a number of Guinean troops wearing civilian garb were already stationed near Freetown by March 23, prompting Brigadier Bangura to demand their withdrawal. Stevens apparently refused to accede to this request and would offer no assurances for future deployment of more Guinean soldiers. According to this report, Bangura then decided to stage a coup, although the actual attack on the prime minister's residence may have been carried out without his prior knowledge. Certainly the breakaway UDP wielded considerable influence over Bangura's decision to intervene militarily. In the court martial of nine army officers that began in early June, Bangura claimed that most of the "actors" who had taken part in the drama were not now in the dock, while some of them were abroad;[32] however, Bangura denied having been offered Le 50,000 by Dr. John Karefa-Smart to stage a coup. For his part, Dr. Karefa-Smart feared being associated with the coup attempt, and on March 24 the leader of the banned UDP boarded a plane for Geneva.

There is one curious aspect to the Bangura affair that merits further research—the heterogeneous tribal composition of the conspiratorial group. Of the nine officers eventually brought to trial on charges of mutiny and incitement to mutiny by violence, there were five Mendes (all but one junior officers), a Kono, a Koranko, and two Temnes. The diversified nature of the conspirators and, in particular, the substantial number of Mende officers would seem to rule out a unitribal explanation for the coup attempt. Mende participation demonstrated unequivocably that Stevens's attempt to strengthen civilian control of the military had not been entirely successful and that this control was only institutionalized at the senior level of the officer corps. Thus although the opposition SLPP formally disavowed any prior knowledge of the coup and condemned the violence associated with it, the involvement of Mende officers—all recruited in Sir Albert's day—suggested that at least certain members of this ethnic group had yet to reconcile themselves to a Stevens government and were prepared to align themselves with Temne officers. Bangura was perhaps the big man par excellence in the Sierra Leone army and, because of his popularity among some junior officers, could attract support for his adventurous schemes from multitribal sources, in exchange for a promise of such sweeteners as future promotions.

As a harsh warning to other potential coupmakers in the army, death sentences were passed on four officers linked to the assassination attempts of March 23. These included Brigadier Bangura, Major S. E. Momoh, Major F. Jawara, and Lieutenant J. B. Kolugbonda, all executed by firing squad on the morning of June 29, 1971. Whether or not these executions would defer future plotters was certainly open to question. One, in fact, could argue that any future coup attempts would be as ruthless as possible in order to guarantee a successful outcome.

Stevens hoped to preserve civilian control of the military by nurturing progovernment cliques of officers and by creating an Nkrumah-type POGR made up of Guinean nationals.[33] The first element in the civilian-control program was of doubtful value because some army cliques may be progovernment one day and antigovernment the next. Also such cliques must be bribed continually, often to the detriment of the country's economic development as scarce financial resources are siphoned off by an unproductive organization. Not content merely to rely upon the loyalties of his force commander and battalion commander, Stevens literally surrounded himself with troops from the "Guinean unit" of the Sierra Leone army. While these were being phased out—the last contingent leaving in mid-1973—he requested and received Cuban assistance to train an APC militia as a counterpoise to the regular army. This militia was later dubbed the Internal Security Unit

(ISU) and absorbed by the Sierra Leone police force. In view of the failure of Nkrumah's POGR and of both Obote's Special Forces and his paramilitary General Services Unit (GSU) to successfully defend their respective leaders, it was open to question whether the Sierra Leone Internal Security Unit could effectively check a determined effort by elements within the army to oust the current regime. Furthermore, as long as the Sierra Leone military organization remained so susceptible to internal divisions and to penetration by civilian political cliques eager to exploit these divisions, further intervention of one form or another was always a strong possibility.

# 12
# CONCLUSION

Throughout our examination of the relationship between civilian and military in Sierra Leone, I have favored a micro- and in some cases a submicro-approach to our material. This has hopefully helped to unravel some of the less obvious features of that relationship, features that normally would be overlooked in cross-national studies of the African military in politics. Within the confines of a case study detailing the interaction between a single battalion army and its sociopolitical environment, the key participants in Sierra Leone's civil-military relations have been identified, how these participants conducted various transactions with one another over a period of time has been demonstrated, and finally some of the more salient political consequences of such transactions have been described. A primary concern has been with the politics of elite competition both within the military organization and also within the total system. Both forms of elite cleavage tend to exercise a mutually reinforcing influence so that the boundaries between intramilitary and intracivilian politics are often highly diffused.

In a limited number of African states of which Nigeria is a prime example, the presence of individual battalions or brigades at separate geographical locations may encourage the conduct of civil-military relations outside the capital city. However in a small state such as Sierra Leone whose technical, economic, and administrative infrastructure remains concentrated almost exclusively in the capital, the relations between civilian and military actors are formed and sustained at a fixed locus. In Freetown—as presumably in Lomé, Kigali, Bangui, and Contonou—some of the principal props of a coup d'état like the radio station and the presidential palace can be easily found within an area of a few square miles. Here too are the spacious homes belonging to government ministers, permanent secretaries, and high-ranking army officers. Being restricted to such a limited physical area, civil-military relations are not unlike normal political relations involving civilian elites living in the capital.

The key figures in Sierra Leone's civil-military relations are easily identified. In that country as presumably in other states with similar social and political characteristics, these include members of both the civilian and military sectors. In the army, three groups sometimes operating separately and at other times together have become involved in political activities. Tiny cliques of junior and senior officers—some who have participated in a number of coup plots, attempted coups, and successful coups—constitute one such grouping. More recently, privates, NCOs, and warrant officers have shown themselves capable of organizing for collective political action. Witness, for example, the privates' mutiny of April 1968, which also involved a number of warrant officers, and the warrant officer-NCO attempted mutiny of October 1970. It now appears that virtually any army group possessed with sufficient daring and capable of wielding guns can perform the role of coup-plotter or coup-maker in an increasingly praetorian society such as Sierra Leone. Thus while coup-leaders in black Africa traditionally have been commissioned officers, one can now expect ambitious NCOs and privates to leave their mark on civil-military relations.

Martin Needler has noted that at least in Latin America, "military coups are not made by the military alone." Rather "the conspirators are in touch with civilian politicians and respond to their advice."[1] Liisa North, again writing on Latin America, specifically Argentina, Chile, and Peru, has argued that "given the officer corps's lack of isolation from the social and political context, we need to examine the specific attempts by the states and by particular social and political groups to manipulate these structures for purposes other than those defined in the ideal of a professional army."[2] It is curious that the available literature on sub-Saharan African military establishments rarely mentions the existing and potential susceptibility of these establishments to external pressures from civilian political factions, although one reason may be that secondary source materials rarely yield the kind of data necessary to validate the existence of such pressures. We have demonstrated that in Sierra Leone, civil-military relations necessarily have implied the continuous interaction of prominent civilians with men in uniform, usually officers. Furthermore, civilian members of both ruling groups and outgroups as well have been portrayed not as highly vulnerable targets of military actions but as prime movers of many of those actions.

The most spectacular example of this phenomenon occurred during the years 1964-1967 when Sierra Leone was ruled by Sir Albert Margai and the SLPP. At that time, during what was ostensibly a period of civilian control of the armed forces, civilian big men from the ranks of the political elites often served as patrons of individual army officers. Intermarriage and close physical proximity between the two groups virtually guaranteed numerous opportunities for interaction. At the time of the March 1967 coups, civilian backers of the effort to maintain the SLPP in power actually outnumbered their military counterparts. In exposing the Bangura coup plot of February 1967, the government blamed the opposition APC for backing the plotters with money and legal advice, and following the abortive coup of March 1971, army leaders of the assassination attempt on Siaka Stevens were linked to members of the outlawed opposition UDP. At the court martial of the first warrant officer implicated in the October 1970 attempted mutiny, the relationship between the mutineers and "opposition politicians" was continually highlighted by the prosecution. One of the mutineers was even said to have been observed driving the car of a former government minister who had joined the UDP.

The potential for the formation of civilian-military cliques has been observed in other African states. In Ghana, Imoru Ayarna, a junior minister under Kwame Nkrumah and later founder of the disbanded Peoples Action Party (PAP) along with Kojo Botsio, once Nkrumah's foreign minister, and John Tettegah, the former leader of the Trade Union Congress, were sentenced to death by a military tribunal in December 1973 for conspiring to influence the commander of the 1st Infantry Brigade to overthrow the Acheampong regime.[3] The sentences, however, were never carried out.

In June 1973 Chad's President Ngarta Tombalbaye placed his army commander, General Félix Malloum, under house arrest, accusing him of plotting to stage a coup backed by certain politicians, one of them being Madame Kalthouma Guembang, head of the women's section of the ruling Chad Progressive Party (PPT).[4] Finally, during the July 1973 coup in Rwanda which resulted in the ouster of a civilian president, Grégoire Kayibanda, the leader of the uprising, Major-General Juvenal Habiyarimana, was said to "represent those Parmehutu [the Parti de l'Emancipation de Peuple Hutu] members from the north of the country who have been increasingly unhappy about the number of cabinet members chosen by Kayibanda from around 'his own hill-' which is in Gitarama in south central Rwanda."[5]

In the Sierra Leone example, it has been possible to observe some of the underlying processes that shaped the formation of civilian-military cliques. The creation of a military elite was hastened by the departure of British army officers in the five years or so after independence, followed by the promotion of Africans to the commissioned ranks. Even though these officers were slow to gain public recognition of their elite status, largely because of their limited education (as of 1971 there was not one staff or command officer in the Sierra Leone army with a university degree) and because of existing civilian prejudices against those opting for a military career, their access to high salaries, car advances, junkets abroad, and comfortable living quarters suggested that these were upwardly mobile men who could not longer realistically be dismissed as noninfluentials. Once having joined the nation's elite if at first only in an economic sense, officers logically ferreted out friends and contacts among civilian politicians. Cross-boundary relationships were nurtured by patron-client ties based upon the notion of reciprocity—the civilian ruling circle gaining physical protection against its internal enemies, real or imagined, and the army officers gaining added status resulting from faster promotions and identification with prominent civilians.

Such patron-client ties would appear to be similar to those observed by René Lemarchand, Eric Wolf and others in their studies of political clientism, which consists of a "more or less personalized, affective and reciprocal relationship between actors, or sets of actors, commanding unequal resources and involving mutually beneficial transactions that have political ramifications beyond the immediate sphere of dyadic relationships."[6] In African political systems, patron-client linkages normally involve the civilian leaders who alone are able to distribute rewards or "patronage" and the peasants and urban workers who receive these rewards, in the form of material assistance and protection against rioters and external aggressors, in return for their willingness to support the ruling group. To the extent that they are still permitted by the modernizers to retain some substantive as opposed to ceremonial functions, traditional authorities may continue to be patrons or, alternatively, to be middlemen between the politicians and their constituents. What should be underlined, however, is that both the patron and the client are locked into a mutual dependency relationship like that binding the SLPP and its army backers.

The analogy between political clientism of the kind described above and that which mediated Sierra Leone's civil-military relations prior to the Lansana coup is not, of course, perfect, owing to the fact that in Sierra Leone it was the patron who ultimately sought the protection afforded by the client who possessed the guns, rather than the other way round. Furthermore, as the civilian patrons found their careers increasingly jeapordized by opposition elements and therefore had to rely more and more upon the army, it was the military men who, in the weeks prior to the March 1967 intervention, began to monopolize both rifles and political resources and were thus in a position to overturn their client status. Nevertheless, as in the more frequently described patron-client relationship, only the actual patron was in a position to distribute rewards under a system of civilian control of the military. Thus in order for the client, the army officer, to rise in the hierarchy of his own organization, it was necessary for him to acquire the benevolent support of a civilian mentor. One Sierra Leonean politician has commented upon the formation of civilian-military cliques in his country and the operation of the patron-client phenomenon:

Here in Africa, many times our troubles stem from the fact that politicians have their relations in the army. And perhaps in order to entrench themselves more, they try to give accelerated promotions to these young people in the army so that in a time of crisis, these relations can come to their aid.[7]

This would seem to be a perfect description of the ways in which civilian and military interacted during the rule of Sir Albert Margai and perhaps to a lesser extent under the present APC government.

The development of civilian-military cliques—united for purposes of mutual aggrandizement—provides the key to our understanding of the intermittent breakdown or threatened breakdown of civilian control of the Sierra Leone army. As civilian-military cliques are formed, it becomes exceedingly difficult for an army officer—particularly one whose indoctrination in the ethos of a professional army may consist of a short training course at the Mons Officer Cadet School—to maintain a sense of perspective towards things political. Even though Sierra Leone officers wear military uniforms, their almost day-to-day contacts with tribal or family brothers in civilian garb inevitably trigger particularistic emotions and a readiness to take sides. Notions of loyalty to an amorphous concept of nation (or state)—at first only tenuously internalized—may disappear altogether, yielding to primordial loyalties when "the chips are down."

For the primary process of civil-military relations in Sierra Leone—that is, cross-boundary clique development—to manifest itself in the form of a coup d'état or countercoup, at least two preconditions are necessary. Intra-army fragmentation, primarily at the officer corps level, constitutes the first precondition. I have shown that with the departure of British officers on secondment to the Sierra Leone army, the officer corps almost immediately disintegrated into minicliques which bickered over the right to occupy the few staff and command positions available. At least in the initial stages, none of these cliques were politically inspired in that they embraced an ideology or openly sympathized with a particular political party. Rather clique formation was essentially a response to uncertainties over the pecking order in the command hierarchy.

The transformation of these cliques into overtly political vehicles and eventually into coupmakers was occasioned by inputs from the civilian sector. During the second Margai administration, the political system itself began to evidence feuding characteristics. The most obvious example of this phenomenon was, of course, the split between Sir Albert Margai and Siaka Stevens—two men who during the late 1950s had joined forces to oppose the conservative policies of Sir Milton Margai. A more subtle but equally divisive struggle was that between followers of Sir Albert and those within the SLPP who opposed his continued leadership of the party. Each of these political groups, especially the anti-Albert factions in the ruling elite, could claim certain army officers as their "relations." Throughout 1966 and in the two and a half months prior to the general elections in mid-March 1967, cliquism in the political system was focused on ever-higher stakes; and cross-boundary linkages, some of which had lain dormant, were awakened. As a result of this development, army cliques were soon politicized and came increasingly to be identified (both through rumor and also through reports in the press) with their civilian counterparts. These officer cliques no longer devoted their energies solely to internal matters of the army organization but instead turned to backing civilian groups even if they had to leave the barracks to do so.

Army takeovers or attempted takeovers in Sierra Leone since 1967 have represented the extension of civilian politics into the military sphere followed by the intrusion of military politics into the civilian sphere. The Bangura coup plot of February 1967 began as a dispute between the force commander and his deputy but was soon made political by the exacerbation of the APC-SLPP struggle in the year prior to the general elections. The Blake-led countercoup resulting in the establishment of the NRC reflected, on one hand, the internal rivalries between Lansana and his immediate subordinates and, on the other, the existence of cleavages within the SLPP. The coup attempt of March 1971 had its origins in Brigadier Bangura's growing sense of isolation from his more junior officers—notably Lieutenant-Colonel Joseph Momoh, whom Bangura felt had unduly aligned himself with his (Momoh's) fellow tribesman, Prime Minister Siaka Stevens. However, only with the appearance of civilian elite instability marked by the split between the "Tonkolili group" and the APC stalwarts did the internal divisions within the Sierra Leone military spill over into the political system.

Samuel Huntington in his *Political Order in Changing Societies* distinguishes between the oligarchical, radical, and mass praetorian models. Thus, "in a praetorian oligarchy politics is a struggle among personal and family cliques; in a radical praetorian society the struggle among institutional and occupational groups supplements that among cliques; in mass praetorianism social classes and social movements dominate the scene." Huntington believes that in Africa there has been a breakthrough from oligarchical to radical praetorianism initiated by the civilian-led political parties and later by the "middle class military officers."[8] However, our data has shown that the interaction of civilian and military elites, at least as far as Sierra Leone is concerned, resembles not so much the radical model as it does the oligarchical. In the radical ideal type, the civilian-backed military coup "differs from the governmental coups of the old oligarchical era because its leadership normally comes from middle-ranking rather than high-ranking officers; the officers are united more by a loyalty to a common purpose than as the personal following of a single leader . . . [and] they normally have a program of social and economic reform and national development."[9] While this description may explain civil-military relations in Algeria, Libya, Egypt, or Ethiopia; it would appear to have less value for Sierra Leone or, for that matter, such states as Upper Volta, Togo, and Dahomey. In Sierra Leone, civil-military relations have involved nothing more or less than a circulation of civilian and military cliques—a musical chairs game acted out by an often bewildering number of actors on the Freetown stage.

The random, often fumbling quality of army intervention in Sierra Leone helped to shape the nature of that country's brief experiment in military government. Since rule by junta has come to represent one of several interrelated aspects of strained civil-military relations in Sierra Leone, it is not surprising that the actual performance of the National Reformation Council should have been directly influenced by the very nature of the March coups. In short, the kind of officer clique formation and disintegration that so profoundly influenced the events of March 21 and 23, 1967, also influenced negatively the administrative capacity of the NRC. Almost from the outset of NRC rule, particularly upon the return of such a relative outsider as Lieutenant-Colonel Juxon-Smith, top-level, effective decision making was severely circumscribed by bickering among individual officers. Just as the anti-Lansana factions had proliferated in the past, so too during the NRC's stay in office did anti-Juxon-Smith cliques appear with startling frequency. When it came time for the NRC to deal with political questions of real substance such as in the case of the proposed return to civilian rule, the regime could not cope with the problem in light of the absence of consensus among council members. Instead of focusing upon constructive approaches to the demilitarization strategy, groups of officers occupied their time by plotting countercoups.

In yet another respect, the style of coupmaking in Sierra Leone was reflected in the NRC's performance. A kind of byproduct of particularistic disputes within the army and the SLPP, the NRC was nothing more than a hastily constructed band of men with little or no political program. Unlike those reformist military regimes that have often appeared in North Africa and Latin America, the coming to power of the NRC resulted from a last-minute impulsive act—the removing of David Lansana as force commander while simultaneously preventing an APC takeover—rather than from a "free officers movement" of long duration. Lacking a concept of how to govern or of how to cultivate public support, the NRC could do little more than flounder from one threat of reprisal against civilians to another. For some NRC members, the regime offered a platform from which they could vent their anger at civilians (particularly Creoles) whom they perceived as having heretofore frowned on the entire military establishment. For others, the regime was a means of thwarting a transfer of power from the ins to the outs and thus permitting these officers to retain their commands. Viewed in this light, the NRC's "politics of reformation" was mere window-dressing, designed to conceal the regime's fundamental insecurity and lack of goals. Certainly the NRC possessed little of the modernizing capacity ascribed to military regimes by such writers as Lucian Pye and Ernest LeFever.

Sierra Leone's brief experiment with military government appears in retrospect to have pleased neither members of the civilian elite nor members of the army officer corps. The first group was alienated by the personal deportment of individual junta representatives and by the failure of the "army boys" to initiate a credible civilian-military dialogue. The members of the National Reformation Council soon became disenchanted both with the delicate task of acquiring legitimacy and began to squabble incessantly among themselves. What has seemed more preferable in the long run to both groups is a system of quasi-civilian control based on elementary notions of reciprocity or trade-offs. During Sir Albert's time, the prevailing modus operandi of civil-military relations required army officers to behave as clients towards their civilian patrons. In the post-NRC era, army officers have become more aware of their political power (even if they may fear to exercise it), and reciprocity has become an operation among equals. Of course, political realities may often produce flaws in the ideal-type, as we observed during the aftermath of the UDP crisis. At that time, an army clique headed by Brigadier Bangura opted to reject the rules of the game only to be thwarted by another, larger clique of officers who perceived no immediate gain from the overthrow of the prevailing system of civil-military relations. For the moment, this system remains intact, albeit at one point Guinean troops had to be called in to buttress it. There certainly exist no guarantees against future intervention as long as civilian cliques persist in feuding among themselves and as long as this behavior is mirrored in the army. Even though Sierra Leone has now become a de facto one-party state as a result of the May 1973 elections, experience elsewhere in sub-Saharan Africa has demonstrated that single-party civilian governments are just as vulnerable to army takeovers as multiparty regimes.[10]

The central purpose of this study has been to elaborate upon the notion that civil-military relations more often than not imply a complex, ongoing process of interaction between a country's civilian and military elites. The well-defined links between the two elites can, during periods of intensified political competition, result in frequent outbursts of military praetorianism. In this way, army intervention has been interpreted as a bastardized form of civilian politics with the added feature of uniformed men carrying guns. I would suggest that the kind of forces that help shape civil-military relations in Sierra Leone must also be at work in the other black African states that resemble Sierra Leone in their political and economic infrastructures. By this I mean states with armies consisting of little more than a few infantry battalions (possessing little or no warmaking capacity), with a tiny interconnected civilian and military elite, and with a preponderance of the country's political activities concentrated in a single area of limited size. Countries which seem to fit into this category are Burundi, Dahomey, Rwanda, Upper Volta, the Central African Republic, Togo, and perhaps even Ghana. Future research would be most helpful if it could clarify the extent to which this group of states evidences patterns of civil-military relations similar to those prevailing in Sierra Leone.

*Postscript:* Beginning on August 2, 1974, the Sierra Leone government authorized the detention of eighty-three civilians and army NCOs. Included in the list were Ibrahim Taqi and Mohammed Forna who, it will be recalled, had been among the founding members of the United Democratic Party and who had been detained in October 1970, only to be released in July 1973. Also included were the former chairman of the National Reformation Council, Andrew T. Juxon-Smith, and the former brigadier and army commander, David Lansana. Fifteen of those detained, including Forna, Taqi, and Lansana, eventually were brought to trial and charged with attempting to overthrow the government by violence. Also accused was a subinspector in the Internal Security Unit and a sergeant in the Sierra Leone police force.

According to the prosecution in the treason trial which commenced on September 10, the plotters, on the night of July 29, had intended to dynamite the residences of acting President S. I. Koroma, acting Vice-President and Minister of Finance C. A. Kamara-Taylor, and Force Commander Brigadier Momoh. President Stevens, it should be noted, was visiting several Eastern European countries at the time the conspiracy was to have been carried out. In actual fact, there was only one explosion, and that was at the home of Mr. Kamara-Taylor at 3:30 AM on the morning of July 30. Fortunately, Mr. Kamara-Taylor escaped injury and was later called as the second witness for the prosecution. Although the evidence presented in support of the government's case was not always very convincing—particularly as far as David Lansana's involvement was concerned—the unsuccessful attempt upon the life of the finance minister cannot easily be discounted. Certainly, as a result of the deliberate exclusion of men such as Taqi and Forna from the mainstream of political life, it is not impossible that they were somehow involved in a civilian-inspired assassination attempt. In any case, on November 16, all of the accused were found guilty of treason and sentenced to death by firing squad.[11]

At the time of this writing, the role of the Sierra Leone army in the latest plot has yet to be fully explained. Nevertheless, it was alleged that one of the plotters, an ex-army lieutenant named Habib Lansana Kamara, tried to persuade an NCO to unlock the armory in order to gain access to weapons. In other testimony delivered at the trial, it was held that Forna, Taqi, and Lansana—together with Juxon-Smith who, curiously enough, was not indicated—had received assurances from certain officers that elements of the army were prepared to provide tactical and material support for the coup. Plans were apparently laid for the creation of military and civilian councils and an eventual return to civilian rule preceded by general elections.[12] It is doubtful that civilians could have sought the elimination of Brigadier Momoh and the others unless they were well aware beforehand that such an action would be backed by cliques within the officer corps and sections of the rank and file.

The government seemed to feel that the army's role was an important one, for shortly after the jury had rendered a verdict in the treason trial, a progovernment newspaper indicated that a court martial of some five NCOs and a private was about to commence.[13] Then in late December 1974, nine soldiers were accused of being involved in the attempted coup of the previous July. The group included three warrant officers, four sergeants, a lance corporal, and a private. The apparent leader of the soldiers was Yaya Seidy Kalogoh who was in charge of training at the army secondary school. Kalogoh and the others had apparently been brought into the conspiracy by David Lansana and ex-lieutenant Lansana Kamara who were acting as go-betweens for Mohammed Forna and Ibrahim Taqi. Seven of the nine soldiers were found guilty of treason by a court martial on January 29, 1975. Then on July 19th, Forna, Taqi and Lansana were hanged along with Lansana Kamara, another civilian, a paramount chief, Bai Makari N'Silk, an NCO and a warrant officer.

Whatever the magnitude of the army's involvement in the latest plot, it is clear that additional strains have been placed on Sierra Leone's civil-military relations and the process of political decay is accelerating. Certainly the potential for further plotting by opposition groups seemed greater than ever and many people were probably beginning to wonder just how much longer Stevens's luck could hold out. Perhaps in recognition of the need to bind the top civilian and military leadership as close together as possible, the Government announced on October 28 that Stevens's tribesman, Brigadier Momoh (together with the commissioner of police, Mr. Kateu-Smith) had been sworn in as a member of parliament and would soon be appointed a minister of state.[14]

# NOTE ON SOURCES
# SELECTED BIBLIOGRAPHY
# NOTES
# INDEX

# NOTE
# ON SOURCES

A case study of civil-military relations in which the researcher requires primary source material to support his hypotheses is not the easiest task to undertake. In the developing states of Africa, governments have become far more sensitive in recent years to the presence of foreign researchers than was the case in the immediate post-independence era. Any scholar attempting to probe the relations between civilian and military elites in a given country has become doubly suspect if only because the subject matter of his inquiry touches upon the most delicate facet of politics. The gathering of data may be hindered by the simple fact that, at least during a period of civilian control of the military, the relations between the two groups are necessarily secretive and therefore beyond public scrutiny. If the army has actually seized power, the conduct of government affairs would normally be based on a system of tight security, with only occasional information "leaks" in the regime-controlled media. In short, civil-military relations are generally conducted behind closed doors, and only during coups and countercoups do these relations receive much publicity. For example, the Ghana coup of February 24, 1966 eventually occasioned the writing of two personal accounts of the proceedings, one by Colonel A. A. Afrifa and the other by Major-General A. K. Ocran. The Nigerian coups of 1966 also succeeded in generating a considerable amount of published material. However, these are exceptions to the general rule.

In a small state such as Sierra Leone, where printed records bearing on political behavior are rather limited, the volume of published data (apart from official newspaper stories) relating to civil-military relations is even more limited. Cartwright notes that in Sierra Leone "the smallness of the political elite and their close inter-linkage meant that a relatively large proportion of interactions could be oral, while the attenuated nature of party organizations further reduced the likelihood that a bare minimum of information would be committed to writing."* In light of such research conditions, a study of civil-military relations in Sierra Leone would have seemed, at least at first, to have represented a rather dubious undertaking.

However, as it turned out, there were a number of compensating factors. In the

*Cartwright, *Politics in Sierra Leone,* p. 284

first place, the research "atmosphere" in Sierra Leone and especially in Freetown was, at the time of the writer's stay in the country, still quite favorable. Unlike Ghana and Nigeria—to mention two other ex-British colonies in West Africa—Sierra Leone since independence has not been studied in any depth. In Freetown, the emphasis of educated Creoles as well as educated non-Creoles on scholarship and on the "pursuit of knowledge for knowledge's sake" is still highly valued and this may have facilitated my task.

In the second place, Sierra Leone has had until quite recently a fairly vigorous opposition press. This press was especially active during the period of Sir Albert Margai and was able to shed considerable light on precoup civil-military relations. In the third place, most of the members of the National Reformation Council were eventually placed on trial for treason, and the hundreds of pages of testimony produced by the various trials provided an invaluable source of data on the motives of the principal actors—both civilian and military—during the various coups of March 1967. Finally, the Ministry of the Interior granted me access to certain unclassified files relating to the NRC period. A number of members of the National Advisory Council and the Civilian Rule Committee were also very helpful in describing the workings of those two bodies and in providing actual documentation. All of this material was supplemented by the usual interviews with key participants in Sierra Leone's civil-military relations. Published materials such as the House of Representatives debates, press releases and government statistical data were also used.

# SELECTED BIBLIOGRAPHY

Just as the incidence of coups d'état in developing countries has shown little sign of abating so too has the literature on civil-military relations particularly with respect to the "tiers monde" become prodigious. The following bibliography makes no pretensions at being definitive, but it does contain a fairly complete listing of recently published and unpublished works relating to the topic of civil-military relations in the developing world with special reference to sub-Saharan Africa.

## BOOKS

Abdel-Malek, Anouar. *Egypt: Military Society: The Army Regime, the Left and Social Change under Nasser.* New York: Vintage Books, 1968.

Afrifa, Colonel A. A. *The Ghana Coup, 24th February, 1966.* New York: Humanities Press, 1966.

Akiwowo, Akinsola. "Performance of the Military Government in Nigeria: 1966 to 1970." Draft of a paper submitted to the Working Party on Armed Forces and Society, 7th World Congress of Sociology, September 14-19, 1970, Varna, Bulgaria.

Ambler, John Steward. *Soldiers Against the State: The French Army in Politics.* Garden City, New York: Anchor Books, 1968.

Andrews, William G., and Ra'anan, Uri. *The Politics of the Coup d'Etat: Five Case Studies.* New York: Van Nostrand Reinhold Company, 1969.

Barker, Peter. *Operation Cold Chop: The Coup that Toppled Nkrumah.* Accra: Ghana Publishing Corporation, 1969.

Bebler, Anton. "Military Rule in Africa (Dahomey, Ghana, Sierra Leone, Mali)." Ph.D. Dissertation, University of Pennsylvania, 1971.

———. *Military Rule in Africa* (Dahomey, Ghana, Sierra Leone and Mali). New York: Frederick A. Praeger, 1973.

Bell, M.J.V. *Army and Nation in Sub-Saharan Africa.* Adelphi Papers, no. 21. London: Institute for Strategic Studies, 1965.

_____. *Military Assistance to Independent African States.* Adelphi Papers, no. 15. London: Institute for Strategic Studies, 1964.

Bennett, Valerie P. "The Foundations of Civil-Military Relations in Ghana: 1945-1962." Ph.D. Dissertation, Boston University, 1971.

Bienen, Henry, ed. *The Military and Modernization.* Chicago: Aldine-Atherton, 1971.

_____. *The Military Intervenes: Case Studies in Political Development.* New York: Russell Sage Foundation, 1968.

Booth, Richard. *The Armed Forces of African States, 1970.* Adelphi Papers, no. 67. London: Institute for Strategic Studies, 1970.

Brill, William H. *Military Intervention in Bolivia: The Overthrow of Paz Estenssoro and the MNR.* Washington, D.C.: Institute for the Comparative Study of Political Systems, 1967.

Brown, Neville, and Gutteridge, William F. *The African Military Balance.* Adelphi Papers, no. 12. London: Institute for Strategic Studies, 1964.

Burggraaff, Winfield J. *The Venezuelan Armed Forces in Politics, 1935-1959.* Columbia, Missouri: University of Missouri Press, 1972.

Colas, John N. "The Social and Career Correlates of Military Intervention in Nigeria: A Background Study of the January 15 Coup Group." Paper read at the Annual Meeting of the Inter-University Seminar on Armed Forces and Society, October 9-11, 1969, Chicago.

Crocker, Chester A. "The Military Transfer of Power in Africa: A Comparative Study of Change in the British and French Systems of Order." Ph.D. Dissertation, The Johns Hopkins University, 1969.

Daalder, H. *The Role of the Military in the Emerging Countries.* The Hague: Mouton, 1962.

Deutsch, Karl W., and Foltz, William J. *Nation-Building.* New York: Atherton Press, 1966.

van Doorn, Jacques, ed. *Armed Forces and Society: Sociological Essays.* The Hague: Mouton, 1968.

Feit, Edward. *The Armed Bureaucrats: Military-Administrative Regimes and Political Development.* Boston: Houghton Mifflin Co., 1973.

Fidel, Kenneth. "Conspiratorial Groups in the Turkish Military: A Morphology." Paper read at the Sixth-third Annual Meeting of The American Sociological Association, August, 1968, in Boston, Massachusetts.

Finer, S. E. *The Man on Horseback: The Role of the Military in Politics.* London: Pall Mall Press, 1962.

First, Ruth. *The Barrel of a Gun: Political Power in Africa and the Coup d'Etat.* London: Allen Lane, The Penquin Press, 1970.

Glickman, Harvey. *Impressions of Military Policy in Tanganyika (East Africa).* Santa Monica: The Rand Corporation, 1963.

_____. *Some Observations on the Army and Political Unrest in Tanganyika.* Pittsburg: Duquesne University Press, 1964.

Goodspeed, D. J. *The Conspirators: A Study of the Coup d'Etat.* London: MacMillan, 1962.

Grundy, Kenneth. *Conflicting Images of the Military in Africa.* Nairobi: East African Publishing House, 1968.

Gutteridge, William F. *Armed Forces in New States.* London and New York: Oxford University Press for Institute of Race Relations, 1962.

_____. *Military Institutions and Power in the New States.* New York: Frederick A. Praeger, 1965.

_____. *The Military in African Politics*. London: Methuen & Co., Ltd., 1969.

Hamon, Leo, ed. *Le Rôle Extra-Militaire de l'Armée dans le Tiers Monde*. Paris: Presses Universitaires de France, 1966.

Howard, Michael, ed. *Soldiers and Government: Nine Case Studies in Civil-Military Relations*. Bloomington: Indiana University Press, 1959.

Huntington, Samuel P. *Political Order in Changing Societies*. New Haven and London: Yale University Press, 1968.

_____. *The Soldier and the State: The Theory and Politics of Civil-Military Relations*. New York: Random House, 1957.

Janowitz, Morris. *The Military in the Political Development of New Nations*. Chicago: University of Chicago Press, 1964.

Johnson, John J., ed. *The Role of the Military in Underdeveloped Countries*. Princeton, New Jersey: Princeton University Press, 1962.

Kilson, Martin. "Politics of the Military in Sierra Leone." Unpublished manuscript, n.d.

_____. "Whatever Happened to the 'African Revolution'?" Unpublished manuscript, March 1967.

Leader, Shelah Gilbert. "Military Professionalism, Intervention and the Disposition to Intervene in Ghana and Mali." Ph.D. Dissertation, State University of New York at Buffalo, 1971.

Lee, J. M. *African Armies and Civil Order*. London: Chatto and Windus, 1969.

LeFever, Ernest W. *Spear and Scepter: Army, Police and Politics in Tropical Africa*. Washington, D.C.: The Brookings Institution, 1970.

Lemarchand, René. "Civilian-Military Relations in Former Belgian Africa: The Military as a Contextual Elite." Paper prepared for delivery at the 1972 APSA Annual Meeting, September 4-9, 1972, Washington, D.C.

Listowel, Judith. *Amin*. London and Dublin: IUP Books, 1973.

Luckham, A. R. "The Nigerian Military: A Case Study in Institutional Breakdown." Ph.D. Dissertation, University of Chicago, 1970.

_____. *The Nigerian Military: A Sociological Analysis of Authority and Revolt, 1960-1967*. London: Cambridge University Press, 1971.

Luttwak, Edward. *Coup d'Etat: A Practical Handbook*. London: Allen Lane, The Penquin Press, 1968.

Martin, David. *General Amin*. London: Faber and Faber, 1974.

Mazrui, Ali. *Violence and Thought: Essays on Social Tensions in Africa*. London: Longmans, Green & Co., Ltd., 1969.

McWilliams, Wilson C., ed. *Garrisons and Governments: Politics and the Military in New States*. San Francisco: Chandler Publishing Co., 1967.

Miners, N. J. *The Nigerian Army 1956-1966*. London: Methuen & Co., Ltd., 1971.

Needler, Martin C. *Anatomy of a Coup d'Etat: Ecuador 1963*. Washington, D.C.: Institute for the Comparative Study of Political Systems, 1964.

Ocran, Major-General A. K. *A Myth is Broken: An Account of the Ghana Coup d'Etat of 24th February, 1966*. London: Longmans, Green & Co., Ltd., 1968.

Panter-Brick, S. K. *Nigerian Politics and Military Rule: Prelude to Civil War*. London: The Athlone Press, 1970.

Payne, Arnold. *The Peruvian Coup d'Etat of 1962: The Overthrow of Manuel Prado*. Washington, D.C.: Institute for the Comparative Study of Political Systems, 1968.

Payne, Richard Harold. "Military Intervention in the Politics of Developing Systems: The African Case." Ph.D. Dissertation, University of Georgia, 1970.

Perlmutter, Amos. *Egypt: The Praetorian State*. New Brunswick, New Jersey: Transaction Books, 1974.

_____. *Military and Politics in Israel: Nation-Building and Role Expansion*. New York: Frederick A. Praeger, 1969.

Pinkney, Robert. *Ghana Under Military Rule, 1966-1969*. London: Methuen & Co., Ltd., 1972.

Shabtai, Sabi. "The Role of the Military in the Process of National Integration in the New States of Tropical Africa." Ph.D. Dissertation, University of Chicago, 1972.

Soláun, Mauricio, and Quinn, Michael A. *Sinners and Heretics: The Politics of Military Intervention in Latin America*. Urbana, Illinois: University of Chicago Press, 1973.

Stepan, Alfred. *The Military in Politics: Changing Patterns in Brazil*. Princeton, New Jersey: Princeton University Press, 1971.

Taylor, Philip B., Jr. *The Venezuelan Golpe de Estado of 1958: The Fall of Marcos Pérez Jiménez*. Washington, D.C.: Institute for the Comparative Study of Political Systems, 1968.

Welch, Claude E., Jr. *Back to the Barracks—Or, Hamlet Revisited*. Unpublished manuscript, n.d.

_____. *Soldier and State in Africa: A Comparative Analysis of Military Intervention and Political Change*. Evanston: Northwestern University Press, 1970.

_____. "The African Military and Political Development." Paper presented at the annual meeting of the African Studies Association, November 2, 1967, New York City.

Whiteman, Kaye. "The Military Regimes of Togo and Dahomey." Unpublished manuscript, London: University of London, Institute of Commonwealth Studies, November, 1970.

Wood, David. *The Armed Forces of African States*. Adelphi Papers, no. 27. London: Institute for Strategic Studies, 1966.

## ARTICLES

Ake, Claude. "Explaining Political Instability in New States." *Journal of Modern African Studies* 11:3 (1973): 347-359.

Bell, M.J.V. "The Military in the New States of Africa." In *Armed Forces and Society: Sociological Essays*, edited by Jacques van Doorn. The Hague: Mouton, 1968.

van den Berghe, Pierre L. "The Role of the Army in Contemporary Africa." In *Garrisons and Governments: Politics and the Military in New States*, edited by Wilson C. McWilliams. San Francisco: Chandler Publishing Co., 1967.

Bienen, Henry. "Public Order and the Military in Africa: Mutinies in Kenya, Uganda and Tanganyika." In *The Military Intervenes: Case Studies in Political Development*, edited by Henry Bienen. New York: Russell Sage Foundation, 1968.

Chick, John D. "Class Conflict and Military Intervention in Uganda." *Journal of Modern African Studies* 10:4 (1972): 634-637.

Clapham, Christopher. "The Ethiopian Coup d'Etat of December 1960." *Journal of Modern African Studies* 6:4 (1968): 495-507.

Cornevin, Robert. "Les Militaires au Dahomey et au Togo." *Le Mois en Afrique* no. 36 (December 1968): 65-84.

Cowan, L. Gray. "The Military and African Politics." *International Journal* 21 (1966): 289-297.

Decalo, Samuel. "Military Coups and Military Regimes in Africa." *Journal of Modern African Studies* 11:1 (1973): 105-127.

_____. "Regionalism, Politics and the Military in Dahomey." *Journal of Developing Areas* 7 (April 1973): 449-478.

Dent, Martin J. "The Military in Politics: A Study of the Relation between the Army and the Political Process in Nigeria." *African Affairs,* no. 3; St. Antony's Papers, no. 21; ed. Kenneth Kirkwood. London: Cambridge University Press, 1969.

Dowse, Robert. "The Military and Political Development." In *Politics and Change in Developing Countries,* edited by Colin Leys. London: Cambridge University Press, 1969.

Dudley, B. J. "The Military and Politics in Nigeria: Some Reflections." In *Military Professions and Military Regimes: Commitments and Conflicts,* ed. Jacques van Doorn. The Hague: Mouton, 1969.

Eleazu, Uma O. "The Role of the Army in African Politics: A Reconsideration of Existing Theories and Practices." *Journal of Developing Areas* 7 (January 1973): 265-286.

Feit, Edward. "Pen, Sword and People: Military Regimes in the Formation of Political Institutions." *World Politics* 25: 2 (January 1973): 251-273.

_____. "Military Coups and Political Development: Some Lessons from Ghana and Nigeria." *World Politics* 20:2 (1968): 179-193.

_____. "The Rule of the 'Iron Surgeons': Military Government in Spain and Ghana." *Comparative Politics* 1:4 (July 1969): 485-497.

First, Ruth. "Uganda: the Latest Coup d'Etat in Africa." *The World Today* (March 1967): 131-138.

Foltz, William. "Military Influences." In *African Diplomacy: Studies in the Determinants of Foreign Policy,* edited by Vernon McKay. New York: Frederick A. Praeger, 1966.

Glentworth, Garth, and Hancock, Ian. "Obote and Amin: Change and Continuity in Modern Uganda Politics." *African Affairs* 72:288 (July 1973): 237-255.

Glickman, Harvey. "The Military in African Politics: A Bibliographic Essay." *African Forum* 2:1 (1966): 68-75.

Gowan, L. Gray. "The Military and African Politics." *International Journal* 21 (1966): 289-99.

Greene, Fred. "Toward Understanding Military Coups." *Africa Report* 11 (February 1966): 10-14.

Gutteridge, William F. "The Political Role of African Armed Forces: The Impact of Foreign Military Assistance." *African Affairs* 66:263 (April 1967): 83-103.

Hippolyte, Mirlande. "Coups d'Etat and Régimes Militaires d'Afrique." *Le Mois en Afrique,* no. 36 (April 1967): 83-103.

Hopkins, Keith. "Civil-Military Relations in Developing Countries." *British Journal of Sociology* 17:2 (June 1966): 165-182.

Horowitz, Donald. "Multiracial Politics in the New States: Toward a Theory of Conflict." In *Issues in Comparative Politics,* edited by Robert J. Jackson and Michael B. Stein. New York: St. Martin's Press, 1971.

Jacob, Abel. "Israel's Military Aid to Africa, 1960-1966." *Journal of Modern African Studies* 9:2 (1971): 165-187.

Levine, Donald N. "The Military in Ethiopian Politics: Capabilities and Constraints." In *The Military Intervenes: Case Studies in Political Development,* edited by Henry Bienen. New York: Russell Sage Foundation, 1968.

Lewis, I. M. "The Politics of the 1969 Somali Coup." *Journal of Modern African Studies* 10:3 (1972): 383-408.

Lissak, Moshe. "Modernization and Role-Expansion of the Military in Developing Countries: A Comparative Analysis." *Comparative Studies in Society and History* 9:3 (April 1967): 233-255.

Lofchie, Michael. "The Uganda Coup—Class Action by the Military." *Journal of Modern African Studies* 10:1 (1972): 19-35.

Luckham, A. R. "A Comparative Typology of Civil-Military Relations." *Government and Opposition* 6:1 (Winter 1971): 5-35.

Makedonsky, Eric. "Les Militaires au Pouvoir à Kinshasha." *Le Mois en Afrique,* no. 38 (February 1969): 24-40.

Newbury, C. W. "Military Intervention and Political Change in West Africa." *Africa Quarterly* 7 (1967): 215-221.

Nordlinger, Eric. "Soldiers in Mufti: The Impact of Military Rule upon Economic and Social Change in the Non-Western States." *American Political Science Review* 64:4 (December 1970): 1131-1148.

Olusanya, G. O. "The Role of Ex-Servicemen in Nigerian Politics." *Journal of Modern African Studies* 6:2 (1968): 221-232.

Perlmutter, Amos. "The Praetorian State and the Praetorian Army." *Comparative Politics* 1:3 (April 1969): 382-404.

Polier, Jonathan Wise. "East Africa: Latin America Revisited?" In *Garrisons and Governments: Politics and the Military in New States,* edited by Wilson C. McWilliams. San Francisco: Chandler Publishing Co., 1967.

Potholm, Christopher P. "The Multiple Roles of the Police as Seen in the African Context." *Journal of Developing Areas* 3 (January 1969): 139-158.

Price, Robert M. "A Theoretical Approach to Military Rule in New States: Reference-Group Theory and the Ghanaian Case." *World Politics* 23:3 (April 1971): 399-430.

––––––. "Military Officers and Political Leadership: The Ghanaian Case." *Comparative Politics* 3:3 (April 1971): 361-379.

Pye, Lucian W. "Armies in the Process of Political Modernization." In *The Role of the Military in Underdeveloped Countries,* edited by John J. Johnson. Princeton, New Jersey: Princeton University Press, 1962.

Sale, J. Kirk. "And Now Nkrumah: The Generals & the Future of Africa." In *Garrisons and Governments: Politics and the Military in the New States,* edited by Wilson C. McWilliams. San Francisco: Chandler Publishing Co., 1967.

Schleh, Eugene P. A. "The Post-War Careers of Ex-Servicemen in Ghana and Uganda." *Journal of Modern African Studies* 6:2 (1968): 203-220.

Spiro, Herbert J. "The Military in Sub-Saharan Africa." In *Garrisons and Governments: Politics and the Military in New States,* edited by Wilson C. McWilliams. San Francisco: Chandler Publishing Co., 1967.

Viratelle, Gerard. "Le Régime Militaire Algérien." *Le Mois en Afrique,* no. 38 (February 1969): 63-78.

Welch, Claude E., Jr. "Cincinnatus in Africa: The Possibility of Military Withdrawal from Politics." In *The State of Nations: Constraints on Development in Independent Africa,* edited by Michael Lofchie, pp. 215-237. Berkeley: University of California Press, 1971.

––––––. "Ghana: The Politics of Military Withdrawal." *Current History* (February 1968): pp. 95-100, 113-114.

––––––. "The African Military and Political Development." In *The Military and Modernization,* edited by Henry Bienen. Chicago: Aldine-Atherton, 1971.

––––––. "Soldier and State in Africa." *Journal of Modern African Studies* 5:3 (1967): 305-322.

Zolberg, Aristide. "Military Intervention in the New States of Tropical Africa: Elements of Comparative Analysis." In *The Military Intervenes: Case Studies in Political Development,* edited by Henry Bienen. New York: Russell Sage Foundation, 1968.

_____. "Military Rule and Political Development in Tropical Africa." In *Military Professions and Military Regimes: Commitments and Conflicts,* edited by Jacques van Doorn. The Hague: Mouton, 1969.

_____. "The Structure of Political Conflict in the New States of Tropical Africa." *American Political Science Review,* 62:1 (March 1968): 70-87.

_____. "The Military Decade in Africa." *World Politics* 25:2 (January 1973): 309-331.

The following is a list of books and articles dealing with those aspects of Sierra Leone politics where the military has been involved in one capacity or another. For a more extensive listing of materials relating to Sierra Leone, see John R. Cartwright, *Politics in Sierra Leone 1947-1967.* Toronto: University of Toronto Press, 1970.

Allen, Christopher. "Sierra Leone Politics since Independence." *African Affairs* 67 (October 1968): 305-329.

Balogun, M. J. "Military Intervention and the Return of Civilian Rule in Sierra Leone." Unpublished paper. Idaban: University of Ife, Institute of Administration, 1970.

Barrows, Walter. "La politique de l'armée en Sierra Leone." *Le Mois en Afrique,* no. 36 (December 1968): 54-64.

Cartwright, John R., and Cox, Thomas. "Left Turn for Sierra Leone?" *Africa Report* 17:1 (January 1972): 16-18.

_____. "Shifting Forces in Sierra Leone." *Africa Report* 13:9 (December 1968): 26-30.

Collier, Gershon. *Sierra Leone: Experiment in Democracy in an African Nation.* New York: New York University Press, 1970.

Dalby, David. "The Military Takeover in Sierra Leone, 1967." *The World Today* 23 (August 1967): 354-360.

Fisher, Humphrey J. "Elections and Coups in Sierra Leone, 1967." *Journal of Modern African Studies* 7:4 (December 1969): 611-636.

K.A.B. Jones-Quartey, "Sierra Leone: Return to Turmoil," *The Legon Observer* 5 (October 9-22, 1970): 11-16.

_____. "Government and Opposition in Sierra Leone—The Clouds Re-form," *The Legon Observer* 5 (November 6-19, 1970): i-viii.

_____. "Government and Opposition in Sierra Leone—The Sources of Conflict," *The Legon Observer* 5 (December 4-17, 1970): i-viii.

The following is a selected list of Government publications which are available to any researcher and relate principally to the period of NRC rule.

1. *Report of the Beoku-Betts Commission of Inquiry into the Sierra Leone Produce Marketing Board with Particular Reference to the Sale of Palm Oil, Rice and Coffee Haulers, Nut-Cracking Machine and the Industrialisation Programme undertaken by the Board during the period January, 1961 to March, 1967 [1968].*
2. *Report of the Beoku-Betts Commission of Inquiry on the Special Coffee Deal of the Sierra Leone Produce Marketing Board, 1967* (1968).
3. *Report of the Dove-Edwin Commission of Inquiry into the Conduct of the 1967 General Elections in Sierra Leone and the Government Statement Thereon* (1967).
4. *Report of the Forster Commission of Inquiry on Assets of Ex-Ministers and Ex-Deputy Ministers* (1968).

5. *Report of the Percy Davies Commission of Inquiry into the Activities of the Free-town City Council from 1st January, 1964 to 23rd March, 1967 and the Government Statement Thereon* (1969).
6. *Report of the Wales Commission of Inquiry into the Conduct of the Immigration Quota Committee from 1st January, 1961 to 23rd March, 1967 and the Government Statement Thereon* (1969).

# NOTES

## 1. CIVIL-MILITARY RELATIONS THEORY AND SUB-SAHARAN AFRICA

1. *Punch,* February 3, 1971, p. 199.

2. Ruth First, *The Barrel of a Gun: Political Power in Africa and the Coup d'Etat* (London: Allen Lane, The Penquin Press, 1970), p. 4.

3. Claude E. Welch, Jr., *Soldier and State in Africa: A Comparative Analysis of Military Intervention and Political Change* (Evanston: Northwestern University Press, 1970), pp. 270-301.

4. First, *The Barrel of a Gun,* p. 362.

5. Ted Gurr, "A Causal Model of Civil Strife: A Comparative Analysis Using New Indices," in *When Men Revolt and Why,* ed. James C. Davies (New York: The Free Press, 1971), p. 296.

6. J. O'Connell, "The Inevitability of Instability," *Journal of Modern African Studies,* 5 (1967), 183.

7. Herbert J. Spiro, "The Military in Sub-Saharan Africa," in *Garrisons and Governments: Politics and the Military in the New States,* ed. Wilson C. McWilliams (San Francisco: Chandler Publishing Co., 1967), p. 264.

8. Rupert Emerson, "Nation-Building in Africa," in *Nation-Building,* eds. Karl Deutsch and William J. Foltz (New York: Atherton Press, 1966), p. 115.

9. William Foltz, "Military Influences," in *African Diplomacy: Studies in the Determinants of Foreign Policy,* ed. Vernon McKay (New York: Praeger, 1966), p. 74.

10. Aristide Zolberg, "The Structure of Political Conflict in the New States of Tropical Africa," *American Political Science Review,* 62 (March 1968), 70.

11. A. R. Luckham, "A Comparative Typology of Civil-Military Relations," *Government and Opposition,* 6 (Winter 1971), 9.

12. Lucian W. Pye, "The Army in Burmese Politics," in *The Role of the Military in Underdeveloped Countries,* ed. John J. Johnson (Princeton: Princeton University Press, 1962), p. 239.

13. Edward Shils, "The Military in the Political Development of the New States," in Johnson, *The Role of the Military,* p. 23.

14. John J. Johnson, "The Latin-American Military as a Politically Competing Group in Transitional Society," in Johnson, *The Role of the Military,* p. 127.

15. S. E. Finer, *The Man on Horseback: The Role of the Military in Politics* (London: Pall Mall Press, 1962), p. 88.

16. Samuel P. Huntington, *Political Order in Changing Societies* (New Haven: Yale University Press, 1968), p. 194.

17. Morris Janowitz, *The Military in the Political Development of New Nations* (Chicago and London: The University of Chicago Press, 1964), p. 68.

18. Amos Perlmutter, "The Praetorian State and the Praetorian Army," *Comparative Politics,* 1 (April 1969), 392.

19. Janowitz, *The Military in the Political Development of New Nations,* p. 71.

20. Samuel P. Huntington, *Political Order in Changing Societies,* p. 245.

21. Henry Bienen, ed., *The Military Intervenes: Case Studies in Political Development* (New York: Russell Sage Foundation, 1968), p. xix.

22. Eric A. Nordlinger, "Soldiers in Mufti: The Impact of Military Rule upon Economic and Social Change in the Non-Western States," *American Political Science Review,* 64 (December 1970), 1148.

23. Mauricio Soláun and Michael A. Quinn, *Sinners and Heretics: The Politics of Military Intervention in Latin America* (Urbana, Illinois: University of Illinois Press, 1973), p. 9.

24. Michael A. Lofchie, "The Uganda Coup—Class Action by the Military," *Journal of Modern African Studies,* 10 (1972), 19-20.

25. Garth Glentworth and Ian Hancock, "Obote and Amin: Change and Continuity in Modern Uganda Politics," *African Affairs,* 72 (July 1973), 248.

26. Aristide Zolberg, "Military Rule and Political Development in Tropical Africa," in *Military Professions and Military Regimes: Commitments and Conflicts,* ed. Jacques van Doorn (The Hague: Mouton, 1969), p. 198.

27. *New York Times,* 21 December 1974 and the *Ethiopian Herald,* 28 November 1974.

28. *New York Times,* 16 December 1974 and *Daho Express, Organe de la Revolution (Cotonou),* 2 December 1974.

29. Ernest W. LeFever, *Spear and Scepter: Army, Police and Politics in Tropical Africa* (Washington, D.C.: The Brookings Institution, 1970), pp. 20-21.

30. J. M. Lee, *African Armies and Civil Order* (London: Chatto and Windus, 1969), p. 3.

31. Ibid., p. 176.

32. Zolberg, "The Structure of Political Conflict," p. 77.

33. First, *The Barrel of a Gun,* pp. 111-121.

34. Welch, *Soldier and State in Africa,* pp. 17-18.

35. Robert Pinkney, *Ghana under Military Rule: 1966-1969* (London: Methuen & Co., 1972), p. 27.

36. Welch, *Soldier and State in Africa,* pp. 49-50.

37. Robert E. Dowse, "The Military and Political Development," in *Politics and Change in Developing Countries,* ed. Colin Leys (Cambridge, England: Cambridge University Press, 1969), p. 222.

38. For an excellent critique of civil-military relations theory which regards the act of the coup d'état as the military reaction to a civilian-dominated political system where things have gone awry, see Samuel Decalo, "Military Coups and Military Régimes in Africa," *Journal of Modern African Studies,* 11 (1973), 105-127. Accord-

ing to Decalo, "the main weakness of attempts to explain military interventions by pinpointing areas of systemic stress is in not placing sufficient weight on the personal and idiosyncratic element in military hierarchies, which have much greater freedom and scope of action within the context of fragmented and unstructured political systems," p. 113.

39. Martin Kilson, "The Grassroots in Ghanaian Politics," in *Ghana and the Ivory Coast: Perspectives on Modernization,* eds. Philip Foster and Aristide R. Zolberg (Chicago and London: The University of Chicago Press, 1971), p. 122.

40. Donald G. Morrison has ranked black African states according to the level of elite instability which they experienced from the date of their independence to 1969. In preparing his table, a numerical weight was assigned to coups d'état (5), attempted coups (3), and plots (1). Of the 32 sub-Saharan African states included in his list, Sierra Leone ranked ninth, below Dahomey, Sudan, Zaire, Togo, Congo (Brazzaville), Burundi, Ghana, and Nigeria, in that order. However, if one takes into account the attempted coup in Sierra Leone of March 1971 and the civilian anti-government plot of July 1974 which apparently indirectly involved elements of the army, then Sierra Leone has definitely moved up the list. See Donald G. Morrison, *Black Africa* (New York: Free Press, 1972), p. 128.

41. John R. Cartwright, *Politics in Sierra Leone, 1947-1967* (Toronto: University of Toronto Press, 1970), p. 4.

42. *West Africa,* 21 March 1964, p. 315.

43. *Proclamation for the Interim Administration of Sierra Leone by a National Reformation Council,* Public Notice No. 28, 25 March 1967.

44. *The London Times,* 14 January 1967.

45. Aristide Zolberg, "The Military Decade in Africa," *World Politics,* 25 (January 1973), 319.


## 2. COLONIAL RULE AND THE SIERRA LEONE ARMY

1. Valerie P. Bennett, "The Foundations of Civil-Military Relations in Ghana: 1945-1962" (Ph.D. diss., Boston University, 1971), p. 68. See also Chester A. Crocker, "The Military Transfer of Power in Africa: A Comparative Study of Change in the British and French Systems of Order" (Ph.D. diss., Johns Hopkins University, 1969).

2. Colonial Office, *Report of the West African Forces Conference, Lagos, 20th-24th April 1953* (London: HMSO, 1954), p. 6.

3. After 1939, the War Office assumed control of the RWAFF, and all expenditures for that force were charged to the British defense vote.

4. Most of those NCOs and warrant officers who eventually qualified for short-service commissions worked in the technical, administrative, or education branches of the RWAFF. The first Sierra Leonean to receive such a commission in 1953 had been employed by the army pay and records office. NCOs assigned to rifle companies were often illiterate and thus not suitable for commissioning.

5. Second lieutenants upon commissioning received in 1958 approximately £ 610 per annum; a graduate upon appointment to the senior service received £ 615.

6. N. J. Miners, *The Nigerian Army 1956-1966* (London: Methuen & Co., Ltd., 1971), p. 44.

7. Martin Kilson, *Political Change in a West African State, A Study of the Modernization Process in Sierra Leone* (New York: Atheneum, 1969), p. 234.

8. *Daily Mail,* 27 October 1956.

9. *West Africa,* 18 June 1949.

10. *Legislative Council Debates, Session 1954-55* (10 December 1954), p. 219.

11. *Legislative Council Debates, Session 1955-56* (1 February 1956), p. 98.

12. *Report of the Commission of Inquiry into the Strikes and Riots in Freetown, Sierra Leone, during February 1955* (Freetown: Government Printing Department), p. 36.

13. *Report of the Commission of Inquiry into Disturbances in the Provinces* (*November 1955 to March 1956*) (London: Crown Agents for Overseas Governments and Administrations on behalf of the Government of Sierra Leone, 1956), p. 209.

14. *Daily Mail,* 21 December 1955.

15. *Commission of Inquiry into Disturbances in the Provinces,* p. 209.

16. *House of Representatives Debates, Session 1957-58* (November 8, 1957), p. 109.

17. Cartwright, *Politics in Sierra Leone,* p. 103.

18. *Commission of Inquiry into the Strikes and Riots in Freetown,* p. 36.

19. *Shekpendeh,* 23 October 1958.

20. *Shekpendeh,* 11 October 1958.

21. *House of Representatives Debates, Session 1957-58* (5 November 1957), p. 73.

22. *Report of the Sierra Leone Police Force for the Year 1958* (Freetown: Government Printer, 1959), p. 4.

23. *Protectorate Assembly, Proceedings of the Eighth Meeting at Bo, 17th, 19th, 20th, 22nd and 23rd October, 1951* (22 October 1951), p. 51.

24. *Daily Mail,* 23 September 1963.

25. *Statement of the Sierra Leone Government on the Report of the Commission of Inquiry into Disturbances in the Provinces* (1956), p. 7.

26. *Daily Mail,* 16 January 1959.

27. *Daily Mail,* 7 March 1959. Cotay's statement was in the form of an appeal to Britain to continue financing the RSLMF after independence on the grounds it was primarily there to benefit British interests. This naturally produced quite a furor in Sierra Leone since Cotay's statement was taken by many as an affront to the country's pending sovereignty.

28. Ibid., emphasis supplied.

29. *Treasury Minute* dated 15th July 1959, relative to the Gift of Tower Hill Barracks, Sierra Leone.

30. Interview with Julius Cole, former Secretary-General of the SLPP, February 1970.

31. *West Africa,* 10 January 1959.

32. W. F. Gutteridge, *Military Institutions and Power in New States* (New York: Frederick A. Praeger, 1965), p. 39.

33. *Shekpendeh,* 11 December 1959.

34. *Report of the Sierra Leone Constitutional Conference: 1960* (Freetown: Government Printer, 1960), p. 10.

35. These rumors prompted an official government statement to the effect that the army was conducting normal training maneuvers in districts adjacent to the border. The Guinean consul in Freetown denied reports of troop movements in his country, claiming that certain elements "do not wish to see Guinea and Sierra Leone in close brotherly embrace." In November, however, Sékou Touré denounced what he termed "anti-Guinea moves in the surrounding territories of Sierra Leone, Portugeuse Guinea and Senegal," claiming that military bases were being constructed in

all three countries. Three weeks later, the Guinean president paid an official visit to Freetown, apparently to attempt to resolve his differences with Sir Milton. Throughout the latter half of the 1960s and into the early 1970s, Sékou Touré would play a significant role in Sierra Leone's civil-military relations.

36. As quoted in Cartwright, *Politics in Sierra Leone*, p. 135.

37. Colonel A. Haywood and Brigadier F.A.S. Clarke, *The History of the Royal West African Frontier Force* (Aldershot: Gale and Polden, Ltd. 1964), p. 483.

38. *Review of Government Departments during 1960* (Freetown: Government Printer, 1961), p. 63.

39. Haywood and Clarke, *Royal West African Frontier Force*, p. 483.

## 3. THE ARMY UNDER SIR MILTON MARGAI

1. *Shekpendeh*, 28 March 1961.

2. Ibid.

3. Samuel Huntington notes that while praetorianism usually refers to the intervention of the military in politics, a "praetorian society" is generally one in which many diverse social forces become politicized. Thus, in such a society, "the wealthy bribe; students riot; workers strike; mobs demonstrate; and the military coup." See Huntington, *Political Order in Changing Societies*, p. 196.

4. The Queen conferred the title of "Royal" on the Sierra Leone Battalion of the RWAFF in October 1959, and she remained the nominal Commander-in-Chief through her representative in Freetown, the governor-general.

5. *House of Representatives Debates, Session 1962-63, II* (November 29, 1962), col. 90. Sierra Leone became the 100th member of the United Nations on 27 September 1961.

6. In June 1962, the government announced that it would not sign a defense pact with Great Britain. The Nigerian abrogation of its defense pact unquestionably influenced Sierra Leone's decision.

7. Zartman has noted that interstate warfare is relatively uncommon in Western Africa because few governments have yet "deemed their goals so important or so pressing as to warrant military measures, nor have they considered such measures to be more effective or more economical than alternative means." See I. William Zartman, *International Relations in the New Africa* (Englewood Cliffs, N.J.: Prentice-Hall, Inc., 1966), p. 91.

8. *West Africa*, 6 January 1962.

9. *African Vanguard*, 24 January 1962.

10. David W. Wainhouse et al., *National Support of International Peace Keeping and Peace Observation Operations, Volume IV, Background Papers, ACDA/IR-161*, prepared for the U.S. Arms Control and Disarmament Agency by the Washington Center of Foreign Policy Research, School of Advanced International Studies, Johns Hopkins University, February 1970, p. 312.

11. Sierra Leone's only casualty in the Congo operation occurred when a member of the contingent was killed in a traffic accident in March 1962.

12. Miners, *The Nigerian Army*, p. 112.

13. *Daily Mail*, 6 May 1962.

14. *Daily Mail*, 8 February 1962.

15. *Speech from the Throne Delivered by His Excellency Sir Henry Lightfoot-Boston, G.C.M.G., J.P. on the occasion of the State Opening of the Fourth Session of the Second Parliament, March 23rd, 1965*, p. 10.

16. "Report of the Currency Conversion of the Bank of Sierra Leone," mimeographed (Freetown: n.d.), p. 1.

17. *House of Representatives Debates, Session 1962-63, II* (December 4, 1962), col. 239.

18. One of these, Lieutenant P. D. Green, resigned from the army in June 1965.

19. *Daily Mail,* 13 October 1959.

20. See *The Staff List* (Freetown: Government Printer, 1960). See also *Army Orders No. 1 of 1965, Royal Sierra Leone Military Forces, November 16, 1965* (Freetown: Government Printing Office, 1965), p. 58.

21. See the *Sierra Leone Gazette,* 5 January 1961.

22. Thomas Hodgkin, *Nationalism in Colonial Africa* (New York: New York University Press, 1957), pp. 156-157.

23. Kilson, *Political Change in a West African State,* p. 234.

24. *West Africa,* 25 January 1964.

25. William Gutteridge, *The Military in African Politics* (London: Methuen & Co., Ltd., 1969), p. 18.

26. Donald Horowitz, "Multiracial Politics in the New States: Toward a Theory of Conflict" in *Issues in Comparative Politics,* eds. Robert J. Jackson and Michael B. Stein (New York: St. Martin's Press, 1971), p. 173.

27. *House of Representatives Debates, Session 1962-63 II* (December 4, 1962), col. 239.

28. Just prior to independence, all of the opposition parties joined with the SLPP to form a "united front." Doyle Sumner and Gideon Dickson-Thomas in separate interviews with John Cartwright, July 1968.

29. Interview with a former senior member of Sir Albert Margai's cabinet, September 1970.

30. Interview with a former permanent secretary in the Ministry of Defence, January 1970. Lansana assumed command of the 1st Battalion in July 1963.

31. Data on the Sierra Leone army is derived from a variety of published sources including newspaper accounts, the parliamentary debates and the *Sierra Leone Gazette* which lists dates of commissioning and promotions. I am grateful to John N. Colas of Washington University (St. Louis) and The American University (Washington, D.C.) for assisting me in determining the ethnicity of individual officers.

32. Cartwright, *Politics in Sierra Leone,* p. 156.

33. As quoted in ibid., p. 137.

## 4. CIVILIAN CONTROL OF THE SIERRA LEONE MILITARY

1. *Daily Mail,* 23 June 1964.

2. *We Yone,* 4 July 1964. *We Yone* was the official voice of the opposition All Peoples Congress (APC).

3. Samuel Huntington, "Political Development and Political Decay," *World Politics,* 17 (1965), p. 394.

4. Brigadier Blackie continued to serve with the Royal Sierra Leone Military Forces in an advisory capacity although, by the time of the army takeover in March 1967, he was no longer in the country.

5. See on this point the testimony delivered at the Forster Commission of Inquiry during the period of military rule as reported in the *Daily Mail,* 8 June 1967.

6. *Daily Mail,* 2 June 1965.

7. One informant claims that Lansana ordered the discharge of the soldier (who

apparently had a satisfactory record) upon learning that he had "insulted" Lady Margai by attempting to overtake and pass her car while driving an army landrover on a Freetown street.

8. *House of Representatives Debates, Session 1965-1966* (March 30, 1965), col. 266.

9. Immanuel Wallerstein, *Africa: The Politics of Unity, An Analysis of a Contemporary Social Movement* (New York: Random House, 1967), p. 165.

10. *Think*, 19 June 1966.

11. *House of Representatives Debates, Session 1965-66* (March 23, 1965), col. 42.

12. From a senior army officer with connections in the Guinean officer corps.

13. Gershon Collier, *Sierra Leone, Experiment in Democracy in an African Nation* (New York: New York University Press, 1970), p. 119, emphasis supplied.

14. In the colonial period, the Bo Government School was usually reserved for the sons and nominees of paramount chiefs.

15. Cartwright, *Politics in Sierra Leone*, p. 166.

16. Interview with Gershon Collier, July 1971. Collier was Sierra Leone's first permanent representative and ambassador to the United Nations. In early 1967, Collier returned to Sierra Leone to serve as chief justice. After the military takeover, he resigned and returned to the United States.

17. Interview with a former Deputy Minister of the Interior, March 1970.

18. Court of Appeal No. 14/70, volume 16—*In the Court of Appeal for Sierra Leone Between—David Lansana and 11 others—Appellants and REGINA—Respondent.* "Appeal from the Judgment Decision of the Honorable Mr. Justice C.O.E. Cole, Acting Chief Justice—given at the Supreme Court, Freetown on Saturday the 18th day of April 1970." *Judge's Summing-Up*, p. 1010. All future references to the *Judge's Summing-Up* will cite the volume and page number. For a further explanation of the treason trial which followed the ouster of the National Reformation Council in April, 1968, see Chapter 11, note 4.

19. P. C. Lloyd, *Africa in Social Change* (Baltimore: Penquin Books, Inc., 1967), p. 152.

20. *Daily Mail*, 29 July 1967. The writer heard the Krio version of this particular story on several occasions.

21. One former cabinet minister explained in an interview how during the years of Sir Albert's rule, this minister did as much as possible to "help" a senior army officer to whom the former was related. This assistance included advancing the officer in question sufficient funds to purchase a new automobile in London. Interview, August 1970. Patron-client relations between members of the military and civilian elites are discussed in Luckham, "A Comparative Typology of Civil-Military Relations," p. 20.

22. Morris Janowitz, "The Military in the Political Development of New Nations," *Bulletin of the Atomic Scientists*, 20; 8 (1964), 9.

23. Robert Blake, "Great Britain: The Crimean War to the First World War," in *Soldiers and Governments, Nine Studies in Civil-Military Relations*, ed. Michael Howard (Bloomington: Indiana University Press, 1959), p. 27.

24. As quoted in Cartwright, *Politics in Sierra Leone*, p. 216.

25. Ibid., p. 217.

26. Ibid., p. 233.

27. The actual announcement to this effect was made on February 8, 1967, on the same day that the nation was informed of the discovery of the Bangura coup plot. Sir Albert stated that "there is no doubt that the majority of the people of Sierra Leone

indicated their support for the One Party Democratic System'' although ''the Government realized that a strong minority, both in the Western Area and the Provinces, were opposed to it.'' Because of this opposition, the prime minister continued, the proposal had been dropped altogether, and the ''present system of a multi-party State'' would be adhered to. See *The Sierra Leonean,* 9 February 1967.

28. See Supplement to the *Sierra Leone Gazette,* extraordinary vol. 97, no. 100 (22 December 1966).

29. Abel Jacob, ''Israel's Military Aid to Africa, 1960-66,'' *Journal of Modern African Studies,* 9 (1971), 179.

30. *Daily Mail,* 1 July 1968, emphasis supplied.

31. Samuel Huntington, *The Soldier and the State, The Theory and Politics of Civil-Military Relations* (New York: Vintage Books, 1957), p. 83.

32. *Daily Mail,* 1 July 1968.

33. *Daily Mail,* 20 March 1965.

34. A. R. Luckham, *The Nigerian Military: A Case Study in Institutional Breakdown* (Ph.D. diss., University of Chicago, 1970), p. 115. See also A.R. Luckham, *The Nigerian Military: A Sociological Analysis of Authority and Revolt, 1960-1967* (Cambridge, England: Cambridge University Press, 1971).

35. Ibid., p. 115.


## 5. DISINTEGRATION OF THE ARMY OFFICER CORPS

1. Reply by Major Charles Blake to cross-examination by David Lansana, *Judge's Summing-Up,* vol. 4, 753-754.

2. Interview with William Gutteridge, September 1969.

3. The Kenyan Government, for one, is apparently well aware of the relationship between the provision of adequate barrack accommodations and a contented military. The most recent Kenya Development Plan states: ''As far as the army is concerned, there is barely enough living accommodation and all the quarters for married Servicemen are of the old one- or two-roomed type . . . . Servicemen have to be housed in barracks, and married men cannot be separated for too long from their families because of lack of accommodation without their morale suffering. A discontented soldier is a bad soldier. There is, therefore, a heavy programme of providing living accomodation.'' (*Kenya Development Plan, 1970-1974* [Nairobi: Government Printer, 1969], p. 554).

4. *Financial Report for the Period July 1966 to June 1967* (Freetown: Government Printing Office, 1969), p. 35.

5. November 1970 interview with an ex-army captain who served on the National Reformation Council, the military government which ruled Sierra Leone from March 1967 through April 1968.

6. *Judge's Summing-Up,* vol. 4, 784.

7. See Miners, *The Nigerian Army,* pp. 90-92.

8. Internal security operations may also undermine army cohesion when one faction of the army sympathizes with those groups which constitute the object of such operations.

9. Interview with a former major in the Sierra Leone army, January 1971.

10. Collier, *Sierra Leone,* p. 119. The problem of boredom and lack of a raison d'être in the armed forces as a condition breeding a coup mentality was discussed recently by Malcolm Macfarlane writing on armed forces in Trinidad, Jamaica and Guyana. He argues that while the Jamaican and Guyanese forces were each given a

particular mission by the civilian government and thus stayed obedient to it, the Trinidad regiment had nothing significant to do and was overshadowed by the police; hence the mutiny in 1970 (and an earlier rampage in 1963). See "The Military in the Commonwealth Caribbean: Study in Comparative Institutionalization," Ph.D. diss., University of Western Ontario, 1974).

11. *Unity,* 22 January 1966.

12. Interview with Ibrahim Taqi, January 1970.

13. In January 1965, the Sierra Leone government arranged for the continued secondment of British officers with technical and administrative skills. The agreement was found to be necessary when the terms of a number of seconded British officers expired in late 1964. (See Public Notice 15, 1965, *Agreement between Sierra Leone and the United Kingdom of Great Britain and Northern Ireland Relating to Arrangements for Secondment of Personnel of the Armed Forces of the United Kingdom to Serve with the Royal Sierra Leone Military Forces, Freetown, January 21st, 1965*).

14. See note 9.

15. *Unity,* 5 March 1966.

16. *We Yone,* 26 March 1966.

17. Ibid.

18. Interview with Gershon Collier.

19. According to *West Africa,* 26 August 1961, Seray-Wurie compiled the best record in his class of 31 cadets at Kaduna.

20. Documented in an interview with one of three cabinet ministers recruited to deal with the army dispute, August 1970.

21. Turay, as we have noted, was deputy commandant and chief instructor at the Benguema Military Academy.

22. Interview with Julius Cole, October 1970.

23. Volume 1, Judge's *Summing-Up,* 582, emphasis supplied.

24. *Think,* 18 September 1966.

25. Interview with a former deputy minister, April 1970.

26. *We Yone,* 26 December 1966, emphasis supplied.

27. *We Yone,* 22 October 1966.

28. *Think,* 18 September 1966.

29. *We Yone,* 10 September 1966.

30. Janowitz, *Military in the Political Development of New Nations,* pp. 72-73.

## 6. COUPS PLOTS AND CORRUPTION: THE WANING INFLUENCE OF THE SIERRA LEONE PEOPLES PARTY

1. *The Sierra Leonean,* 9 February 1967.

2. W. Arthur Lewis, *Politics in West Africa* (New York: Oxford University Press, 1965), p. 13.

3. Bank of Sierra Leone, *Annual Report and Statement of Accounts for the Year Ended 31st December 1966,* p. 52.

4. Interview with Brian Quinn, February 1971. Mr. Quinn served as the IMF's resident representative in Freetown during the "stabilization program" imposed under Sir Albert Margai and later under the National Reformation Council.

5. Rattan J. Bhatia et al., "Stabilization Program in Sierra Leone," International Monetary Fund, *Staff Papers* (November 1969), p. 505.

6. *Report of the Dove-Edwin Commission of Inquiry into the Conduct of the*

*1967 General Elections in Sierra Leone and the Government Statement Thereon* (Freetown: Government Printing Office, 1967), p. 15.

7. According to the Forster Commission of Inquiry, Kai-Samba and Jusu-Sheriff used their office to acquire unlawful assets of Le 108.20 and Le 61 respectively. Clearly neither belonged in the same league as their party leader when it came to using public revenue for private gain. See *Report of the Forster Commission of Inquiry on Assets of Ex-Ministers and Ex-Deputy Ministers* (Freetown: Government Printing Office, 1968).

8. Kilson, *Political Change in a West African State,* p. 273 and Cartwright, *Politics in Sierra Leone,* pp. 125-137.

9. Cartwright, ibid., p. 201.

10. *We Yone,* which revealed details of the coup plot four days before the official government statement noted in its issue of February 4, 1967: "It is understood that the dissatisfaction in the army has nothing to do with politics but with the administration of the army. Brigadier Lansana has been charged by his fellow officers with crimes ranging from unbrotherly conduct to nepotism and tribalism."

11. As reported in *Unity,* 8 July 1970.

12. *Unity,* 3 March 1967, described Seray-Wurie as the man "who let the cat out of the bag."

13. Luttwak argues that the so-called "machine parties" which normally lack a base of mass support represent no threat to coupmakers. Thus, "even if the machine has a base of mass support, its leadership, being a coalition of local power structures without a national 'presence,' will not be able to mobilize it." In the case of Sierra Leone, however, cross-boundary civilian-military linkages between the SLPP "machine" and the armed forces, hampered the ability of conspiratorial groups to conduct their operations in secrecy and thus, at least in the case of the February 1967 coup plot, the bonds between SLPP "notables" and senior army officers permitted the ruling party to neutralize rebellious factions within the RSLMF. See Edward Luttwak, *Coup d'Etat, A Practical Handbook* (London: Allen Lane, The Penquin Press, 1968), pp. 130-134.

14. *We Yone,* 11 February 1967.

15. *Think,* 15 February 1967.

16. *Africa Research Bulletin,* 1-28 February 1967, p. 715.

17. *Judge's Summing-Up,* vol. 6, 1082-1084.

18. Arnold Payne, *The Peruvian Coup d'Etat of 1962: The Overthrow of Manuel Prado* (Washington, D.C.: Institute for the Comparative Study of Political Systems, 1968), p. 59. Martin C. Needler also notes that coups d'état in Latin America have increasingly occurred around election time. See Martin C. Needler, "Political Development and Military Intervention in Latin America," in *Reform and Revolution, Readings in Latin American Politics,* eds. Arpad von Lazar and Robert R. Kaufman (Boston: Allyn and Bacon, Inc., 1969), p. 237.

19. See for example, Cartwright, *Politics in Sierra Leone,* pp. 238-254; David Dalby, "The Military Takeover in Sierra Leone, 1967," *World Today,* 23 (August 1967), 354-360; Humphrey J. Fisher, "Elections and Coups in Sierra Leone, 1967," *Journal of Modern African Studies,* 7 (December 1969), 611-636; Christopher Allen, "Sierra Leone Politics Since Independence," *African Affairs,* 67 (October 1968), 305-329; Walter L. Barrows, "La Politique de l'armée in Sierra Leone," *Le Mois en Afrique,* 36 (December 1968), 54-64.

20. Barrows, ibid., p. 56.

21. See on this point, Dick Simpson, "Ethnic Conflict in Sierra Leone" in *The*

*Politics of Cultural Sub-Nationalism in Africa,* ed. Victor A. Olorunsola (New York: Anchor Books, 1972), pp. 153-188.

22. Cartwright, *Politics in Sierra Leone,* p. 248.
23. *Judge's Summing-up,* vol. 4, 710.
24. *Judge's Summing-Up,* vol. 4, 713.
25. *Judge's Summing-Up,* vol. 5, 884 and *Dove-Edwin Commission,* pp. 12-13.
26. *Dove-Edwin Commission,* p. 19.
27. *Judge's Summing-Up,* vol. 3, 496.
28. *Judge's Summing-Up,* vol. 2, 259.
29. Peter Tucker, the secretary to Sir Albert Margai, claimed in an interview with John Cartwright on August 10, 1968 that "the Army majors under Lansana were plotting to take power even before the election; it was Lansana who was holding them back."
30. *Judge's Summing-Up,* vol. 4, 710.
31. Interview with Major S. B. Jumu in Accra, February 1971.
32. The fact of army officers backing particular candidates in the general election produced at least one curious anomaly. David Lansana is said to have supported an independent, Dr. Kobba, against Sir Albert's favorite, Maigore Kallon, in Kailahun Central (Lansana's home constituency). When news of Kallon's unopposed return reached the army commander, he is reported to have flown into a rage. According to Decalo, during the March 1970 general elections in Dahomey which produced the ill-fated "triumvirate" experiment, military factions participated openly in illicit voting activities "on the side of their favored candidate." See Samuel Decalo, "Regionalism, Politics and the Military in Dahomey," *Journal of Developing Areas,* 7 (April 1973), 470.
33. *Judge's Summing-Up,* vol. 4, 752.

## 7. COUPS AND COUNTERCOUPS: THE FALL OF THE SLPP.

1. Michael F. Lofchie, "The Uganda Coup—Class Action by the Military," *Journal of Modern African Studies,* 10 (1972), 28.
2. *Daily Mail,* 24 March 1967.
3. On SLPP methods of falsifying election returns, see Christopher Allen, "Sierra Leone Politics Since Independence," p. 320.
4. *Dove-Edwin Commission,* p. 14.
5. I am grateful to Professor D. Owen of Fourah Bay College who monitored the radio broadcasts in the days preceding the military takeover and who provided this writer with data on the election results.
6. *Dove-Edwin Commission,* p. 24.
7. Cartwright, *Politics in Sierra Leone,* p. 253.
8. Among the qualities Luttwak considers essential to the successful execution of a coup d'état is: "instant personnel management at the radio-television station in order to persuade its technical staff to cooperate with . . . " the army. See Luttwak, *Coup d'Etat,* pp. 148-149.
9. *Judge's Summing-Up,* vol. 2, p. 274.
10. *Judge's Summing-Up,* vol. 3, p. 498.
11. *Unity,* 20 March 1967.
12. APC supporters, particularly those who belong to the party's youth league, often wear red tee-shirts to indicate their loyalties.

13. *Judge's Summing-Up*, vol. 5, p. 856. The Flagstaff guards were under the command of a Mende lieutenant, Emile Gbassa.

14. *Judge's Summing-Up*, vol. 5, p. 984.

15. *Judge's Summing-Up*, vol. 2, p. 284.

16. *Dove-Edwin Commission*, p. 18.

17. *Judge's Summing-Up*, vol. 2, p. 286.

18. Dr. Sarif Easmon, *Sierra Leone General Elections: Constitutional Crisis* (mimeo: n.d.), p. 1.

19. In early February, Lieutenant Norman, a Mende, became Sir Henry's aide-de-camp after the arrest of Captain F.L.M. Jawara, a northerner. Prior to serving under Sir Henry, Norman had been Lansana's personal driver and second in command of "B" company. He was thus a good choice to do Lansana's bidding at State House.

20. As quoted in *Think*, 21 March 1967.

21. The exact figures were: 286,585 for the APC; 231,567 for the SLPP; 129,429 for the Independents.

22. *Dove-Edwin Commission*, p. 24.

23. *Judge's Summing-Up*, vol. 2, p. 316.

24. *Judge's Summing-Up*, vol. 6, p. 1027, emphasis supplied.

25. *Dove-Edwin Commission*, p. 16.

26. Interview with Sembu Forna, November 3, 1970. Forna is now a minister in the APC government under Siaka Stevens.

27. *Judge's Summing-Up*, vol. 3, p. 649.

28. Interview with Gershon Collier.

29. In 1967, the deputy commissioner of police was an Englishman and the assistant commissioner of police, a Temne.

30. *Judge's Summing-Up*, vol. 5, p. 914.

31. *Judge's Summing-Up*, vol. 3, p. 514.

32. *Judge's Summing-Up*, vol. 4, p. 653.

33. See Peter Barker, *Operation Cold Chop: The Coup that Toppled Nkrumah*. (Accra: Ghana Publishing Corporation, 1969), pp. 31 and 117.

34. *Judge's Summing-Up*, vol. 2, p. 185.

35. *Daily Mail*, 22 March 1967.

36. *Unity*, 23 March 1967.

37. In reply to a question in the House of Representatives in July 1968, Siaka Stevens stated that nine deaths were recorded in the period March 21-23, 1967 (*Daily Mail*, 18 July 1968). Earlier in an address to the nation, the APC prime minister claimed that "some forty peaceful citizens were killed in cold blood," during Lansana's takeover (*Daily Mail*, 1 June 1968).

38. While votes were being counted, a number of paramount chiefs were taken at gunpoint to Sir Albert's Freetown residence and told to declare for the SLPP.

39. Transcribed from the author's tape recording of Lansana's radio broadcast.

40. Christopher Clapham, "The Context of African Political Thought" in *Journal of Modern African Studies*, 8:1 (April 1970), pp. 12-13.

41. Finer, *The Man on Horseback*, p. 171.

42. Transcribed from the author's tape recording of Leigh's radio broadcast.

43. *Judge's Summing-Up*, vol. 4, p. 715.

44. Ibid., p. 716.

45. Interview with S.B. Jumu.

46. *Judge's Summing-Up*, vol. 4, p. 777.

47. Interview with S.B. Jumu.

48. *Judge's Summing-Up*, vol. 4, p. 719.

49. Ibid.

50. *Judge's Summing-Up,* vol. 3, p. 631.

51. Transcribed from the author's tape recording of Blake's radio broadcast.

52. Valerie P. Bennett, *The Foundations of Civil-Military Relations in Ghana,* p. 11.

53. Ibid., p. 290.

54. *New Statesman,* 31 March 1967, p. 428, emphasis supplied.

55. *Commission of Inquiry into the Strikes and Riots in Freetown,* p. 58.

56. Robert Price, "Military Officers and Political Leadership: The Ghanaian Case," *Comparative Politics,* 3 (April 1971), 362-363.

## 8. THE NATIONAL REFORMATION COUNCIL ASSUMES OFFICE

1. *Proclamation for the Interim Administration of Sierra Leone by a National Reformation Council,* in *Sierra Leone Gazette,* 25 March 1967.

2. Transcribed from a tape recording of the NRC broadcast of March 25. According to Section 2(1) of the NRC Proclamation, "All of the provisions of the Constitution of Sierra Leone 1961, which came into operation on the 27th of April 1961, which are inconsistent or in conflict with this proclamation or any law made hereunder shall be deemed to have been suspended with effect from the 23rd day of March 1967." On 31 March 1967, the NRC issued a decree which permitted the publication of newspapers provided certain rigid conditions were met. Under the terms of the decree, no newspaper could make any references to the banned SLPP and APC. Statements in any way critical of the NRC or of any of its members were also forbidden. No newspaper, furthermore, could publish "any statement, rumour or report" likely "to cause fear or alarm to the public or to disturb the public peace." The law would also be invoked against any newspaper publishing reports which might "encourage or promote or stir up feelings of ill-will and hostility between different tribes or nationalities or between persons of different religious faiths in Sierra Leone." The *Daily Mail* continued to operate throughout the life of the military regime. See NRC Law No. 4, *The Newspaper Law* (1967), dated March 31, 1967.

3. A cartoon in the *London Times* of 29 March 1967 showed a group of army officers, members of a newly formed military government, gathered around a table. One officer is heard to exclaim: "Gentlemen, the first item on the agenda is to decide who is to be leader today."

4. *West Africa,* 15 April 1967.

5. After Lansana, Bangura, and Genda, Juxon-Smith was the next most senior officer in the RSLMF; he had been promoted to lieutenant colonel in June 1966.

6. See Juxon-Smith's testimony during his trial on charges of treason, as reported in *Unity,* 2 July 1970.

7. *West Africa,* 15 April 1967.

8. It will be recalled that Major Turay had been sent into exile the previous year for his anti-Lansana activities.

9. See a letter reported to have been written by Davidson Nicol to the NRC on March 24, 1967 as reprinted in *The Express* (Freetown), 14 October 1968.

10. Interview with a former permanent secretary with close connections to the SLPP. July 1970.

11. *London Times,* 29 March 1967. The tribal and regional alignment of the National Reformation Council was now as follows:

Lieutenant-Colonel Andrew T. Juxon-Smith (Creole/Sherbro—Western Area)

Police Commissioner Leslie William Leigh (Susu/Liberian—Western Area)
Assistant Commissioner of Police Alpha Kamara (Temne—Northern Province)
Major Abdul Rahman Turay (Temne—Northern Province)
Major Sandi Bockarie Jumu (Mende—Southern Province)
Major Augustine Charles Blake (Sherbro—Southern Province)
Major Bockarie Kai-Samba (Mende—Eastern Province)
Captain Sahr James Foyah (Kissi—Eastern Province)

Foyah was appointed the eighth member of the NRC in early April. He was initially designated a member "with special responsibility in the N.R.C. Secretariat"; however, he later took up duties in the Department of the Interior.

12. This story was confirmed by several well-placed sources.

13. *Judge's Summing-Up,* vol. 4, p. 721.

14. Turay was a logical choice for this post for, at the time of his being recalled from England, he was pursuing a degree course at Cambridge University.

15. Lucian W. Pye, "The Legitimacy Crisis," in *Crises and Sequences in Political Development,* ed. Leonard Binder et al. (Princeton, New Jersey: Princeton University Press, 1971), p. 144.

16. *London Times,* 29 March 1967.

17. Kenneth Grundy, *Conflicting Images of the Military in Africa* (Nairobi: East African Publishing House, 1968), pp. 15-23.

18. Grundy, *Conflicting Images,* pp. 15-16.

19. Transcribed from a tape recording of a speech made by the NRC chairman upon his arrival at Lungi Airport on March 28.

20. *Daily Mail,* 29 March 1967.

21. From a transcript in the possession of Professor Humphrey Fisher of the School of Oriental and African Studies, University of London. I am grateful to Professor Fisher for providing me with transcripts of Juxon-Smith's press conferences and other important speeches.

22. *Daily Mail,* 1 April 1967.

23. Fisher transcripts, see note 21.

24. National Reformation Council, *Decree 15.*

25. National Reformation Council, *Decree 23.*

26. As quoted from a memorandum entitled "Mammy Queens and Chiefdom Councils," dated May 20, 1967, from the Provincial Commissioner, Northern Province, to the Secretary, Department of the Interior.

27. *NRC Directive to the Provincial Commissioners,* dated July 7, 1967.

28. *NRC Directive to the Provincial Commissioners,* dated April 5, 1967.

29. *Daily Mail,* 17 October 1967. In areas with large so-called "stranger" populations, as in Freetown where a large number of Fulas from Guinea work as petty traders, both the colonial administration and its successor governments have often appointed a tribal headman who performs political and quasi-judicial functions.

30. Huntington, *Political Order in Changing Societies,* pp. 245-246.

31. Anton A. Bebler, "Military Rule in Africa (Dahomey, Ghana, Sierra Leone, and Mali)" (Ph.D. diss., University of Pennsylvania, 1971), p. 48.

32. As quoted in Martin J. Dent, "The Military and Politics: A Study of the Relation between the Army and the Political Process in Nigeria," in *African Affairs* no. 3, ed. Kenneth Kirkwood (St. Antony's Papers, no. 21) (London: Oxford University Press, 1969), p. 121.

33. *Daily Mail,* 29 July 1967.

34. *Daily Mail,* 27 March 1967.

35. Robert E. Dowse, "The Military and Political Development," in *Politics and*

*Change in Developing Countries,* ed. Colin Leys (London: Cambridge University Press, 1969), p. 231.

36. Kwame Nkrumah, *Class Struggle in Africa* (London: Panaf Books Ltd., 1970), p. 42.

37. G. Glentworth and I. Hancock, "Obote and Amin: Change and Continuity in Modern Uganda Politics," *African Affairs,* 72 (1973), 253.

38. *Daily Mail,* 9 August 1967.

39. As quoted in a letter from the provincial commissioner, Northern Province, to the district commissioner, Bombali District, dated June 2, 1967.

40. *The Sierra Leonean,* 27 April 1967.

41. Brief prepared for the visit of Major Sandi B. Jumu to the Eastern Province (located in the files of the office of the Provincial Commissioner, Kenema), n.d.

42. Interview with a former member of the NRC, November 1970. It should be noted here that chiefdom disputes for many years have been an important feature of rural politics in Sierra Leone. Walter Barrows has studied the impact of national, two-party politics upon the institution of chieftaincy in the Kenema district of Mendeland. According to Barrows, conflicts between several families with dynastic claims to rule and between paramount chiefs and certain "out" groups in a particular chiefdom have often been exploited by the national parties. Thus, just as the Paramount Chief "is pressured to support the party in power, the opposition faction within his chiefdom is inclined toward rival parties."

Victor Minikin has drawn precisely the same conclusions in an analysis of political participation in the Samu and Soa chiefdoms. Based on his observations, Minikin found that when the SLPP was in power from 1951 to 1967 it recruited traditional authorities as its allies or brokers in the provinces, while rival parties such as the APC and the Kono Progressive Movement "modelled themselves on similar lines, basing their organization on the chiefdoms also, but usually working through the enemies of the chiefs." The APC has not really modified this technique since it assumed office in April 1968 following the overthrow of the National Reformation Council; but with the complete atrophy of the SLPP in recent years and the emergence of a defacto, one-party system in Sierra Leone, the situation has undoubtedly changed. Local chiefdom disputes may no longer be the appropriate vehicle for translating national political issues into a "language" that the rural population can readily understand. See Walter L. Barrows, The Position of the Contemporary Mende Chief, unpublished paper, 1971; Walter L. Barrows, *Grassroots Politics in an African State: Integration and Development in Sierra Leone* (New York: Africana Publishing Company, 1975); and Victor Minikin, "Indirect Political Participation in Two Sierra Leone Chiefdoms," *Journal of Modern African Studies,* 11 (1973), p. 130.

43. As quoted in a letter from the provincial commissioner, Southern Province, to the secretary, Department of the Interior, dated July 25, 1967.

44. Advisory Council No. 6, *Resume of Minutes of the Advisory Council held in Parliament Chambers from 18th to 21st September 1967, Appendix C,* p. 1.

45. Akinsola Akiwowo, "Performance of the Military Government in Nigeria: 1966 to 1970" (Draft of the paper submitted to the Working Party on Armed Forces and Society, 7th World Congress of Sociology, September 14-19, Varna, Bulgaria, 1970), p. 17.

46. Jon Kraus, "Ghana, 1966" in William G. Andrews and Uri Ra'anan, *The Politics of the Coup d'Etat—Five Case Studies* (New York: Van Nostrand, 1969), p. 123.

47. Pinkney, *Ghana Under Military Rule,* p. 39.

48. In an independence anniversary message, Juxon-Smith clearly erred when he described the National Advisory Council as a "unique venture in the history of military regimes wherein a group of civilians from all over the country, experts in various fields, have been invited to get together, to deliberate and advise us on the running of the government of this country." *The Sierra Leonean,* 27 April 1967.

49. *Daily Mail,* 31 March 1967.

50. Interviews with Dr. Sarif Easmon, February 1970 and Sembu Forna, November 1970.

51. Anyone closely associated with Sir Albert Margai, especially any of the "Flagstaff House boys," were not invited to join the advisory council.

52. Forster Commission, p. 44.

53. *Daily Mail,* 15 and 16 August, 1967.

54. *Daily Mail,* 27 July 1967.

55. Ibid., 30 June 1967.

56. *The Sierra Leonean,* 18 May 1967.

57. National Reformation Council, *Decree 65.*

58. B.J. Dudley, "The Military and Politics in Nigeria: Some Reflections" in *Military Professions and Military Regimes: Commitments and Conflicts,* ed. J. van Doorn, p. 216.

59. Bebler, *Military Rule in Africa,* p. 84.

60. Gutteridge, *The Military in African Politics,* p. 155.

## 9. OPPOSITION TO THE NATIONAL REFORMATION COUNCIL

1. Claude E. Welch, Jr., "The African Military and Political Development" in *The Military and Modernization,* ed. Henry Bienen (Chicago: Aldine-Atherton, 1971), p. 228.

2. One possible exception to this rule—Mobutu Sese Seko and Zaire's MPR, founded in April 1967.

3. "Memorandum from the Sierra Leone Bar Association," mimeographed (Freetown, April 3, 1967). The Sierra Leone Bar Association has traditionally been dominated by Freetown Creoles and was unquestionably pro-APC.

4. "Memorandum delivered to the NRC on Friday, March 31, 1967, by the Teaching Staff of Fourah Bay College," mimeographed (Freetown).

5. "An Open Letter from Members of the Senior Staff of Fourah Bay College to the National Reformation Council," mimeographed (Freetown, April 18, 1967).

6. "Memorandum from the Senior Staff, Njala University College, to the Chairman of the National Reformation Council," mimeographed (Njala: May 1, 1967).

7. *Unity,* 7 April 1967.

8. *Daily Mail,* 12 April 1967. In a press conference, Juxon-Smith claimed that copies of the bar association memorandum had been discovered as far away as Kono in the Eastern Province.

9. Interview with Mrs. Nancy Steele, secretary of the National Congress of Sierra Leone Women (affiliated with the APC), 17 May 1970 and *Unity,* 29 April 1967.

10. *Daily Mail,* 2 May 1967.

11. "Introduction to the College Annual Report of the Principal," mimeographed (Fourah Bay College, University of Sierra Leone: September 1966-August 1967).

12. At the time of the swearing-in of the judges, Jones expressed doubts as to the legality of the whole NRC venture and later on demanded that the army hand over power to the APC without further delay.

13. Advisory Council no. 6, Appendix C, p. 2, emphasis supplied.

14. *Judge's Summing-Up,* vol. 4, p. 654.

15. Interview with a former army captain who served in the NRC's Department of Interior, December 1970.

16. *Judge's Summing-Up,* vol. 4, p. 656.

17. See note 15.

18. Interview with a former secretary-general in the NRC Secretariat, April 1970.

19. In April 1967, Major Blake was promoted to lieutenant-colonel and Juxon-Smith became a full colonel. In late July, more promotions ensued. Jumu and Kai-Samba achieved the rank of lieutenant-colonel, Blake became a full colonel, and Juxon-Smith announced that he was a brigadier—all of this after Blake had initially pledged not "to enchance the social standard" of the NRC members.

20. Interview with a former member of the NRC, September 1970.

21. Ibid.

22. On April 26, 1967, the eight army officers detained on February 8 in connection with the coup plot were released. Seven were reinstated in the army at their former rank and seniority. Colonel Bangura was retired from the army and sent off to Washington to serve as counselor and head of Chancery. Lansana had been released somewhat earlier and became consul-general at the Sierra Leone Mission in New York.

23. *Unity,* 28 July 1970.

24. Interview with a junior officer who served on the NRC, January 1970.

25. On June 16, Major Turay announced that he was quitting the NRC in order to resume his studies at Cambridge. Turay promised to give the council "his unflagging support and loyalty until such time as that body ceases to be the government of this country." In actuality, Turay had long since become disenchanted with the antics of the NRC chairman and had decided to bail out of what he regarded as a losing proposition. On June 29, Major Koroma succeeded Turay as the NRC member with responsibility for the Department of Education.

26. Interview with an army officer who served on one of the commissions of inquiry established by the military government, February 1970.

27. Pinkney, *Ghana Under Military Rule,* p. 59.

28. *Statement on the Budget for 1967/68, Broadcast by Colonel A. T. Juxon-Smith, Chairman, National Reformation Council on 30th June 1967* (Freetown: Government Printer, 1967), p. 3.

29. Interview with Brian Quinn, February 1971.

30. Interview with S. B. Jumu, January 1971.

31. *Daily Mail,* 27 March 1967.

32. From transcripts provided by Humphrey Fisher.

33. Interview with a former secretary, Department of the Interior under the NRC, August 1970.

34. Interview with a former secretary-general in the NRC Secretariat, June 1970. On June 8, the NRC created a second post of secretary-general in the Secretariat. Peter Tucker was designated secretary-general I and Mr. A. K. Hyde, secretary-general II. Tucker was later dismissed, and Hyde became the Sierra Leone ambassador in Washington. In January 1968, G.L.V. Williams became secretary-general I and M. L. Sidique, secretary-general II.

35. Memorandum from the NRC Secretariat: "Complaints of Disrespectful Behavior on the part of Provincial Administrative Officers," dated April 24, 1967.

36. "NRC Directive on Misbehavior in the Civil Service," dated August 5, 1967.

37. See note 35.

38. "NRC Directive," dated March 5, 1967.
39. Interview with a former district commissioner in the Eastern Province, October 1970.
40. See note 33.
41. See note 34.
42. Interview with a former provincial commissioner in the Northern Province, July 1970.
43. There are already indications from the experience of other countries that army officers and civil servants may lose their initial fondness for one another. Several months after the January 1972 coup in Ghana, there were already "many complaints from the Ghanaian public service against treatment meted out to them by members of the armed forces; . . . public servants who were late to work were 'drilled,' a humiliation to which reductions in rent on government bungalows and the reintroduction of the vehicle-maintenance allowance does not reconcile them." *Africa Report,* May 1972, p. 6. Daalder, for one, has described some of the strains which can develop within the military-civilian administrative alliance: "Both the range and mass of bureaucratic duties make it impossible for the military to replace the civilian administrators completely. The most they can do, therefore, is to insert military personnel into civilian offices, to supervise and control their performance. But this adds a new layer in government. It complicates the channels of communication. It may decrease the rapidity by which decisions can be taken on all but the highest level. Confusion may result." See H. Daalder, *The Role of the Military in the Emerging Countries* (The Hague: Mouton, 1962), p. 22.
44. *The Freetown Bulletin,* mimeographed and distributed anonymously in mid-April 1967.
45. Advisory Council, "Terms of Reference," mimeographed, n.d.
46. Advisory Council, no. 5 *Resume of Minutes of the Advisory Council held in Parliament Chambers from August 21st to 29th, 1967,* Appendix B and C, mimeographed.
47. Ibid., Appendix D.
48. "Memorandum from the Chairman of the National Reformation Council to the National Advisory Council," mimeographed, n.d.
49. Ibid.
50. Interview with F. Minah, October 1970. Minah served on the National Advisory Council.
51. Advisory Council, no. 5, p. 5.
52. Advisory Council, no. 6, Appendix C, p. 2.

## 10. THE NRC AND THE POLITICS OF DEMILITARIZATION

1. Major-General A. K. Ocran, *A Myth is Broken* (London: Longmans, Green & Co. Ltd., 1968), p. 94.
2. *West Africa,* 16 July 1973.
3. Amos Perlmutter, "The Praetorian State and the Praetorian Army," *Comparative Politics,* 1 (1969), 392.
4. *Unity,* 27 April 1967.
5. *The Sierra Leonean,* 8 June 1967.
6. Ibid., 8 June 1967.
7. *Daily Mail,* 24 August 1967.
8. *London Times,* 29 March 1967.
9. Claude E. Welch, Jr., "Back to the Barracks—Or, Hamlet Revisited" (unpublished manuscript, n.d.), p. 13.

10. *Daily Mail*, 2 May 1967.

11. "Stabilization in Sierra Leone," *IMF Staff Papers* (November 1969), p. 512.

12. Bank of Sierra Leone, *Annual Report and Statement of Accounts for the Year ended 31st December 1967*, p. 14.

13. *Statement on the Budget for 1967/69, Broadcast Speech by Col. A. T. Juxon-Smith*, p. 5.

14. Bank of Sierra Leone, *Annual Report and Statement of Accounts for the Year ended 31st December 1968*, p. 9.

15. *The State of the Nation—Address Delivered by the Chairman, National Reformation Council, Brigadier A. T. Juxon-Smith on the occasion of the Opening Session of the Civilian Rule Committee on Wednesday, 21st February 1968* (Freetown: Government Printer, 1968), p. 8.

16. Ibid., p. 9, emphasis supplied.

17. *Report of the meeting of Paramount Chiefs held in Bo*, March 25, 1968 (located in the files of the Bo District Office).

18. *Daily Mail*, 11 March 1968.

19. *Dove-Edwin Commission*, p. 1. The membership of the commission included Mr. Justice G. F. Dove-Edwin, Captain T. W. Caulker of the Sierra Leone army, and Mr. T. M. Kessebeh, a superintendent of police.

20. Ibid., p. 19.

21. Ibid., emphasis supplied.

22. "Statement of the National Reformation Council on the Report of the Commission Appointed to Inquire into the Conduct of the Last General Elections Held on the 17th and 21st Days of March, 1967," *Dove-Edwin Commission*, pp. 1-5.

23. *Confidential Report of the National Advisory Council to the Chairman of the NRC*, mimeographed, September 21, 1967.

24. Interview with Sembu Forna, November 1970.

25. See the letter from Siaka Stevens to the NRC, dated October 19, 1967; see also the letter from Sir Henry Lightfoot-Boston to the Chairman of the NRC, dated October 9, 1967.

26. Siaka P. Stevens, *Statement on the National Reformation Council*, mimeographed (London: November 17, 1967).

27. As quoted in *The State of the Nation*, p. 10.

28. Commissioner Leigh stated during the treason trial that it was he who originated the idea of setting up a "Citizens Committee" to consider how the NRC might extricate itself from direct military rule. See *Judge's Summing-Up*, vol. 4, p. 658.

29. *The State of the Nation*, p. 10. The secretary to the Civilian Rule Committee, V. E. Younge, believed that the committee was made cumbersome in size in order to "ensure its failure" as there would be "too much disagreement." Interview with V. E. Younge, January 1970.

30. Like its predecessor, the National Advisory Council, the Civilian Rule Committee met in the Parliament Building. None of the meetings were open to the public.

31. As quoted in the *Minutes of the Meeting of the Civilian Rule Committee held on Wednesday, February 21st, 1968*, mimeographed.

32. *Memorandum Submitted Jointly by the Representatives of the All Peoples Congress and the Sierra Leone Peoples Party, February 21st, 1968*, mimeographed, emphasis supplied.

33. Ibid.

34. *Minutes of the Meeting of the Civilian Rule Committee held on Monday, February 23rd, 1968*, mimeographed.

35. *Minutes of the Meeting of the Civilian Rule Committee held on Monday, February 26th, 1968,* mimeographed.

36. *Minutes of the Meeting of the Civilian Rule Committee held on Friday, March 1st, 1968,* Appendix A, mimeographed.

37. Interview with S. B. Marah, October 1970. Marah served as one of the six SLPP representatives on the Civilian Rule Committee.

38. *Report of the Civilian Rule Committee Appointed by the National Reformation Council, dated March 20th 1968,* mimeographed.

39. During the first Margai government, the APC was often associated with Guinea partly because of Sir Milton's coolness toward political developments in that country and partly because of the APC's socialist pretensions. In October 1962, for example, the APC was accused of receiving substantial Soviet aid during the recent general elections, some of it in the form of weapons and landrovers channelled through Guinea. When Sir Albert came to power, he cultivated the friendship of the Guinean president in order to boost his (Sir Albert's) radical image abroad; and the APC-Guinean links began to turn sour.

40. While in London, Stevens met with a number of MPs in an attempt to persuade the British government to disavow its support for the NRC and instead to recognize the APC's claim that it was the "legitimate government" of Sierra Leone.

41. Stevens is said to have been extremely embittered by Sékou Touré's impromptu efforts to save the Margai regime and thus was only persuaded at the last minute to join the other APC sympathizers in Conakry.

42. According to Ibrahim Taqi, the NRC would not grant Stevens safe passage back to Freetown so he was unable to attend sessions of the Civilian Rule Committee. Stevens, however, did correspond with the committee. See "Letter from Siaka Stevens to the Civilian Rule Committee," dated February 21, 1968. Interview with Ibrahim Taqi, September 1970.

43. Davidson Nicol, "Introduction to the Annual Report," *Annual Report, 1967-1968* (Freetown: University of Sierra Leone, Fourah Bay College, 1968).

44. As quoted in the *Minutes of the Meeting of the Civilian Rule Committee held on Thursday, February 29th, 1968,* mimeographed.

45. Ibid.

46. Interview with V. E. Younge.

47. As appears to be the case, for example, in Uganda.

48. *Daily Mail,* March 25, 1968.

49. Interview with a senior army officer, October 1970.

50. Ibid.

51. *Judge's Summing-Up,* vol. 4, p. 658.

52. On January 16, 1968, Captain F. Jawara replaced Captain D.D.K. Vandi as "Member of the NRC with special responsibility in the Secretariat." According to the *Daily Mail* of January 17, 1968, "This was in keeping with the NRC policy of bringing junior officers into the NRC for three month periods to enable them to acquire insights into the working of the council and the secretariat." Jawara, it will be remembered, was one of the eight officers arrested on February 8, 1967 when Sir Albert was still in power.

53. *Judge's Summing-Up,* vol. 4, p. 660.

54. On June 6, 1968, *Unity* published what it claimed were secret minutes of a meeting of junior and senior army officers held at the Wilberforce Officer's Mess on February 2, 1968. No one has ever disputed the authenticity of these minutes.

55. *Judge's Summing-Up,* vol. 4, p. 660.

56. *Judge's Summing-Up,* vol. 4, p. 725.

57. *Judge's Summing-Up,* vol. 4, p. 662.

58. First, *The Barrel of a Gun,* p. 5.

59. Lieutenant Colonel Jumu received an early warning of the impending mutiny and managed to slip across the border into Liberia. He eventually made his way to Ghana. Since that time, attempts by the APC to extradite Jumu have ended in failure.

60. According to a senior army officer.

61. *West Africa,* 4 May 1968.

62. *Judge's Summing-Up,* vol. 4, p. 662.

63. *Daily Mail,* 19 April 1968.

64. Ali A. Mazrui, *Violence and Thought, Essays on Social Tensions in Africa* (London: Longmans, Green & Co. Ltd., 1969), p. 21, emphasis supplied.

65. Genda had been appointed Sierra Leone's ambassador to Liberia in August 1967.

66. *Daily Mail,* 20 April 1968.

67. *Daily Mail,* 22 April 1968. In its enabling decree, the National Interim Council was "charged with special responsibility to effect a speedy restoration of a Civilian Government."

68. Salia Jusu-Sheriff in an interview with John Cartwright, July 21, 1968.

69. As part of the terms for handing over to the APC, the army rank and file received promises of a substantial boost in pay.

70. *Speech by Colonel John Amadu Bangura, Chairman of the National Interim Council to Elected Members of Parliament on the Return to Civilian Government on the 26th of April 1968,* mimeographed.

71. The APC held seven portfolios (including the premiership, interior, external affairs, information), the SLPP five portfolios (including most of the lesser ministries such as health); the Independents, two portfolios; and the Paramount Chiefs, three.

72. *Broadcast Talk by the Chief Justice, Mr. Banja Tejan-Sie, Officer Performing the Functions of the Governor-General, April 26, 1968,* mimeographed.

73. S. E. Finer, *The Man on Horseback,* p. 191.

74. Claude E. Welch, Jr., "Cincinnatus in Africa: The Possibility of Military Withdrawal from Politics" in *The State of Nations: Constraints on Development in Independent Africa,* ed. Michael F. Lofchie (Berkeley: University of California Press, 1971), p. 217.

## 11. CIVIL-MILITARY RELATIONS UNDER SIAKA STEVENS AND THE ALL PEOPLES CONGRESS

1. *New York Times,* 28 March 1971.

2. *Daily Mail,* 14 June 1968.

3. In July 1969, Genda became Sierra Leone's ambassador to the Soviet Union. For this officer, diplomatic exile had become a kind of annual ritual.

4. On April 18, 1970, Brigadier Lansana, Commissioner William Leigh, Major Blake, Major Kai-Samba, and Lieutenant Norman with five civilians were found guilty of treason and sentenced to hang. On July 30, in a separate trial, Juxon-Smith was also found guilty and received the death sentence. Then in May 1971, the Sierra Leone Court of Appeal ruled that all of the charges against these men had been improperly drawn up and that the proceedings which had been conducted in the Supreme Court were therefore a "nullity." The government immediately detained Lansana and the others under state of emergency regulations but never filed any new

charges. In late November of 1971, Kai-Samba, Leigh, and Blake together with S. B. Daramy, George Panda, and Thomas Decker were pardoned and released. By the end of 1973, all of the officers and civilians connected with the coups of March 1967 had been released, including Lansana and Juxon-Smith.

5. As quoted in the *Express,* 16 August 1968.

6. "Speech from the Throne, Delivered by His Excellency Banja Tejan-Sie on the occasion of the State Opening of the Third Session of the Third Parliament," (June 12, 1970), p. 9.

7. *House of Representatives Debates, Session 1969-70* (June 30, 1969), p. 32.

8. Most of the army officers involved in these operations were of northern extraction.

9. *House of Representatives Debates, Session 1969-70* (July 1, 1969), p. 15.

10. This was the way one APC Minister described the Sierra Leone army. *House of Representatives Debates, Session 1968-69* (June 24, 1968), col. 704.

11. "Speech from the Throne," p. 9.

12. This was Captain D.D.K. Vandi who had served briefly with the NRC and who was allowed to remain in the army, apparently because he had family ties with a certain APC politician.

13. By March 1970, the twenty-eight seats "won" by the SLPP in 1967 had been reduced to twelve as a result of by-elections. The APC's parliamentary overall majority increased from thirty-two to fifty-one seats. There were also nine paramount chiefs who customarily support the government of the day. Having gone into the opposition—officially on June 10, 1969—the SLPP could no longer tap the financial resources of the government as it had done when Sir Albert Margai was in power.

14. The Sierra Leone Provincial Organization, *Unity for Progress,* mimeographed, n.d.

15. See John Cartwright and Thomas Cox, "Left Turn for Sierra Leone?" *Africa Report,* 17 (January 1972), 16.

16. Mohammed Bash-Taqi, Stevens's Minister of Development, and the elder brother of Ibrahim Taqi also resigned and joined the "Tonkolili group."

17. In August 1970, the APC's national executive had moved that Sierra Leone should become a republic with a strong, centralized presidency. See Mohammed Forna's letter of resignation dated September 12, 1970, as quoted in the NDP newspaper, *Probe, Special Edition,* "The Folly of Siaka Stevens," mimeographed, Freetown, n.d.

18. Ministry of Information, *Press Release 163/70,* mimeographed.

19. *UDP Press Release,* mimeographed.

20. The Directorate of the Democratic Civil Resistance Movement, *Release,* distributed anonymously in Freetown, October 20, 1970, mimeographed, p. 2.

21. Ministry of Information, *Press Release 160/70,* "Allegations Against the Security Forces," mimeographed.

22. Actually, Colby had visited Wilberforce Barracks at the army's request in order to discuss the possible sale of US-manufactured communications equipment for use by the RSLMF. Sesay never appeared for the meeting.

23. *Unity,* 15 December 1970.

24. *Unity,* 12 December 1970.

25. The Directorate of the Democratic Civil Resistance Movement, *Release,* p. 2.

26. UDP Overseas, *The Sierra Leone Political Crisis: 1970,* mimeographed (London: November 1970), p. 8.

27. *West Africa,* 2 April 1971.

28. Ibid.

29. The Guinean High Command in Conarky as quoted in note 27.

30. Ibid.

31. When announcing the signing of the mutual defense treaty with Sierra Leone, Guinean radio referred to a resolution which was passed at the special session of the OAU Council of Ministers held in Lagos to discuss the November 22, 1970 invasion of Guinea. At that session it was decided to encourage the setting up of regional and subregional defense organizations. Meanwhile, on December 22, 1970, Sierra Leone's parliament resolved that the Government "enter into immediate negotiations with the Government of the Republic of Guinea and the Republic of Liberia, its next door neighbors, with a view to concluding mutual defence arrangements in the context of an all African Defence Organization under an African High Command." Liberia evidenced little interest in the proposal so that Sierra Leone and Guinea concluded their own arrangements. Under the terms of the pact between the two countries, they agreed to combine their forces to defend each other against any form of attack, "from wherever it came."

32. *Daily Mail,* 23 June 1971.

33. On Monday 19 April 1971, Sierra Leone became a sovereign republic within the British commonwealth. Siaka Stevens was made president of the Republic and S. I. Koroma became vice president and prime minister. Under the new constitution, the presidency was of the executive type. For more details on the altered constitutional arrangements, see Cartwright and Cox, "Left Turn for Sierra Leone?"

## 12. CONCLUSION

1. Martin C. Needler, "Political Development and Military Intervention in Latin America" in *Reform and Revolution,* ed. Arpad von Lazar and Robert P. Kaufman, p. 233.

2. Liisa North, *Civil-Military Relations in Argentina, Chile and Peru* (Berkeley, California: Institute of International Studies, 1966), p. 2.

3. *West Africa,* 7 January 1974.

4. *West Africa,* 9 July 1973. When Tombalbaye was overthrown in April 1975 by a military coup, Malloum was released from house arrest and assumed leadership of the new government. See Chapter 1.

5. *Africa Report,* 18 (September-October 1973), p. 55.

6. René Lemarchand and Keith Legg, "Political Clientelism and Development, a Preliminary Analysis," in *Comparative Politics,* 4 (January 1972), p. 151.

7. Commonwealth Parliamentary Association, *Verbatim Report of the Proceedings of the First Conference of the Commonwealth Parliamentary Association, African Region,* 28th April-29th April, 1969, Lusaka, Zambia.

8. Huntington, *Political Order in Changing Societies,* pp. 197, 198, 200.

9. Ibid.; pp. 201-202.

10. As a result of Sierra Leone's third general election since independence, held on May 11, 1973, the country has become a defacto one-party state although the SLPP is still, technically speaking, in the opposition. The United Democratic Party remains banned although all of its former leaders, including Ibrahim Taqi and Mohammed Forna, have been released from detention. At the time of the May 11 election, all but five of the eighty-five regular seats in the expanded parliament had been declared unopposed for the ruling APC. The twelve paramount chiefs who sit in the parliament were also elected unopposed. Of the five remaining seats for which voting was held on May 11, four were won by the APC. An independent, Mr. Desmond Luke, won the fifth seat in the Freetown West Three constituency. He is

now the minister of external affairs.

11. "Treason Trial Special," Government Information Services, November 16, 1974.

12. *We Yone,* 17 November 1974 and "Sierra Leone Treason Trial Verdict," *Africa,* 41 (January 1975).

13. *We Yone,* 20 November 1974.

14. *Africa Research Bulletin* (October 1-31, 1974), p. 3394.

# INDEX

111; role in March 1967 military seizure of power, 125, 129-131, 133, 137, 142; participation in National Reformation Council, 161-165 passim, 167, 171, 182, 189, 194, 195-196

Jusu-Sheriff, Salia, 96, 131, 200

Juxon-Smith, Andrew T., 28, 77, 78, 84-87 passim, 133; assumes chairmanship of National Reformation Council, 140-141; political philosophy of, 144-147, 149, 151-153, 155, 158, 159, 162-165 passim, 166, 168, 169, 170, 173, 176-178 passim, 180-182 passim, 184-187 passim, 188, 191, 193, 194; opposed by other senior members of NRC, 195-196; arrested in privates' mutiny of 17 April 1968, 197, 201-203, 207, 227

Kai-Samba, Bockarie, 65, 67, 68, 88, 89, 96; origins of opposition to Sir Albert Margai and David Lansana, 101, 109-111 passim; role in military intervention of March 1967, 114, 125, 129-134 passim, 137, 138; participation in National Reformation Council, 142, 144, 147, 149, 155, 167, 177, 182, 188, 195-197 passim, 207

Kai-Samba, Kutubu, 67, 71, 96, 110, 116, 131, 153, 171, 178, 208

Kallon, John, 98, 119, 167, 168

Kallon, Maigore, 68

Kamara, Alpha, 126, 133, 165, 167, 194

Kamara, A. O., 99, 100

Kamara, Habib Lansana, 228

Kamara, Morlai, 198

Kamara-Taylor, C. A., 123, 189, 210, 227, 228

Kanu, M., 132

Kapaka, Manna, 116

Karefa-Smart, John, 35, 36, 55, 97, 210-212, 213, 215, 216

Kargbo, Benedict, 212, 213

Kayibanda, Grégoire, 221

Kengenyeh, John, 206

Kenya, 6

Kerekou, Mathieu, 176

Kershaw, Richard, 136

King, R. G. O., 67, 189

King, Sam, 214

Kolugbanda, J. B., 216

Kono Progressive Movement (KPM), 34

Koroma, M., 68, 106, 167

Kuyateh, Ahmed, 215

Kuyeembeh, J., 53

Lamizana, General Sangoulé, 176

Lansana, David, 20, 21; early career of, 29-30; linkages with the SLPP leadership, 29, 45, 46, 52, 57, 58, 61, 62-65, 68-69, 73, 77, 80, 82-91 passim, 93, 94, 96, 98, 99-102 passim, 104; role in March 1967 military intervention, 106-112, 114-129 passim; arrested by Majors Blake, Jumu, and Kai-Samba, 129-134 passim, 135-137, 207, 227, 228

Lee, J. M., 14-15

LeFever, Ernest, 14

Leigh, William, 103, 124, 125, 126, 129 passim, 141, 142, 148, 163, 165, 167, 195, 196, 207

Lewis, W. Arthur, 95

Libya, 2, 3, 225

Lightfoot-Boston, Sir Henry, 43, 115, 116, 121-126 passim, 130-131, 183, 184

Lloyd, P. C., 69

Lofchie, Michael, 12

Luckham, A. R., 78

Macauley, Berthan, 68, 69, 103, 123-125 passim, 131, 168

Magba-Kamara, A. B., 68, 106

Malagasy Republic, 3, 4

Malloum, Félix, 3, 221

Mammy Queens, 146

Margai, Albert, 29, 34, 52, 55, 83-90 passim; attitudes toward civilian control of the military, 57-62, 134-135; linkages with David Lansana, 62-64, 136; support for a single party system and a republican constitution, 71-72; favors increased Mendeization of the army, 73-76;